DECODING THEORYSPEAK

Existentialism; Urbanism; Aporia; Deontic; Tabula Rasa; Hyperspace; Heterotopia; Metareality; Structuralism ...

BUT WHAT DOES IT ALL MEAN?

The unique language used in architectural theory, in either speech or writing, can appear daunting and confusing, particularly to new architectural students.

- Definitions of over 200 terms
- Clearly cross-referenced
- Illustrated throughout

Decoding Theoryspeak provides an accessible guide to the specialized language of contemporary design for the next generation of thinkers, architects and design leaders. An essential pocket-sized resource for students and practitioners alike.

Enn Ots is a practicing architect and teacher with 40 years of theoryspeak experience. Since 1979 he has been an associate professor at the Florida A&M University School of Architecture while maintaining an architectural practice. He conducts design/build workshops, as well as teaching theory and undergraduate design studio. Prior to 1979, he was an architectural researcher and designer in Winnipeg and Toronto, Canada.

This book is dedicated to the late Tom Porter who made it possible. He was a true friend.

DECODING THEORYSPEAK
An illustrated guide to architectural theory

ENN OTS

With contributions by:

Michael Alfano Jr.
Jonathan Hale
Craig Huffman
Beth Lewis
Byron Mikellides
Alessandra Orlandoni
Tom Porter

Routledge
Taylor & Francis Group

LONDON AND NEW YORK

Published 2011
by Routledge
2 Park Square, Milton Park, Abingdon, Oxon, OX14 4RN

Simultaneously published in the USA and Canada
by Routledge
270 Madison Avenue, New York, NY 10016

Routledge is an imprint of the Taylor & Francis Group, an informa business

© 2011 selection and editorial material, Enn Ots; individual chapters, the contributors

The right of Enn Ots to be identified as author of this work has been asserted by him in accordance with sections 77 and 78 of the Copyright, Designs and Patents Act 1988.

Typeset in DIN by Saxon Graphics Ltd, Derby
Printed and bound in Great Britain by
TJ International Ltd, Padstow, Cornwall

British Library Cataloguing in Publication Data
A catalogue record for this book is available from the British Library

Library of Congress Cataloging-in-Publication Data
Decoding theoryspeak : an illustrated guide to architectural theory / Enn Ots ; with contributions by Michael Alfano Jr. ... [et al.].
p. cm.
1. Architecture—Philosophy. 2. Architecture—Terminology. I. Alfano, Michael. II. Title. III. Title: Illustrated guide to architectural theory.
NA2500.O78 2010
720.1'4—dc22
2010013651

ISBN13: 978-0-415-77829-9 (hbk)
ISBN13: 978-0-415-77830-5 (pbk)
ISBN13: 978-0-203-84190-7 (ebk)

Contents

Illustrations
Unless indicated otherwise, all illustrations are by Enn Ots.

List of contributors

Michael Alfano Jr., AIA, is an architect and urban designer. He is an Associate Professor and a founding member of the Florida A&M University School of Architecture. His research and teaching focus is in architectural theory and urban design.

Jonathan Hale is an architect and Associate Professor at the Department of Architecture and Built Environment, University of Nottingham. He is course director for the interdisciplinary MA in Architecture and Critical Theory. He is the author of numerous articles and books. He is also a founder member of the international subject group, Architectural Humanities Research Association (AHRA).

Craig Huffman is an award winning architect and Associate Professor of Architecture at Florida A&M University. He has lectured and exhibited his work throughout the United States, contributed essays on design and theory in two books, and has had work published in *Competitions Magazine*.

Beth Lewis, AIA, LEED AP, Associate Professor in the School of Architecture at Florida A&M University teaches architecture design, sustainable construction and green building design. She is active in the state and local leadership of AIA and the US Green Building Council.

Byron Mikellides is an environmental psychologist and Emeritus Professor at the School of Architecture, Oxford Brookes University and visiting professor at the School of Architecture, University of Cyprus. He is the co-editor of *Colour for Architecture* (1976) and author of *Architecture for People* (1980).

Alessandra Orlandoni is an architect and designer based in Florence, Italy. She has collaborated on numerous cultural projects as curator, coordinator and consultant. Her writings have been published in several international publications. From 2002 to 2005, she was Professor of Interior and Exhibition Design at the Industrial Design and Fashion Design Departments of the Florence Architecture University.

Tom Porter, the late author and color consultant was Visiting Professor at Montana State University (2006-2008) and visiting fellow at Oxford Brookes University. He has authored numerous books, including *Archispeak* (2004), the first volume in this series.

Acknowledgements

This volume would not have been possible without the generous contributions of the following individuals:

Definitions·

Michael Atrano Jr, Jonathan Hale, Craig Huffman, Beth Lewis, Byron Mikellides. Alessandra Orlandoni, Tom Porter

Illustrations·

Andy Beckham, Louis Hellman, Thor Mann, Karl Ots, Janice Ratner, Karen Williams, Tom Yohe

I would like to also thank my graduate assistants, Jeffrey Smiley and Cheryl Callender for their efforts. Special thanks are due to Alexey Ots for his editorial assistance.

Enn Ots

Preface

Language is the house of Being. In its home human beings dwell. Those who think and those who create with words are the guardians of this home.

Martin Heidegger

The discourse on theory streams along in all of its convoluted complexity, largely unnoticed by the average practitioner of architecture. If the articles get too complex, simply no one will read them.

Arie Graafland

Theoryspeak is the second volume in the "Speak" series. It was not planned to be a series, but after *Archispeak* was complete, more terms kept coming up during design studio reviews and in general discussions with students. Since most of these additional terms seemed to be in the area of architectural theory it seemed appropriate to supplement *Archispeak* with *Theoryspeak*. Together they provide an introduction to over 550 architectural design and theory terms. As the expected reader is anyone who has a newfound interest in design theory, an effort has been made to ensure that each term is accessible and understandable without relying on prior knowledge of related terms and concepts. Towards that end, it has been important to avoid the pedantic and obscure, yet at the same time to not trivialize or minimize the full meaning and importance of the selected term.

Introduction

The first half of the twentieth century witnessed the rise and fall of modernist architectural dogma, espousing what many regarded as cold-hearted rational rules for problem solving through form generation. Few members of the public appreciated the resulting break from the past. In the effort to find an alternative to modern architecture, the architectural academy imported European structuralist philosophy and recast it as architectural theory. The profession and the academy was receptive, as they had been alerted by the publication of Robert Venturi's "gentle manifesto on non-straightforward architecture," *Complexity and Contradiction in Architecture* (1966), along with other grumblings about the poverty of modernism from Peter Blake and others.

The project of the new structuralist architectural theory was to restore meaning in architecture through the metaphor of language. The discipline of semiology provided the methodology for this effort. Unfortunately it relatively quickly turned on itself and "deconstructed." In the movement away from this short-lived flirtation with structuralism, critical theory became of interest to purveyors of architectural theory in the 1990s. Long-neglected issues such as feminism, cultural theory, and globalization became the topics of the day within the academy.

In the twenty-first century, the academic interest in critical theory has been largely replaced by a messier, earthier, more technical, yet humanistic, interest in experimental and experiential architecture. The focus is on building skins, digital media, sustainable design, and new forms of digital practice. There is a renewed pragmatism within a changed environment of ethical practice. Architects are getting their hands dirty again. This shift away from the more esoteric theories of the previous decades was aided by the eventual acceptance by designers of twentieth-century paradigm changes in the sciences. Biological sciences, complexity and chaos theory, string theory, and non-Euclidean spatial conceptions are some of the current influences on the thoughtful designer. The execution of the resulting architectural waves, folds, and blobs has also been made possible by advances in digital technologies. Terms such as "blobmeister" and "biomimicry" have joined the lexicon of design talk. Emergent, non-Cartesian form, inspired somewhat by Deleuzian philosophy, and made possible by the computer, is the magazine-worthy architecture of the day.

It has also been a time of reinvention of the process of delivering architecture. Parametric design using building information modeling (BIM) and integrated practice are thrusting the architect into the unfamiliar role of working with total transparency in a fully cooperative design process that is global. Thus, the twenty-first century has started out by shifting from critical theory to critical practice. This critical practice has also been described as the new pragmatism. Eventually the most significant current development will prove to be the production of sustainable architecture. The state of the natural world has now swept architects into the environmental crisis, reluctantly at first, but now with apparent enthusiasm, as clients demand it. Unlike the energy crisis of the 1970s, the entire design community is now involved. The stakes are higher. We are not as naïve as the earlier "back to the earth" movements that became associated with the "Woodstock generation."

Is this an odd time for the introduction of a glossary of theory terms? Hardly, the past 20 years have seen a dramatic change in the theory and practice of architecture. The "Speak" series, including this volume, is a timely effort at helping to navigate the specialized jargon found in current design literature.

Absence/presence

When Structuralists and Post-Structuralists make the apparently outrageous claim that every object is both a presence and an absence, they mean that an object is never fully there – it is there to the extent that it appears before us, but is not there in so far as its being is determined by its relation to the whole system of which it is part, a system that does not appear to us. — Donald Palmer

There is no presence. There is no absence. There is only the difference between them, always and already in movement. — Michael Benedikt

The notion that a work of architecture can have a simultaneous quality of *absence* and *presence* is part of the late twentieth century Structuralist effort at placing designed objects within their larger contexts. For them, the quality of *absence* was relative to our unconscious understanding of the missing. The quality of *presence* was simply what we have before us, no more. The discipline for understanding these notions was borrowed from linguistics, a well-developed philosophical science, having been initiated by de Saussure in the first decade of the twentieth century. The qualities of *absence* and *presence* are not only significant to the Structuralists. Phenomenologists have an interest in the presentness of the object, devoid of the *absence*. What matters most to them is the raw reality of the experience of the object before them. In other words, the immediate *presence* of the object is what is truly real.

A building with presence, with a kind of mute awareness of its doors left ajar and windows open, finally seems attentive to our presence. — Michael Benedikt

Post-modern style architects confronted *absence* by overtly sampling architectural artifacts from the past. The intent was to restore meaning to a mute modern architecture. This attempt at the removal of the *absence*, by being more evident and literal may have been one of the downfalls of post-modern architecture, particularly as practiced by less talented second-tier designers. The deconstructivist architecture that briefly followed the post-modern architectural style abandoned all references to the implicit structures that form the *absence*. What were being "deconstructed" were the underlying artificial structural constructs that Structuralists contended formed the *absence*. In the twenty-first century the project of post-deconstructivism has been to rediscover the absent structures that fall within the agenda of critical theory. Socio-political and economic contexts are once again acknowledged. In a twist of fate, the current digital blob and fold advocates seem to be most interested in an aggressive *presence* at the expense of *absence*. Their references to context are typically missing. This is illustrated by the Grande Arche at

Figure 1: La Grande Arche, Paris

La Defense in Paris, which has a strong presence due to the *absence* of context, and even the middle of the building itself (Figure 1).

Space – The presence of absence. — Bernard Tschumi

See also: **Critical theory** • **Deconstructivism (Archispeak)** • **Emptiness** • **Silence** • **Structuralism.**

Abstraction

According to Plato, words name concepts, ideas, which are abstractions. — Donald Palmer

Modern architecture attempted to strip itself of the outward trappings of "Classical" style. This process of reduction was called abstraction. — Peter Eisenman

Modern architecture employed many forms of *abstraction*, including the elevation of function to the status of form giver. As illustrated in Figure 2, abstraction in modern architecture can even reduce the building to its bare bones. To abstract is a fundamental human need. *Abstraction* allows one to confront the complexities of raw reality through a process of sorting, labeling, cataloguing, and denying those aspects of our world that do not fit the invented schema. Newtonian space is a powerful *abstraction* that relates directly to classical and modernist architecture, just as the abstraction we call non-Euclidean space can be regarded as one of the hallmarks of twenty-first century architecture. An interesting twist to contemporary architectural form abstractions is the use of the folds, twists, and blobs derived from nature. Architecture has moved from the simplistic notion of "form follows function" of modern architecture to an even greater level of *abstraction*. "Form" is no longer the primary concern of a meaningful and ethical green digital architecture. "Function" is declared a dead end, as it has proven to be too transitory and arbitrary.
    Ironically, the growing use of digital media has made it possible to cyber simulate the visible world with less *abstraction*. The virtual world is becoming more real with each new massive multiplayer online game. The digital design process, however, has abstracted the physical act of design. The designer no longer has an intimate relationship with her design media. It is housed in the virtual world, which she can only observe through the looking glass. Occasionally, in response to the client's need for a physical manifestation of the design, traditional physical models are still produced. With the use of rapid prototyping machines, even these physical models are produced without the intimate involvement of the designer. Physical models are still favored by many clients, even though they are more abstract than a fully rendered digital model. For group viewing situations, physical models are in the round and thus easier to use for fund raising and general promotional purposes.

See also: **Abstraction** • **Blob architecture (Archispeak)** • **Blobitecture** • **Digital architecture** • **Fold** • **Form** • **Prototyping**

Further sources: Ballantyne (2002: 34); Colebrook (2006: 99); Gausa (2003: 21, 24) Johnson (1994: 331) Lefebvre (in Hays: 174)

Figure 2: Franklin Court:

Accident   ▮

I hate perfection. I think perfection is boring. Instead, there is something beautiful about accident, when things never completely fit.
— Winka Dubbeldam

Many of the world's most important discoveries have been made as a consequence of what is often termed the "happy accident." Examples are Johann Aloys Senefelder's discovery of the lithographic printing process in 1798 after accidentally spilling bacon fat on to a stone surface, the Victorian William Henry Perkins stumbling upon mauve, the first aniline dye, when attempting to create artificial quinine in the 1860s, and among the most famous, Isaac Newton's observation of an apple falling from a tree which led to his musings on the nature of gravity. Indeed, accidents have led to the discovery of countless innovations both great and small, from the chocolate chip cookie and the Post-It note to penicillin, ink jet printers, and polycarbonates. The amount of discoveries due to *accident* varies extensively across the disciplines – pharmacology and chemistry probably represent the fields where such serendipitous discoveries occur more frequently.

History, of course, does not document accidental exposures of information, which could have resulted in a new discovery, and we are justified in suspecting that they are many. However, one aspect of such discoveries is that their discoverers agree upon one common point of view. That is, while prejudice and preformed concepts present the greatest obstacle, a receptively open mind is required on the part of the inventor or scientist to detect the importance of information that is suddenly and accidentally revealed.

While examples abound in art, *accident* can also play a key role in architecture, where some designers purposefully employ misadventure as part of their design process. Perhaps the most vivid architectural example can be found in Bernard Tschumi's competition-winning design for the Parc de la Villette in Paris (see Figure 3). Here, Tschumi used serendipitous techniques to superimpose point, line, and field, each planned to have "accidental" intersections. As each layer was supposedly developed without regard for the others, the results are surprisingly productive. Will Alsop is another architect who, unusually, arriving at his architectural designs via painting, is constantly open to the incidence of *accident* and chance. He describes a stain on a drawing accidentally left behind by a wine glass as having the potential to open up the imagination to a whole new world of possibility. There is also the legendary story of Frank O. Gehry crumpling up some paper and throwing it into the trash, only to retrieve it later and use it as the form of inspiration for one of his buildings. TP

Figure 3 Parc de la Villette

Many of those who allow *accident* to play a part in their design process believe that *accident,* like chance, is a fine thing. — Tom Porter

See also: **Ad hocism • Constraints • Creativity • Defamiliarization • Unselfconscious form**

▌Ad hocism

Design, essentially a collage, where every part of a building, or each element of a building-complex, is designed with scant regard to the whole, and often involves disparate parts taken from catalogues — Charles Jencks

… assemblage occurs in architectural design when models and diagrams are quickly fabricated from junk materials to symbolize the components and relationships of an idea. — *Archispeak*, p. 10

Ad hocism is a common and longstanding method of construction among informal settlements throughout the world. Unfortunately, these unsafe and unsanitary developments are going to grow in number and size as political and environmental catastrophes continue in the developing world. In the developed world, ad hoc construction has a less ominous future. The current do-it-yourself (DIY) movement has resulted in widespread ad hoc design without a conceptual compass. In addition to the DIY world, the profession of architecture is flirting with ad hoc design. In this "green" era of recycling materials, ad hocism is growing as a design/build methodology. Programs such as the Rural Studio at Auburn University (Figure 4), and similar efforts at other schools of architecture, are becoming incubators for future ad hoc designers. The design/build movement using recycled materials is following in the footsteps of Bruce Goff. In referring to the Bavinger House (1957), Jencks describes Goff as

Figure 4: Rural studio

"the master of ad hoc building, or the 'Army and Navy Surplus Aesthetic,' using any conceivable leftover materials."

In addition to architecture, towns and cities have developed in an ad hoc manner, controlled only by the need for defense and the patterns of supplied infrastructure and natural features. This is particularly true of places that have evolved over a very long period of time. In contrast, modern towns have been carefully planned since the start of the twentieth century. Howard's *Garden Cities* (1902) was an early example of the movement away from ad hoc town growth. However, as a reaction to the sterility of the planned community, efforts are now underway in these artificial communities to simulate *ad hocism* through contrived variation of colors, roof types, and other applied elements. This type of planned *ad hocism* is of course no *ad hocism* at all. American pragmatism, as demonstrated by Thoreau's cabin at Walden Pond, is a better example of ad hoc design and construction in the United States.

See also: **American pragmatism • Assemblage (Archispeak)**

Aesthetics

The study of the feelings, concepts, and judgments arising from our appreciation of the arts or of the wider class of objects considered moving, or beautiful, or sublime. — *Oxford Dictionary of Philosophy*

... esthetics as an umbrella term is used for qualities possessed by an artifact or building after it has been designed. — Paul-Alan Johnson

Vitruvius popularized the discussion about architectural aesthetics with his prescriptions for beauty (eurhythmy) and arrangement (diathesis). *Aesthetics* was an important part of the ensuing classical architecture, with its careful and explicit canons of proportion, symmetry, the orders, etc. Classical aesthetics endured for most of the history of western culture. Modern aesthetics began in the eighteenth century with the publication of David Hume's "Of the Standard of Taste" (1737). Modern architectural dogma rejected formal *aesthetics* as a valid concern for the designer. The break occurred with the advent of societal modernism, and its rejection of all things deemed to be irrational and unscientific. As a result, architectural aesthetics became a lost art.

For a brief period in the twentieth century there was an attempt to resurrect classical aesthetics, but the effort was not often based upon scholarship, but rather uninformed sampling of historical elements. The commercialized post-modern architecture that was produced by less talented architects resulted in discrediting architectural aesthetics once again. In an ironic twist, occasionally modern buildings were being updated to post-modern by the addition of classical motifs. The bank shown in Figure 5 had a plywood pediment added in the late 1980s to update it to the aesthetic of the day. Unfortunately it was too little too late, and the building is once again out of date.

In the twenty-first century the influence of popular culture and its preoccupation with image has created a renewed interest in aesthetic as a fashion statement. The result is that, as in all fashions, the accepted *aesthetics* shift as the consumer industry and social media promote the new "look." Thus, popular neo-modern taste has shifted attention way from any formal prescriptions for beauty and elegance towards the hip-hop aesthetic or the chunkiness and strangeness of the biomorphic. The difficulty is that fashions change quickly. As it takes a work of architecture several years to go from initial concept to completed building, there is an increasing danger that the building will already be considered to be old fashioned the day it has its grand opening.

... architectural creations cannot be detached from intention either in their creation or their interpretation ... aesthetic autonomy is therefore a myth. — Paul-Alan Johnson

See also: **Beauty • Post-modernism (Archispeak) • Sublime**

Further sources: Ballantyne (2002: 18); Harries (1998: 4, 17, 21); Johnson (1994: 399); Lang (1987: 179)

Figure 5: Bank aesthetic transformation from "modern" to "post-modern" with the addition of some plywood

▌Aletheia

The impossibility of something, being true. — *Oxford Dictionary of Philosophy*

For Greek thought the nature of knowing consists in aletheia. — Martin Heidegger

Algorithm   9 | A

The Greek term *aletheia* refers to the problem of truth, including the impossibility of something being true, regardless of the soundness of the arguments to the contrary. A strong argument for an impossible truth, combined with the difficulty of determining what "ought to be" (deontics), sometimes causes the designer to be misled into thinking results are valid. This may be particularly true when a sophisticated cyber-based design process has been employed. Upon further investigation the project is often revealed to be less thought out than the representation implies. The evidence may be hidden behind a very convincing fully rendered and animated digital model. Sometimes the design proposal is an elaborate answer to the wrong question, or a critical parameter that disqualifies the solution has been omitted. If the right questions had been asked, the truth of the answers to those questions may have shown that the solution under consideration was alethetic. This is a common problem that students encounter with their class design projects, which often present good answers to the wrong questions. *Aletheia* can only be prevented in the studio if logical analysis and honest argumentation are emphasized in the design process. Parametric design is only as useful as the specific parameters that are being selected to be addressed. "I did it because I always wanted to do a pyramid," or "because Gehry did it" may not be good enough. Peter Eisenman demonstrated a more interesting application of reverse *aletheia* to architectural design in the interrupted arch at the 1989 Wexner Center for the Visual Arts (Figure 6). The arch is true, despite the impossibility of it being so.

In our era of "hidden persuader" we are incessantly, and unknowingly, confronted by television hucksters who are presenting sound arguments for impossible truths. The "Sham Wow" does an impossibly good job of cleaning up spills, despite evidence to the contrary.

See also: **Deontics • Parametric design**

Further sources: Heidegger (in Leach 1997: 121)

Figure 6: Wexner Center for the Visual Arts

Algorithm

The term algorithm simply means a series of steps. Today, as modeling, representation, and fabrication technologies shift from manual to automated processes, the issue of algorithm is pressing ...
— Benjamin Aranda and Chris Lasch

In recent years there is an increasing trend in architecture to exploit the ability of algorithmic design to produce complex forms by implementing relatively simple and easy formulas. — Sawako Kaijima

Design has tried to get hold of the immense performative power of algorithms for almost a decade. — Sanford Kwinter

In the past, *algorithms* have been closely associated with the specialized fields of mathematics and computer programming. However, with the widespread popularity of spreadsheet programs such as Microsoft Excel, the use of the *algorithm* has spread to general use in the business and academic worlds. With the growing use of digital parametric design tools, such as building information modeling (BIM), the development and use of *algorithms* has become a part of the architect's everyday duties. Spreadsheet-based inputs, as well as other types of *algorithms,* are important to many of the functions of a BIM. Also, as architects become increasingly involved in the CAD/CAM cycle, facility with *algorithms* as scripting will be necessary.

The spread of *algorithms* may have a downside. The science fiction specter of machines using self-generated *algorithms* to design and manufacture other machines, including architecture, may not be that far off. The implications for architects may be particularly disturbing, as they become bystanders. Even today, there is a danger that the architect may be forced to relinquish control over the BIM to professional BIM managers who are not designers, but more closely resemble the accountants who are most comfortable dealing with *algorithms*. The tyranny of algorithmic, parametric design is a real concern. The immeasurable will suffer. The fascination with the complex shapes possible due to *algorithmic* design may supplant more pressing design concerns. In the future we may be blessed with an increasingly interesting architecture that comes complete with lawsuits for lack of functionality, cost overruns, and damages due to water intrusion. That future may have already arrived with infamous projects such as Gehry's STATA and Libeskind's Denver Art Museum.

See also: **Building information modeling: BIM • Craft • Parametric design**

Figure 7: Piazza d'Italia

Allusionism

Allusion – an indirect reference to something. — *Webster's Unabridged Dictionary*

Allusionism was an approach to post-modern architectural design that attempted to provide clues for communicating the narrative of the work. It can take on a variety of forms, from explicit references to particular fragments from earlier buildings, to the wholesale sampling of iconic buildings from the past. The Pantheon has been a popular subject for creating the allusion of ancient Rome. Charles Moore's Piazza d'Italia is perhaps the most aggressive and overt example of post-modern *allusionism*. Its design concept includes an elaborate fountain in a stone urban plaza that in plan view is a literal map of Italy. The fountain also has a complex, curved backdrop that is a riot of classical Italian architectural references (Figure 7).

Allusionism has not disappeared with the demise of post-modernism in architecture. The Beijing Olympic stadium, the "Bird's Nest," is a testament to that. Although it was not Swiss architecture firm Herzog & de Meuron's intention to reference a bird's nest, it was a happy accident that the allusion resonated with the Chinese client group. As architects venture ever more into blobs and folds, the public will increasingly look for allusions, intended or not. Alsop's "Big Blue," Calatrava's bird wings, and Erskine's "Ark" are just some of the well-known architectural allusions. Looking for allusions is part of human nature. After all, we have all looked at clouds to see Homer Simpson or a duck's head.

See also: **Blob architecture (Archispeak) • Blobitecture • Fold • Post-modernism (Archispeak)**

Figure 8: The Portland Building

Alterity   ▮

Term used in postmodern writing for the "otherness" of others, or sometimes the otherness of the self. — *Oxford Dictionary of Philosophy*

Alterity is the philosophical principle of exchanging one's own perspective for that of "the other." It applies to the discipline of architecture as it involves the challenge of designing for others in their "otherness." In order to do so successfully, it is necessary to "put yourself in the other person's shoes." Although architects are often accused of designing buildings to assuage their own egos and personal agendas, most architects truly listen to their clients and place the user's needs above their own. Clearly there are a few starchitects who are first and foremost involved in gaining more notoriety through the production of ever more extravagant and photogenic architecture. They are promoting their brand with the blessings of their client/patron. As we move still more quickly from one "ism" to the next, these iconic "star" works will quickly seem dated and naïve. We already devalue the cutting-edge post-modernist (PoMo) work from the 1980s as old-fashioned. The iconic Portland Municipal Services Building (1982) by Michael Graves looks decidedly out of date (Figure 8). The deconstructivist architecture that followed "PoMo" is now also out of fashion. How long will the media and the public's fascination with blobs and folds last? Their novelty is already wearing off, as we become even more entrenched in the pragmatism of the green movement. Considering that buildings are physically capable of remaining sound for much longer than the 30 years since 1980, architecture with a strong commitment to a particular style may not be in the best interests of the client. To be sustainable, perhaps buildings should be able to keep up with the times through built-in mechanisms for updating. In this age of concern of the efficiency of resource allocation, buildings should not be discarded prematurely. The "other" has become not just the client/user but also the environment.

See also: **Branding** • **Deconstructivism (Archispeak)** • **Green building (Archispeak)** • **Greenscaping** • **Post-modernism PoMo (Archispeak)** • **Starchitect** • **Style**

▌Ambivalence

The simultaneous existence of conflicting emotions.
— *Webster's Unabridged Dictionary*

Univocal space now yields to a space decidedly ambivalent in its physical and virtual manifestations. Not only because it is functionally non-predetermined, but also substantively hybrid. A building can be a garden, a garden, a building. — Manuel Gausa

Architectural *ambivalence* has the connotation of "betweenness," an architecture that is neither "fish nor fowl." It resides in the indeterminacy of a building's purpose and meaning. Unlike the functionalist attempts of twentieth-century modern architects to force form to follow function, twenty-first-century architects are more ambivalent about the relationship between form and function, or perhaps the definition of "function" has evolved. Architecture has become somewhat loose-fitting and non-specific to the particulars of usage at any given time. The acceptance of the dynamic and unpredictable nature of architecture's technological, social, and economic context has created the realization that the custom-designed building, with its clear and single purpose and tailored accommodations, is doomed to early demolition. On the other hand, buildings that are "light on their feet" have a greater chance of survival. Architecture as a beneficial setting for human occasions, without shaping and limiting those occasions, may be the appropriate civic architecture of the twenty-first century. The techniques for achieving this loose fit must avoid dreary universal space. Mies van der Rohe, one of the promoters of universal space (Figure 9), aptly demonstrated the flaw in this solution with his 1968 master work – the Neue Nationalgalerie in Berlin, a building that could only display most of its art treasures in the basement due to the lack of suitable accommodations for sunlight-sensitive art in the "flexible" main hall. In *Words and Buildings* (2000), Adrian Forty quotes James Sterling is as being "sick and tired of the boring, meaningless, non-committed, faceless flexibility and open-endedness of the present architecture (1984)."

The challenge before us is to design ambivalent space that is relieved of its ambivalence by our participation. Responsive technology may provide the means for converting a space that is ambivalent, and waiting for our collaboration, to restore it to univalence.

See also: **Betweeness • Functionalism • Indeterminate architecture**

Figure 9: Crown Hall

American pragmatism

Pragmatism insists that since our limited human efforts at inquiry can never achieve totality, we must settle for sufficiency, which is ultimately a practical rather than theoretical matter, so that prioritizing practical over theoretical reason is an inescapable part of the human condition. — Immanuel Kant

If it looks like a duck, quacks like a duck, waddles like a duck, it must be a duck. — popular American truism

The development of *American pragmatism* can be attributed to the "pioneer spirit" that came with the taming of the vast wilderness of eighteenth-century America. The romantic myth of the rugged and independent American cowboy on his horse smoking a Marlboro cigarette persists. Thoreau, Whitman, Roosevelt, and Wright come to mind when American cultural pragmatism is invoked. An interesting expression of *American pragmatism* can be found on the campus of Rice University, where Cesar Pelli designed Herring Hall (1984) to conform to the strictly mandated brick cladding, only to switch back to bare concrete as soon as the surface is no longer visible from the path through the campus (Figure 10). The final irony is that the building is a steel frame structure.

Today the archetypical "ugly American" is still a brash no-nonsense, all-business pragmatist. In the architecture business, *American pragmatism* translates into a singular desire for an "in your face" architecture that "works" at the level of cost and performance. The current globalized form of digitally based design practice suits the methods of the pragmatic architect. Building information modeling (BIM), driven by spreadsheets and other accounting methods, places emphasis on the performance of architecture bolstered by sophisticated and hidden "number crunching."

Form is at the mercy of the pragmatic parameters that the architect has released to the other members of the "integrated" team for insertion into the BIM. The architectural values that count above all have become cost, schedule, and function. If care is not taken to keep the team committed to a broader agenda, the digital design machine may swallow up the nascent cultural and humanistic concerns of a critical theory-based architectural discourse. Perhaps as the technology matures, it will eventually accept and value cultural and critical parameters as valid algorithms that reset the balance between positive and normative concerns. *American pragmatism*, as it spreads worldwide and matures, may still remain the underpinning of a sustainable, yet humanistic architecture.

See also: **Algorithm • Building information modeling: BIM • Form • Integrated practice • Machines •Parametric design • Pragmatism.**

Further sources: Broadbent (in Nesbitt 1996: 127) Jencks (2007: 210); Sharr (2007: 10)

Figure 10: Herring Hall

▌Anthropomorphism

The representation of human form. — *Oxford Dictionary of Philosophy*

The turrets of the house are the ears, the furnace is the stomach and the windows are, as usual, eyes. — Carl Jung

The anthropomorphic way, which humanizes the world and interprets it by way of analogy with our own bodies and our own wills, is still the aesthetic way; it is the basis for poetry, and is the foundation of architecture. — Geoffrey Scott

Drawing upon the human body as the inspiration for architectural form dates back to the ancient Egyptians. Vitruvius continued the tradition, when he documented in Book Three, Chapter one, the proper proportions for temples based on the human form. Most Renaissance critics, including Leonardo da Vinci, famously translated his prescription for ideal building proportions in drawings of the "Vitruvian man." Charles Jencks describes the importance of the human body metaphor to the Renaissance architect in *The Language of Post-Modern Architecture* (1977). Jencks also illustrates several examples of "face buildings." The apartment building illustrated in Figure 11 is unmistakably another overt face building.

The human body was inscribed both into plan and elevation of churches, and the metaphor was taken so seriously that Bernini was even criticized because his piazza for St Peter's resulted in a contorted figure with mangled arms. — Charles Jencks

In the search for acceptance, post-modern architects resorted to body metaphors that even bordered on the obscene. Stanley Tigerman's Daisy House (1976), which uses the almost literal form of the phallus as its floor plan, is perhaps the most extreme case. With the growing interest in biomimicry, combined with the form manipulations available today, the human body can now appear in the round. It may be the ultimate achievement of blobitecture.

Figure 11: Face building in Helsinki, Finland

See also: **Anthropomorphic (Archispeak)**
• **Biomimicry • Eroticism • Facadism •**
Morphogenic design •Nature • Phallocentrism •
Physiognomic properties

Further sources: Agrest (1993:173); Jencks (1995)

Aporia

A serious perplexity or insoluble problem.
— *Oxford Dictionary of Philosophy*

It is time to embrace, rather than try to resolve, the *aporias* associated with our human condition since the nineteenth-century.
— Alberto Pérez-Gómez

Aporia (or apory in English) simply means that there is a series of individually plausible statements that collectively form an inconsistent proposition. The term is from the Greek meaning "without passage." *Aporia,* and related concerns, go back to pre-Socratic times and have persisted throughout the history of philosophy, gaining renewed interest especially with Jacque Derrida and his followers in the twentieth century. The pervasiveness of *apories* throughout human inquiry has led skeptics, ancient and modern, to propose abandoning the entire cognitive enterprise. The aporetic method is associated with the Socratic method of raising problems without providing solutions. Even when there is some sense of a direction of inquiry that could yield results, the aporetic method requires that one assume the affectation of not knowing where to begin or what to say. The method persists up to the present, especially in the deconstruction of texts, which often uncovers their aporetic nature. Theodor Adorno, a founder of critical theory, refers to *aporia* in his discussion of utopia and order. He argues that utopia must be free of order, yet the banning of order becomes an order. With the declining interest in academic theory, and post-structuralist theory in particular, terms such as *aporia* will return to the obscurity they deserve. If this means there is a return to a form of twenty-first-century functionalism, then we must be once again aware of the pitfalls associated with hoping to resolve inconsistent and contradictory demands through reasoning. At least the aporetic method has shown us that this is seldom likely.

See also: **Critical theory • Deconstructivism (Archispeak) • Functionalism (Archispeak) • Post-structuralism (Archispeak)**

Architectonic

In philosophy: Architectonic studies the systematic structure of our knowledge. — *The Oxford Guide to Philosophy*

In biology: the arrangement, or pattern of arrangement, of cells in a body tissue, organ, or structure. — *Princeton's online dictionary*

Architects and their critics do not use the term *"architectonic"* – everyone else does. As with the term "architecture" itself, the widespread general use of the word has robbed it of its usefulness within architectural discourse. The populace has co-opted it to describe many everyday objects. The term now refers to high-end modern furniture and other household items that are simple, angular, and occasionally elegant (Figure 13). Thus, being *architectonic* is most associated with Bauhaus and mid-century modern styles. In most cases, being described as *architectonic* is considered elitist, and thus a high compliment. As architecture continues to evolve from the clean, angular forms of early twentieth-century modernism to the messy, blobular forms of the twenty-first century, will the popular understanding of *architectonic* follow suit? Will the Michelin Man eventually be considered *architectonic*? It is unlikely, as the term is well entrenched in other disciplines such as philosophy and biology. It will simply become more remote from architecture.

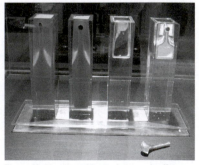

Figure 12: Alessi's architectonic tea and coffee towers: Wiel Arets

See also: **Architecture • Beauty • Blob architecture (Archispeak) • Blobitecture**

Archi-philosophy

Philosophy: Thinking about thinking. — *Oxford Guide to Philosophy*

... due to Peter Eisenman's links with philosophers such as Derrida and Rajchman, there is a resulting false suggestion of projective arch-philosophy. — Arie Graafland

A collection of mostly French, German, and Italian philosophical tracts,
were introduced into the American Academy through departments
of comparative literature and were immediately recognized by all as
a wondrous new mode of contemporary thought. In Europe, Jacques
Derrida and Gilles Deleuze were philosophers, but in America they
became theorists. — Michael Speaks

What constitutes architectural philosophy or "archi-philosophy"? The
answer is not an easy one. Michael Speaks describes classical
architecture as philosophy based, modern architecture as manifesto
based, architectural post-modernism as theory based, and the current
era in architecture as intelligence based. Thus, the era of architectural
philosophy was relatively short, from approximately 1966 to 1990.

It is probably a good thing that the marriage did not last, as philosophers
and architects appeared to be a dubious pairing. After all, philosophers have
less to lose if they are wrong. There now appears to be a backlash against
the dense and obtuse one-way dialogue that occurred when scholarly
architects attempted to mine the writings of academic philosophers for
nuggets of architectural grounding. It was an awkward process, as evidenced
by the difficulty that even a fan of architecture like Jacques Derrida had in
collaborating with his admirer, Peter Eisenman. Fortunately, architectural
thinkers in the twenty-first century appear to have little patience for the
esoteric musing of European philosophers, except perhaps for the down-
to-earth prescriptions of Gilles Deleuze and Felix Guattari.

In the twenty-first century, archi-philosophy is being replaced by "plain
talk" intended to restore the direct relevance of theory to architectural
practice. Archi-philosophy of linguistics, and its post-structuralism, is
replaced by archi-biology and archi-topology, among other "ologies." The
deconstruction of archi-philosophy was needed in order to provide the
freedom that has been accorded the twenty-first-century designer. It helped
to wipe the slate clean, which was encumbered by classical, modernist,
and post-modernist rules and rituals. However, despite a clean slate, there
still seems to be some room for philosophy "lite" in the broadest sense.
After all, philosophy, even demoted to "theory," is still the business of
thinking about how we understand the world, and thus ponder the deeper
and wider implication of our actions as an architect. This is particularly
important at this time, as we no longer have the luxury of contemplating
the nature of meaning. The challenge before us now is the contemplation
of the meaning of nature. As we spiral towards the inevitable exhaustion of
the planet, architects are reluctantly embracing the utilitarian philosophy
of "do what we have to" in order to survive as the human race. Thus, the
new archi-theory is perhaps that of utilitarianism and pragmatism.

Utilitarianism claims that our obligations depend on an impersonal
assessment of the consequences of our actions, and if we have a
choice between doing more for strangers or less for ourselves and/or
our friends and relations, we must give preference to the strangers.
— The Oxford Guide to Philosophy

See also: **American pragmatism • Ethics • Post-structuralism (Archispeak)**

Further sources: Deleuze (in Ballantyne 2007: 15); Scruton (1979: 266)

Architectural determinism

We shape our buildings, thereafter they shape us.
— Sir Winston Churchill

The reason for architecture is to encourage people ... to behave, mentally and physically, in ways they had previously thought impossible. — Cedric Price

... the city of Le Corbusier, the former city of deliverance is everyday found increasingly inadequate. — Colin Rowe and Fred Koetter (1976), *Collage City*

Figure 13: Downtown Chicago

Architectural determinism involves the belief that there is a direct cause/ effect relationship between architecture and human behavior. In its most extreme form it has been called social engineering. *Architectural determinism* is one of the most significant miscalculations of the modern movement. Deterministic design was not confined to architecture. The modern city was seen as deliverance from the ills of the medieval city by changing the behavior of its inhabitants. Le Corbusier and Frank Lloyd Wright's sanitized and suburbanized high-rise visionary megaschemes were hoped to be the answer. Sprawling American cities, modeled on Corbusier's vision, have occasional downtown high-rises, but with virtually no one living in them (Figure 12).

The most striking example of the failure of these social engineering projects was the ill-fated Pruitt Igoe development in St Louis. It was modeled after the Unite´ de Habitation by Le Corbusier, with skip floor elevator stops, and wide dark corridors that became indefensible settings for undesirable activity – rather than the positive social interaction spaces that they were intended to be. Charles Jencks marks the demolition of the Pruitt Igoe housing project as the moment of death of modern architecture, a gross oversimplification that he exploits for dramatic effect. Although the hope that architecture could directly lessen social and psychological ills has faded, the value of architecture as the setting for human life remains. In the twenty-first century, the dominant goal of architecture seems to be to entertain. Perhaps the determined ability to shock, amaze, amuse, and inspire through aggressive, digitally produced form can be regarded as the architectural determinism of the day. Somehow it doesn't seem as noble as housing workers.

See also: **Behavior and environment • Form • Functionalism (Archispeak)**

Architectural positivism   ■

Positivism seeks to discover the immutable universal laws that govern the universe by using observation, experimentation and calculation.
— *Dictionary of Critical Theory*

We can see a clear relationship between the Modern Movement's desire to find its architectural forms in the material "facts" of the design problem and the Logical Positivist desire to find its scientific truths in the "facts" of empirical sense. — Mark Gelernter

After the orthodox Modern Movement became discredited in the 1960s, it was generally agreed that positivism was a naïve and incomplete way to seek knowledge. The rejection of pure positivism created a vacuum. The alternative that emerged may have been just as naïve. The reactive rise of subjectivity as a legitimate source of truth in architecture was bolstered by architectural phenomenology and related spiritual quests that aspired to know the immeasurable and unknowable. The project was to describe a "quality without a name." Inevitably that description robbed the quality of its un-namable quality.

In the twenty-first century, the anti empiricist approach of the late twentieth century is being threatened by the intrusion of the computer into the design process. There is once again the danger of a "tyranny of the measurable." To feed the many algorithms that must be scripted to drive the parametric modeling system, hard numerical data is needed, as the computer tolerates fuzzy feelings poorly. These early years of the digital design revolution may mark the unintended return of *architectural positivism*. Subjective, indescribable input need not apply. Beauty, elegance, and the sublime take a back seat to functional and environmental performance. Engineering triumphs over architecture; form follows facts, not essences. Fortunately, once the architect's digital tools have evolved beyond their current beta stage, we may once again be able to insert the entire architect into the design process.

See also: **Algorithm • Beauty • Parametric design • Phenomenology • Sublime**

Further sources: Agrest (1993: 125); Colquhoun (2002: 12); Gelernter (1995: 251); Perez-Gomez (1984: 6)

Architectural presentness   ■

Presentness is grace. — Michael Fried

An architecture that for the sake of presentness renders itself uninhabitable and in this respect comes to resemble a ruin – an anti architectural architecture. — Karsten Harries

Michael Benedikt, in *For an Architecture of Reality* (1987), describes the quality of *architectural presentness* as equivalent to stage presence. He postulates that architecture achieves this power through honesty about itself that is timeless. He probably felt compelled to produce the publication because for a time in the twentieth century we lost sight of an honest *architectural presentness*.

The project of post-modern architecture required that the narrative embedded in the architecture be intellectually decoded, rather than felt at a visceral level. Presentness was lost to a preoccupation with striving for meaning through mining the past. Phenomenology came to the rescue, with its concern for the gut-level, immediate experience of the timeless moment. Presentness once again became a central concern, as it had been throughout the classical period in architecture. As expressed by Harries above, an architecture of presentness is not driven by a concern for function. As a result, it may more resemble a monument or a work of sculpture than what is traditionally considered to be architecture. This is amply demonstrated by the strength of Cincinnati's Lois and Richard Rosenthal Center for Contemporary Art by Zaha Hadid (2003) (Figure 14).

The current crop of digitally produced blobitecture has this quality of *architectural presentness*. It is unapologetic for its bold shapes and colors. It has stage presence, even if it may be somewhat intimidating and even unapproachable.

The presentist maintains that only presently existing objects and presently occurring events are real, thereby excluding from reality past and future objects and events. — *The Oxford Guide to Philosophy*

See also: **Blob architecture (Archispeak)** • **Blobitecture** • **Meaning** • **Phenomenology (Archispeak)** •**Postmodernism (Archispeak)**

Further sources: Gadamer (in Leach 1997: 134); Harries (1998: 216, 251)

Figure 14: Cincinnati Art Museum

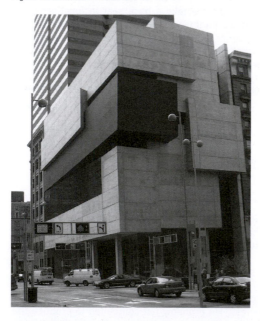

Architectural psychology   ∎

Architectural psychology, environmental psychology, man/woman (people)–environment studies, human factors of design, or the ontoperivantic aspects of psychostructural environics, call the study what you may, has been concerned primarily over the past 40 years in making better and more humane environments. These preoccupations also have strong and varied undertones, and appeal to the social and behavioral sciences, including psychology, sociology, neurophysiology, geography, and anthropology.

Prior to 1970, there were very few books from mainstream psychology or sociology which designers found inspiring or relevant to the practice of their profession. Those that existed included: Ervin Goffman's *Behavior in Public Places* (1963); Richard Gregory's *Eye and Brain* (1966); Edward Hall's *The Hidden Dimension* (1966); and Michael Argyle's The *Psychology of Interpersonal Behavior* (1967).

A body of specialized knowledge in *architectural psychology* began to evolve in the 1970s. Important publications included Proshansky, Ittelson, and Rivlin's book, *Environmental Psychology*, David Canter's *Psychology for Architects*, James Gibson's *Ecological Approach to Visual Perception*, Neil Prak's *Perception of the Visual Environment*, Charles Moore's *Body Memory and Architecture* (Bloomer and Moore 1977), Raymond Lifchez's *Rethinking Architecture*, and Byron Mikellides' *Architecture for People*.

In addition to the above books, there have been many conference papers published, as well as scholarly articles in the psychological and the architectural journals on *architectural psychology*. Primary journals in the field include the *Journal of Environmental Psychology, Environment & Behavior*, and the *Architectural Psychology Newsletters*. To support the varied academic community involved in the development of *architectural psychology*, international organizations such as IAPS, EDRA and PAPER were established.

In the fields of urban design and city planning, Kevin Lynch's *The Image of the City* (1960), and Terence Lee's work on mental mapping applications were significant landmarks of what was to follow. Defensible space and territoriality also became important concepts in urban design and architecture due to the pioneering work of Nico Tinburgen, John Calhoun, Robert Ardrey, and Konrad Lorenz. Later, Oscar Newman and Alice Coleman made significant contributions to new concepts of defensible space, surveillance, and vandal-proof architecture.

In the 1970s, schools of architecture introduced the subject in various guises ranging from human aspects of design, to courses in *architectural psychology*, or as part of history and theory. Other developments in education included Terence Lee and David Canter offering the first MSc course in environmental psychology outside the context of a school of architecture at the University of Surrey, and in Lund, Sweden the first Department of Theoretical and Applied Aesthetics was formed.

When we look at architectural practice, a considerable amount of this research has gone unnoticed. Some architects are skeptical about its value in design (Figure 15), and as a consequence, design awards are given primarily for imagination and originality at the expense of the users' health and wellbeing. Niels Prak's 1984 book *Architects, the Noted and the Ignored* provides us with a useful analysis of the self-image and self-esteem of the professional as opposed to the user. Despite the current emphasis on architectural technology, a growing number of established and up-and-coming architects with a conscience are offering us hope for the future when they combine contemporary parametric, digital, "green" design with a concern for people's needs. BM

See also: **Aesthetics • Behavior and environment • Functionalism • Proxemics (Archispeak) • Psychological needs • Universal design • User • Wayfinding**

Figure 15: Psychology and Architecture depart

Architectural theory

My contention is that "theory" – the attempt to decide architectural right and wrong on purely intellectual grounds – is precisely one of the roots of our mischief. — Sir Geoffrey Scott, 1924

Most of what is called theory in architecture is either hypothesis incapable of being tested, or is a model of such simplicity that it lacks explanatory power. — Paul-Alan Johnson

Theory is relatively new to architecture, as it only emerged in the second half of the twentieth century. Prior to that, classical architecture was based upon canons, or established rules. In rejection of these classical rules, modern architects published dogmatic manifestos that could seldom be considered theoretical. Often they were recipes for the making of an architecture that interjected political and social agendas into value positions about the honesty of the materiality of the result. Today most of these manifestos seem naïve, and even silly.

In the 1970s and 1980s, following the era of modern architecture, there was a relatively brief period of post-modern thought in architecture. During that time, theory came into its own as an academic discipline, particularly at America's northeastern ivy-league schools of architecture. Leading gurus included Peter Eisenman at Yale University, and Bernard Tschumi at Columbia. Unfortunately, much of what was produced remained scattered "theory for theory's sake." The suspension of the MIT Press architectural theory publication *Assemblage* in 2000 marked the end to this era of rampant *architectural theory*.

In contemporary "critical" and "green" discourse, architectural theory is becoming clarified and redefined as "intelligencing" (Michael Speaks). Chatter, tweets, blogs, and so on have been added as fodder for the intelligence needed to design well. The flood of "chatter" is so immediate and overwhelming that the task of mining useful intelligence from the informational deluge requires that artificial intelligence filters be applied to the incoming noise. Making design sense of the received intelligence will still require the intervention of an architect, even if the cyber machine does most of the heavy lifting. Does it mean that the era of reflection is over, as there is now only time for reacting? That may be a problem, as architectural theory may be an important beacon we can't afford to ignore in our hurry-up-and-perform world.

Architectural theory is no discipline. — Mark Linder

See also: **Artificial intelligence • Classicism • Intelligence • Manifestos**

Further sources: Colquhoun (2002: 11); Harries (1998: 286); Lang (1987: 12); Scruton (1979: 4)

Architecture   ▮

A bicycle shed is a building; Lincoln cathedral is a piece of architecture. — Sir Nikolaus Pevsner (1943)

There is no architecture without a concept or an idea. Concept – not form, as some would suggest – is what distinguishes architecture from mere building. — Bernard Tschumi

Architecture is a word that has spread beyond the boundaries of the profession and into the public realm. Everyone who makes something happen is now referred to as an architect. There are more Google hits for *architecture*, as it relates to computer architecture, than for architecture – the building design profession. *Architecture* has even been transformed into a verb. One can now "architect."

Today, an architect is one who manages information, designs web sites, and decides foreign policy –in short someone who organizes things, and does it within an ever more complex and interconnected global field. — Bernard Tschumi

Students enroll in schools of architecture not knowing exactly what it is. Some still think it is producing AutoCAD drawings of houses; others have unrealistic hopes of being the next Frank Gehry or another starchitect du jour.

Whereas "Architecture" may be a term lost to the exclusive use of the profession, the term "architect" is jealously guarded. To protect the turf of the licensed architect, there is a legal definition of "architect" in most jurisdictions. In the United States and Canada, only those who have been issued an official government architectural license, based on educational and other qualifications, are permitted to call themselves "architects." The legislated goal is to protect the health, safety, and welfare of the public. The system is flawed. Frank Lloyd Wright was not qualified to be an architect in Florida, even though he was near the end of his long and productive career. Tadao Ando, a self-taught world-class architect, may not call himself an architect in most US jurisdictions, even though he has been awarded the American Institute of Architects Gold Medal, along with similar honors from France, Great Britain, Turkey, Japan, and so on. He has even been awarded the Academy Award for architecture – the Pritzker. The architect, as a local legal entity, may become obsolete with the growth of globalized team practice. *Architecture*, as distinct from engineering, may follow suit, as we follow our current pragmatic, digitally driven, problem-solving, green building agenda.

For the general public and students of architecture, the term *architecture* will remain without a single, simple definition. Its meaning will continue to be variable, relative to the purpose of its usage.

See also: **American pragmatism • Ethics • Starchitect**

Further sources: Antoniades (1990: 288); Ballantyne (2002: 11, 174); Borden (2000: 6); Gausa (2003: 56); Harries (1998: 12, 214); Johnson (1994: 75, 117); Sharr (2007: 37)

Armature

Any means of bracing or stiffening a weak part. A framework used by a sculptor to support a figure being modeled in a plastic material
— *Webster's Unabridged Dictionary*

Architecture should cut the third-party process and address itself directly to the manufacturers who elaborate (produce) the armatures and surfaces of the project right from the design process.
— Winka Dubbeldam

In a general sense, an *armature* is anything that provides an underlying structure on which to attach the primary material(s) of an assembly. It is a common term in sculpture and increasingly in architecture. Metaphorically, *armature* can refer to anything that provides something to hang things on to – a framework. In cutting-edge architecture the *armature* has replaced the "frame" as the support system for the non-Euclidean structures associated with digital blobitecture. The post and lintel have become a curved strut. Pliable surface materials, such as the micro-thin metal skins favored by the current generation of blob designers, require complex armatures to support and smooth the non-Euclidean soft forms that bubble up. In the now iconic Experience Music Project (EMP) by Frank O. Gehry (2000), the armatures

are exposed to the public (Figure 16). As demonstrated by the EMP, the individual armature pieces can be unique, unlike the repetition preferred in the design of old-fashioned steel beam grids. This is possible due to the CNC tools used for the design and manufacture of the complex three-dimensional shapes.

Once the term *armature* becomes a popular word in general architectural discourse, its loss of meaning through overuse is only a matter of time. The following statement by Thom Mayne evidences this devaluation; "These

Figure 16: EMP armatures

armatures became part of a larger generative fabric that departed from conventional construction techniques." He was referring to door handles.

See also: **Blob architecture (Archispeak) • Blobitecture • Fabric architecture**

Artificial intelligence (AI)   ∎

Recently, computer researchers in architecture ... have attempted to develop ... algorithms of design that try to assimilate design with artificial intelligence systems. — Paul-Alan Johnson (1994)

Artificial intelligence is the effort to cyber-replicate the human mind. It generated great interest when it began in the late 1950s, including the establishment of several research institutes, most notably at MIT. It also spawned science fiction stories and movies about self-learning and self-replicating machines that eventually destroy humankind as an inferior, parasitic life form.

Despite its promising start, and subsequent omnipresent and unnoticed success in many facets of contemporary society, *artificial intelligence* has only recently started to have a significant impact on architectural design. Building information modeling (BIM) is increasingly employing AI applications as it evolves into a mature technology. The implications for architectural design are profound. As the machine acquires human-like reasoning ability, it may supplant much of what the architect is still tasked to do, including creative problem solving and the generation of form. Currently, architects and other members of the integrated practice team provide the algorithms and parameter inputs to the BIM. Eventually, with the increased integration of AI, the computer will self-generate many of its inputs. No one can predict what will happen then. We are already using AI extensively in our day-to-day activities without realizing it. It is in the background, toiling away to allow us to search rapidly on the Internet, or to shape our database profiles maintained by Amazon, and the data-mining activities of every other large-scale retailer. *Artificial intelligence* is a major tool in the arsenal of America's Homeland Security operations and other covert spying efforts. Perhaps even practice will one day consist mostly of AI-generated architecture, as design increasingly relies upon intelligence and algorithmic design. Without our notice, AI tools will surreptitiously replace the critical functions traditionally performed by architects. Has it already happened?

See also: **Associative design • Building information modeling: BIM • Expert systems • Integrated practice • Parametric design**

Associative design   ∎

Associative design is based on "parameters" (variables) and "constraints." While the "parameter" defines the values of the elements, a "constraint" defines the relation between them, thus dictating their behavior. Associative parametric software has so far mainly been used to produce and construct amorphous forms.
— Dr. Ami Ran

Associative design is an emerging computer-based design technique. It moves parametric design to the next level. The Berlage Institute in Rotterdam has been conducting a studio in associative design, and by default, has emerged as a leader in the utilization of associative design. It has been exploring the potential for *associative design* as a technique for the automated generation of multiple planning possibilities. It is essentially a brainstorming technique using a cybernetic brain. Much like the 1970s Zwicky box that evaluated all permutations and combinations, *associative design* is comprehensively analytical. As each alternative is generated, a formal, digitally based evaluation system is applied to "score" it. The system is inefficient in that most alternatives are not worthy of evaluation, but the computer does not care. The danger in the system is that the measures of performance must be carefully conceived, and relative weights must be applied to each parameter as they foretell the results. Another difficulty inherent in the *associative design* process is the assignment of quantities to unquantifiable aspects of a design. Also, each criterion function, parameter weighting, and aggregation routine must be carefully scrutinized as they are often poorly expressed or manipulated to ensure a desired outcome – a self-fulfilling prophecy. Not since the Design Methods movement in the 1970s has the design of an evaluation system been so explicit.

As we incorporate *associative design* into our design routines, and thus move ever more into the unfamiliar world of the logic of parametric building information models, cyber-challenged architects will be rendered ever more mute and thus out of the "do" loop. Their fate will be in the hands of the more computer-savvy members of the so-called integrated project team. Eventually they must adapt or step aside.

See also: **Building information modeling: BIM • Constraints • Integral design • Parametric design**

Atopia

A society without territorial borders – a no-place. — Vittorio Gregotti

Principle of oriented atopia; that is; principles of settlement based on something other than the idea of place. — Vittorio Gregotti

The creation of "place" has been a central concern of architectural design for most of the twentieth century. Despite the modest efforts by architects, the spread of *atopias* has been unabated. It has taken many forms. Cities such as Las Vegas have aggressively pursued the creation of an everyplace that is no-place (Figure 17). The endless suburban sprawl of most American cities is another example of *atopia*. The same fast food joints, gas stations, motels, and strip malls, along bland suburban commercial corridors make them indistinguishable from each other.

The entire World Wide Web may be considered an *atopia*. With the viral proliferation of social networks such as Facebook, the entire concept of a society has been rendered placeless. Another atopical development is the growth of multi-territorial corporate entities such as the mega banks and PepsiCo, that have no place associations, but rather claim everyplace as their place. We have become more aware of these "too large to fail" entities due to the current worldwide recession, caused by the world financial system – a system with no territory of its own. Thus the twenty-first century is promising to be a period of redefinition of place as the place of no place and everyplace – the real is becoming the virtual, place has become extra-geographical. The world is de-territorialized, as predicted by Gilles Deleuze. The "Nowhere Man" in the Beatles song is the twenty-first-century man.

Post-modern hyperspace has finally succeeded in transcending the capacities of the individual human body to locate itself, to organize its immediate surroundings perceptually, and to cognitively map its position in a mappable external world. — Fredric Jameson

See also: **Deterritorialization/reterritorialization** • **Globalization** • **Heterotopia** • **Hyperspace**

Further sources: Gregotti (1996: 75)

Figure 17: Luxor Hotel and Casino, Las Vegas

Aura   ▌

An invisible atmosphere supposedly arising from and surrounding a person or thing. — *Webster's Unabridged Dictionary*

I have tried to identify a condition in architecture that resists interpretation, a condition I have referred to as an aura or a "presentness." The architectural *aura* involves the eye and the body differently than does a written text. — Peter Eisenman

Familiar to the eighteenth-century English picturesque architect, the term *aura* had little usage until the media theorist Walter Benjamin reintroduced the concept of *aura* in the early twentieth century to describe the effect on the viewer of traditional art objects. He concluded that *aura* arises from the unconscious understanding of the significant historical, cultural, and personal aspects of a place or object. Other than Peter Eisenman's use of the term, *aura* has not become a part of the architectural lexicon, even though it can refer to an indefinable experience of a place. Jacques Derrida, on the other hand, has described the follies in Bernard Tschumi's Parc de la Villette in terms of *aura*. Perhaps its mystical, paranormal connotations have kept it out of the conversation for the rest of us. One would expect a phenomenologist to employ the term, as it is primarily describing a feeling. In contrast to the lack of interest from architecture, there is considerable interest in the creation of aura in the design of gaming and virtual reality. This is not surprising, as in the pre-virtual world, descriptions of *aura* were often used to create a dramatic atmosphere in literature. Victorian romance novels led the way.

It was a hazy sunrise in August. The denser nocturnal vapors, attacked by the warm beams, were dividing and shrinking into isolated fleeces within hollow ... — Thomas Hardy, *Tess of the D'Urbervilles* (1891)

As architecture evolves beyond the current preoccupation with shape, skin, and environmental pragmatics, perhaps the creation of building aura will return as a design parameter, as it was with the Gothic cathedral.

See also: **Absence/presence • Uncanny – unheimlich • Virtual reality (Archispeak)**

Authenticity

Living in full acknowledgement of our finitude is the key to being authentic or rather the key to authentic being. — Martin Heidegger

... mythicizing – classicist postmodern architects inevitably find themselves at one remove from any authentic reality ...
— Michael Benedikt

There is no place for authenticity because we do not know any more what authenticity means. We do not have any examples or definitions.
— Manuel Gausa

In our media-saturated times the effort to maintain an unspoiled and authentic culture seems futile. In our world of the knock-off Gucci and Rolex, where imitation is the sincerest form of profitability, can *authenticity* in architecture exist, and if so, will we know it when we see it?

Clearly, any individual act of architecture has become so contaminated by outside influences that it is most authentic when it is created as a mere building, unselfconscious and unspoiled by design affectations and foreign influences. Archetypical elements such as roof, wall, floor, and door, when derived from longstanding design habits, can become an authentic folk architecture. This may be the closest thing left to *authenticity* in architecture. However, deliberately designed folk architecture easily becomes Disneyesque.

Phenomenological experiences of the authentic have been subverted in our hyped world. Popular culture has become too popular. Umberto Eco's 1986 essay, *Travel in Hyperreality*, describes almost all of Florida as inauthentic. It is a trend that is spreading with each "theme city" (Figure 18). The understanding of *authenticity* may need to be revised. For example, is a virtual world authentic? As the Sony Wii draws us increasingly into the virtual world as an active participant, is the interaction authentic as we swat the virtual tennis racket in our living room?

Perhaps we should abandon all efforts at trying to be authentic. The very act of trying renders the result contrived, and thus inauthentic.

See also: **Allusionism • Archetypical image (Archispeak) • Architecture • Caricature • Cliché •Disneyfication • Fictional architecture • Hyperrealism (Archispeak) • Myth • Naked architecture • Phenomenology**

Further sources: Leach (in Ballantyne 2002: 96); Sharr (2007: 103)

Figure 18: New York, New York, Casino Hotel, Las Vegas

Autonomous architect

The notion that the architect is an autonomous professional, a sort of solitary artistic and engineering genius, has been a myth from the beginning. A work of architecture is also not autonomous. Globalization, multicultural practice, and our media-saturated times, make it impossible for autonomous architecture to be produced. Encumbered by client and user inputs, codes and regulations, political and social contexts, cost limitations, public opinion, and so on, the architect is a highly regulated servant to the particulars of each project. Howard Roark, Ayn Rand's autonomous hero architect in her homage to selfhood, *The Fountainhead* (1943), has misled many students who enroll in schools of architecture in order to become the independent genius starchitect responsible for single-handedly producing autonomous architecture.

The starchitect media phenomenon that places all of the credit for published work on the shoulders of one individual perpetuates the myth of the *autonomous architect*. The starchitect's vision only becomes a reality due to the backroom support team of architects, engineers, technicians, and others, that comprise the starchitect's firm, plus the subservient architectural "firm of record." They are the enablers that make the illusion possible. Essentially the starchitect is the front person. The team learns how to place the starchitect's signature on the work. Thus, with the complicity of the media, the public is led into thinking of it as the work of one individual. As the profession moves ever more into integrated practice and the reliance on building information modeling, the myth of the *autonomous architect* may fade away. Already most newer firms are avoiding the use of the names of the firm's partners as the name of the practice. Future Systems, Foreign Office Architects, UN Studio, Asymptote, Fat, and so on are examples of the firms that are resisting the temptation of promoting a starchitect as their brand. It also sends the message that the production of architecture is a team sport, and not the creation of the genius of an *autonomous architect*.

See also: **Branding • Building information modeling: BIM • Globalization • Integrated practice • Starchitect**

Further sources: Johnson (1994: 182); Vidler (2008: 58)

Babel Tower

If the Tower of Babel furnishes architecture with a paradigm, this paradigm carries a warning: as we all know, the tower could not be finished – the center would not hold. By confusing the builders' languages and scattering them abroad... God inflicted on them the fate they had sought to avoid. — Karsten Harries

(Burj Khalifa) the anorexic Tower of Babel that does reach up into the heavens. — Aaron Betsky

In the *Tower of Babel* fable, Noah's descendents were attempting to build a tower that reached the heavens. They were unable to complete the project because they were eventually unable to communicate with each other. It was God's punishment for their impertinence. The story was unclear about how high they would have to go to succeed. We may find out, as we seem to be still trying to build buildings to reach the heavens. One wonders what the punishment will be this time. Despite the wake-up call of the Twin Towers, the race to be the tallest has recently been on the upswing. The current leader is SOM's Burj Khalifa tower, reported to be over 2,650 feet, or half a mile tall. It appears that Frank Lloyd Wright's mythical mile-high tower may be a reality yet.

Perhaps another aspect of the Babel myth also bears heeding. It is an appropriate cautionary tale for the building information modeling (BIM) generation. Everyone working together on the same model from different professional values, cultures, and jargons could result in the reenactment of the communication breakdown that occurred at Babel. As large, multinational project efforts shift from being spearheaded by American firms to being locally managed and directed, the challenge of overcoming the cultural and language barriers will grow. Babel reincarnated as BIM could cause a reassessment of the process of twenty-first-century integrated practice, including the consideration of a shared international language, and rules and procedures of practice.

See also: **Building information modeling: BIM • Globalization • Hyperbuilding • Integrated practice**

Further sources: Harries (1998: 140)

Banal

I like boring things. — Andy Warhol

Many people like suburbia. By dismissing Levittown, modern architects ... reject whole sets of dominant social patterns because they don't like the architectural consequences.
— Robert Venturi in *Learning from Las Vegas* (1977)

In our search for the unique we all make or find the same things; desiring en masse the authentic and the exceptional, it all turns out banal. — Winy Maas

Unoriginal and commonplace, the very definition of *banal*, is the fate of most buildings. The background building is ignored by the critics but is an important and necessary work of architecture. *Banal* architecture is the background that is needed in order for foreground buildings to shine as landmarks. Every jewel needs a setting. *Banal* does not necessarily imply bad. As Steven Izenour and the Venturis famously proclaimed in *Learning From Las Vegas* (1977), there is value in the ugly and the ordinary as a reflection of the truth of the American suburban condition – the low-density sprawl of Levittown. Banality reigns. It is familiar, and thus comfortable, for most of its occupants. The desire to live in the same architecture as your neighbor is universal. As the appreciation of high-design architecture is still the domain of the initiated, everyone else is perplexed. The problem became most evident during the era of modern architecture. Modern international-style buildings, hailed by critics at the time, now form the *banal* backgrounds of industrialized cities around the world (Figure 19). Unfortunately, it is hard to imagine that the colorful and aggressively foreground blob building of the more recent past will become *banal*. They are more likely to simply become sad reminders of a short-lived mannerist, neo-baroque, pop architectural style. Like the glitz

and glitter of 1970s Las Vegas, they will be regarded as pathetic and dated as they become trite and age badly. As "green" building becomes the norm, the *banal*, modest, background building may become respectable once again. After all, the dominant architectural agenda will be to humbly do the right thing and not necessarily to impress. It may ultimately be the age of banality in architecture in a good way.

See also: **Blob architecture (Archispeak) • Blobitecture • Cliché • Fabric architecture • Green building (Archispeak) • Heterotopia • Ugly and ordinary**

Figure 19: Toronto in 1974: Banal modernism

Baroque   ∎ **B**

....**defined as "complex forms characterized by grotesqueness, extravagance, or flamboyancy" describes ... Frank O. Gehry's Experience Music Project ...** — Joseph Rosa

The affinity between the baroque age and our own goes deeper than the formal complexity common to both ... — Herbert Muschamp

The *baroque* is most associated with the historical style in architecture that occurred in Europe in the seventeenth and eighteenth centuries. The Renaissance baroque style consisted of exuberant decoration, expansive curvaceous forms, undulating façades, large-scale sweeping vistas, and spatially complex compositions that often employed ovals in plan. The *baroque* space was carved and subtractive, rather than assembled and additive.

In reaction to the visual excesses of the baroque style of architecture, plus the movement towards rationalism in all things, the neoclassical and gothic revival styles that followed the *baroque* eventually resulted in the most extreme anti-baroque style of all – modern architecture. The dogmatic modern architecture style did not become popular, as the humanity and richness of the baroque persisted in the public appetite.

Recently, the term *baroque* has become understood as transcending a particular style and denoting instead an ideology that rejects the paucity of unadorned, rectilinear form and space, and thus the modern "international style" of architecture.

Some of the above characteristics of historical *baroque* architecture, and urban planning, could be describing the current crop of blob and fold architecture. Digitally generated architecture facilitates curvature and spatial complexity (Figure 20). It is making the task of creating *baroque* architecture easier than it was in the Renaissance. Perhaps in our never-ending need for labels, this installment of architectural style could become known as the twenty-first-century neo-baroque.

See also: **Blob architecture (Archispeak)** • **Blobitecture** • **Digital architecture** • **Fold**

Figure 20: Greg Lynn: Alessi coffee and tea set

▌Beauty

It is amazing how complete the delusion is that beauty is goodness.
— Leo Tolstoy

Nothing is really beautiful unless it is useless; everything useful is ugly, for it expresses a need, and the needs of man are ignoble and disgusting ... — Theophile Gautier (1825)

"Functionalism" has many forms. Its most popular form is the aesthetic theory that true beauty in architecture consists in the adapting of form to function. — Roger Scruton

In Eisenman's work and in other recent theory, beauty is reemerging in the context of opposition to the sublime (grotesque). — Kate Nesbitt

The word beauty remains proscribed in modern professional debate today only as a vestige of Puritanism.
— Inaki Abalos and Juan Herreros

Since the Renaissance, architects have been uncomfortable with the burden of beauty. During the twentieth century, it was barely mentioned and seldom embraced. Louis Kahn was one of the only prominent twentieth-century architects to dare to mention the word. His dictum: "Design is not making beauty, beauty emerges from selection, affinities, integration, love" stands as a recipe for modernist beauty. With Venturi's legitimization of the "ugly and the ordinary," the burden of beauty was lessened. Perhaps thankfully *beauty* is now seen as old-fashioned and dispensable; an obstacle to the perception of the more profoundly moving aesthetic values of the sublime and the uncanny.

Today's architectural students have little interest in qualities such as *beauty* and elegance. They regard these as "old school," out of step with the aesthetic that celebrates pseudo grunge styling, alongside an emerging ecological fashion movement in architecture towards retro "junkstyle." The popularity of anti-beauty merchandise like the youth-oriented anti-aerodynamic "cube" automobiles is testament to the sea change that has occurred in consumer goods (Figure 21).

Influenced by the curved-form opportunities provided by digital design tools, the language associated with the search for architectural form has evolved from the traditional terms "*beauty*, scale, and proportion" to "smooth, supple, and morphed." The leader in the current design revolution is Apple. Its "designed" versus "engineered" product line has started to influence the appearance of all of the other consumer electronics products. Such staid companies, as Dell, Samsung, and Nokia, have even discovered color. It is a brave new world.

Beauty... withers under the edicts of today's aging architectural revolutionaries who man the review boards and have achieved aesthetic certainty.
— Robert Venturi's parting words in *Learning from Las Vegas* (1977)

See also: **Aesthetics • Elegance (Archispeak) • Junkspace • Purism • Sublime • Ugly and ordinary • Uncanny – unheimlich**

Further sources: Abalos (in Gausa 2003: 79); Hale (2000: 52); Harries (1998: 229); Johnson (1994: 402); Scruton (1979: 25) Vittamo (in Leach 1997: 151)

Figure 21: Boxy car

▌Behavior and environment

Behavioral science research provides the basis for environmental designers and clients asking ... what patterns of behavior presently exist and what ones should exist... — Jon Lang

The science of studying the effects of environment on behavior is known variously as environmental psychology, man–environment relations (MER) or environment/behavior studies (EBS). It was based on the 1950s research findings of B. F. Skinner and other early behavioral psychologists. Environmental psychology was a growth industry for architectural academics in the 1960s and 1970s. Some schools even switched their program names from "architecture" to "environmental design." UC Berkley was a leader in that regard. There was the promise of architectural research becoming a legitimate social science – or at the very least providing scientific credibility to architectural decision making. The project of MER was to improve the behavior of the participant in the environment in an act of architectural determinism. The effort was doomed, as it was based on a simplistic model of our relationship to our environment. The stimulus/response causal relationship that was assumed was naïve. It turned out that the human species is not as easy to condition as Pavlov's dogs. Behaviorism was the precursor to functionalism in psychology, just as MER was the scientific side of functionalism in architecture. Even though remnants of MER still exist through groups such as the US-based Environmental Design Research Association (EDRA), they are a fringe group with little audience other than themselves. However, with reawakened twenty-first-century interest in building performance, concern for the effective and efficient human use of space may resurrect the study of *behavior and environment*. It is to be hoped that this time around the effort will be better integrated into the culture of architectural production. The promise of a responsive architecture that is capable of adapting to changing environmental and human needs may spur on a renewed interest in the relationship between *behavior and environment*. In the future architecture won't try to change behavior, but rather be changed by behavior.

See also: **Architectural determinism** • **Event space** • **Evidence-based design** • **Responsive architecture**

Further sources: Lang (1987: 213)

▌Betweenness

Traditional oppositions between structure and decoration, abstraction and figuration, figure and ground, form and function could be dissolved. Architecture could begin an exploration of the "between."
— Peter Eisenman

The Middle Path; it gives vision, gives knowledge, and leads to calm, to insight, to enlightenment. — Buddhism's Noble Eightfold Path

The concept of *betweenness* harkens back to Hegel's dialectic. *Betweenness* could be considered analogous to synthesis – the mediation between thesis and antithesis. Instead of viewing architectural theory as a contest between two opposing views, *betweeness* embraces the middle ground. The suggestion is that perhaps Cartesian dualism is not an intrinsic human condition. *Betweenness* does not suggest compromise, but rather a third way that is a middle way with no concessions. The notion has Buddhist undertones – the Noble Eightfold Path to Enlightenment – the Middle Way. How one finds this middle way may be the problem. Peter Eisenman attempted to literally illustrate his concept of betweeness with the white scaffolding of the Wexner Center (1989) (Figure 22). It mediates between the old and the new without a reference to either one. However, the scaffolding at the Wexner may just be a third way and not *betweenness*. In order to truly achieve betweeness may require a modest response, a synthesis that enfolds the essence of both oppositions.

Figure 22: Wexner Center

See also: **Ambivalence • Chora (Archispeak) • Dualism (Archispeak) • Scaffolding**

Further sources: Goldblatt (in Ballantyne 2002: 156, 167)

Bilbao effect

The *Bilbao effect* is the notion that one building can transform the fortunes of an entire region. For example, when Frank Gehry's Cubism-inspired Guggenheim Museum opened in Bilbao in the Basque region of Spain in October 1997, the building seemed to act as a magnet for literally thousands of visitors (Figure 23). Indeed, in its first year, the museum attracted a greater number of visitors than the entire population of the city. The Guggenheim functioned as the centre piece of an ambitious EU-funded city-wide regeneration program – a makeover involving other signature architects such as Norman Foster, Santiago Calatrava, and Cesar Pelli, who, seemingly overnight and after years blighted by terrorism, transformed the hitherto drab and declining industrial port into a popular cultural destination. However, although Gehry himself vehemently disputes the notion that one building can cause this phenomenon, it is the mental icon of his swirling titanium and glass structure that remains synonymous with the whole idea of the "*Bilbao effect.*" Since the success of Bilbao, other cities around the world have sought a similar impact, mainly using the competition system to commission "look at me" museum designs and attract top-drawer architects to create keynote buildings in the hope that people will come.

One such city is Toronto, which, eager to shake off its rather pedestrian architectural image and increase tourism, attracted various starchitects including Daniel Libeskind, Frank Gehry, and Santiago Calatrava to inject some diversity to its urban blandness. One memorable building that induced a "Toronto effect" is Will Alsop's Sharp Center for the Ontario College of Art & Design – a huge crossword-puzzle-covered flying box supported on multicolored wonky legs (Figure 24). Described by Robert Ivy, editor-in-chief of *Architectural Record*, as one of the iconic buildings of the twenty-first century, since its opening in 2004 it has been shown that the existence of this building has dramatically increased visitor levels to the city.

However, the numbers visiting various new major city buildings around the world have, following a novelty phase, fallen as quickly as they had increased. The jury, according to Witold Rybczynski, is still out on the long-term effect of any Bilbao phenomenon on the way in which tourists choose their destinations. Meanwhile, he writes, the real *"Bilbao effect"* is its major influence on the way that clients, especially those procuring designs for major museums around the world, choose their architects. TP

See also: **Blobitecture • Fashion • Image • Starchitect**

Figure 23: Guggenheim Museum, Bilbao Spain

Figure 24: Sharp Center

Building Information Modeling: BIM

Building information modeling (BIM) is an object oriented digital representation of a building, and unlike traditional computer aided drafting (CAD) technologies, building information modeling (BIM) is not a collection of discrete lines on a screen, but a compilation of integrated and dynamic data that describes the physical and functional aspects of a building and its components that are shared and accessed throughout the entire project team. — Joann Gonchar

Building information modeling (BIM) has the potential to fundamentally change the entire enterprise of making architecture. It moves the production of buildings from a series of separate design efforts, and contractual document sets, to a single, integrated team effort supported by a digital model. The model serves as the repository for design parameters and related design responses generated by project participants. As a design tool, it provides the opportunity for the evaluation of the cost/benefit of alternatives under consideration. It is essentially an advanced "value engineering" tool that avoids the painful process of post-design cuts because of cost overruns. To achieve this capability, *BIM* encompasses systems evaluation software platforms, which can be used to provide area calculation and materials quantities, in addition to evaluating lighting, structural stresses, or even LEED compliance. It can also be used to visually evaluate the digital model from infinite sectional planes and perspective views. The advantage of an integrated model is that, as a change is made in one part of the model, the rest of the resulting changes are made automatically. The *BIM* also eventually serves as a three-dimensional, on-demand construction document.

As described above, one of the fundamental differences between *BIM* and computer-aided drafting (CAD) technologies is that CAD uses a series of discrete lines with very low-level attributes, whereas *BIM* is predominately object-based, with the objects having very high-level attributes that embed associative information about object identities and behaviors. Ironically, it is the malleability of the discrete lines in CAD technologies that makes it very easy to draw whatever can be imagined. This can be seen as a disadvantage of *BIM* as there are predetermined constraints built into *BIM* technologies. It is these preconceived constraints that cause some to believe that *BIM* sometimes forces architects to do things that they do not want it to do. Another concern is that there is a potential blurring of duties and responsibilities between construction management and architecture. The forced collaboration raises the fear of a power grab for project control, with the architect marginalized. Issues of liability are also paramount. To address these issues, the American Institute of Architects in November 2007 released an *Integrated Project Delivery Guide*. The document outlines best practices for collaboration between owners, designers, consultants, and contractors, with *BIM* as the facilitating technology. We still have to wait and see how all of this unfolds. The adoption of *BIM* is still in its early stages.

See also: **Associative design • Integrated practice • Parametric design**

Biomimicry

The study of the structure and function of biological systems as
models for the design and engineering of materials and machines.
— *The Free Dictionary*

One of the great advances in thought in our own era came when a
connection was formed between the processes of nature and the world
of form. — Sanford Kwinter

For the past 20 years there has been a renewed interest in the lessons
that nature can teach the designer. From the pioneering work of d'Arcy
Thompson in the early twentieth century, through the theoretical and built
works of the Japanese Metabolist group at mid-twentieth century, natural
forms and processes have been of interest to architects throughout
history. Even the Greek temple is believed to be a mimesis of the sacred
olive grove. The more recent manifestation of *biomimicry* has extended the
metaphor to include an emphasis on architectural process and technology,
in addition to form. Janine Benyus (1997) lists the following *biomimicry*
principles: run on sunlight using only the energy you need; fit form to
function; recycle everything; and reward cooperation and diversity.

Frei Otto (1982) rationalized his lightweight tent and pneumatic
structure as "bionic." The reference was more associated with the process
of form finding than the question of function fitting. The notion that
designing is based upon a constant search for "how nature would do it" has
a renewed relevance in the greening of twenty-first-century architecture.
The rejection of form simply following function, plus the 1990s emergence
of blobitecture and the fold is certainly a continuation of the tradition of
biomimicry. Bionic is cool again, decades after Steve Austin, television's
bionic man. The potential of bionic architecture remains to be seen. As
a cutting-edge aspect of *biomimicry*, biomimetic design concentrates on
the replication of the adaptation and survival mechanisms of biological
organisms. The skin of a building may one day function very much like
the human skin, able to heal itself, react to protect its host from the sun,
wind, and rain, all while providing an attractive outward appearance.
Perhaps this current experimentation with dynamic, responsive skins
is just on the surface. Biology has many more lessons for architecture,
as new technologies provide the means and materials. Nanotechnology
promises to be a key element in the development of architectural
bionics. One can imagine a multitude of nano-sensors that are tied to
nano-machines actively
adjusting a building form
and surface to respond to
level of occupancy, internal
environmental needs, and
external weather conditions.
Unlike the unique, but
failed, bionic skin of Jean
Nouvel's Institut du Monde
Arabe (1987) (Figure 25),
with its inoperable 30,000
light-sensitive diaphragms,

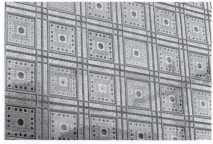

Figure 25: Institut du Monde Arabe

the technology of the twenty-first century will have a better chance of supporting bionic architecture: a brave new world.

See also: **Anthromorphism • Biomimicry • Blob architecture (Archispeak)**
• Blobitecture • Fold •Metabolism (Archispeak) • Morphogenetic design •
Responsive architecture

Further sources: Kruff (1994: 436)

Blobitecture

The most interesting example is the development of "isomorphic poly surfaces" "meta-clay" "meta balls" or "blob" models.
— Greg Lynn (1993)

Digital technology has made blob like forms buildable while streamlining the design process from concept to fabrication.
— Joseph Rosa

Crapitecture. — Sir Peter Cook

Figure 26:
The EMP

It has been more than ten years since the landmark Experience Music Project (EMP) by Frank Gehry opened in Seattle (Figure 26). It is significant that it occurred at the beginning of a new century. Perhaps it was an early harbinger of what will be the hallmark of the twenty-first century. Just as the nineteenth century has been characterized as the industrial century, and the twentieth as the modern century, the twenty-first may be eventually known as the organic century. The architecture of an organic century will not consist of rectilinear, Euclidean boxes, but rather isomorphic poly surfaces – blobs. *"Blobitecture,"* as it was labeled by the late *New York Times* writer William Safire, rose up as a result of Greg Lynn and others experimenting with shapes on the computer.

Blobitecture has great appeal to the student and architect searching for a foothold in fame. It is a profound break with the history of architecture, a history that had become soiled by the histrionics of modernism, and subsequently the self-indulgence of post-modernism. As a measure of its success, schools as prestigious as Tu Delft and Columbia now offer courses in *blobitecture*.

Time will tell if blobs will become passé, and thus render another generation of architectural forms old fashioned. Already the shock value has worn off.

What we usually call avant-garde forms are often only new for an instant and then quickly become "arriere-garde" forms. — Odile Decq

See also: **Blob architecture (Archispeak) • Fold • Parametric design • Post-modernism (Archispeak)**

Further sources: Gausa (2003: 84); Lynn (in Malgrave 2008: 543); Rosa (2003: 33)

▌Blur

Blur is a state of the gaze; tool that permits the joining of the analogical and the synthetic world; bonding agent between the virtual world and the real. — Enric Ruiz-Geli

Blur challenges the orthodoxy of high resolution by presenting a formless, featureless, scaleless, depthless, spaceless, massless, and surfaceless space. Upon entering the fog mass, visual and acoustic references are erased, leaving only an optical whiteout and the white noise of pulsing fog nozzles. — Elizabeth Diller

Popularized by Diller and Scofidio's 2002 temporary "Blur Building" pavilion, blurring is a common activity we all understand. We *blur* when we lose focus. We "blur the lines" when we combine things and deny their separateness. Thus the term *blur* has also become a term used to describe the action of developing a continuum, as illustrated in the following statement by Thom Mayne "I am trying to *blur* or find a continuous flow between the generic and the specific." Its application to architecture at first seemed strange and ethereal. It broke through a conceptual barrier, that of the necessity of materiality in architecture. Just as John Cage's 1952 silent composition "Four, thirty-three," marked a shift in what could be considered music, so the Blur Building expanded the definition of what can be considered to be "architecture." It opened up the possibility of a soft architecture that was free from materiality.

However, the most prevalent, and thus consequential, blurring might be the blurring of the distinction between the virtual world and the "real." Reality television, Wii video gaming, and buildings that consist of flat-panel digital display walls, *blur* the boundary between the virtual and the real. Cyber representation, including building information modeling (BIM), evolves into "Holodeck" levels of architectural simulation. *Star Trek*'s Starship Enterprise virtual reality time-travel device may eventually become the ultimate blurred architecture. Avatars will be representing us in the blurred virtual reality of digital hyperspace.

See also: **Building information modeling: BIM • Soft architecture**

Further sources: Ruiz-Geli (in Gausa 2003: 88)

Bracketing ▮

According to Husserl, we can describe the objects in our minds as phenomena only after we have bracketed their existence. By bracketing the objective world, one suspends judgment about the existence of things around us. — *The Oxford Guide to Philosophy*

A principle problem within phenomenology is our ability to access the intrinsic, when the world is a bombardment of the extrinsic. In order to peel back the layers of our existence, it is necessary to filter out the noise that is unrelated to the naked reality of the experience of the phenomena at hand. The challenge is to focus on the essence without the distractions of the world around us, the excess. In the architectural arena this means that the parameters introduced to create a "real" architecture must be carefully reduced to only those that draw out the intrinsic presence of the work. This is achieved by placing strict brackets around acquired intelligence. This is easier said than done. We can hardly shut out the noise of the rest of our full existence as we search for essences. Buddhist monks spend a lifetime trying to achieve a connection with the intrinsic without the extrinsic, a state of nothingness. For the rest of us, *bracketing* is perhaps only experienced when we encounter a "first impression."

Architects, by their training and conditioning, are ill equipped to severely bracket their thoughts to focus uncluttered on the intrinsic nature of the object in question. They are by necessity broad and critical thinkers, and typically not very good at suspending judgment. The quick conceptual gesture sketch that comes before the rational mind takes over may be the easiest, and most underrated, window into the phenomenal reality of the desired architecture. Frank Gehry famously and unapologetically uses this *bracketing* technique.

See also: **Bracketing • Intelligence • Phenomenology (Archispeak)**

Braids ▮

Braids are spatial loops; transgressive trajectories; nodes and crosses; virtual bonds and links of movement, but also superimposed messages ... — Manuel Gausa

Braids play an important role in topology. By closing braids we obtain knots or links. A knot is an embedded closed curve in the 3-dimensional space and a link is a disjoint union of embedded closed curves. — Toshitake Kohno

In the bag of tricks of the new digital architecture, *braids* are one of the new spatial ordering devices that have emerged from non-Euclidean mathematics and physics. Other forms that are inspirational include nanotubes, buckiballs, the double helix, torus (doughnuts), weavings, Moebius strips, and crystals. Daniel Libeskind, in particular, has adopted the crystal as the appropriate form for the museum. To date, his crystals trying valiantly to pose as museums have graced Denver and Toronto.

Braids may have their greatest application in the development of building enclosures. In a reversion to primitive, low technology, the braiding of grasses, including bamboo, might be a viable "green" technology to be considered as the use of oil-based materials becomes increasing unsustainable. At the high end, one could also consider Calatrava's Turning Torso in Malmo, Sweden and the Turning Tower, Dubai to be strands of braid architecture.

Spiraling, packing, weaving, blending, cracking, flocking, tiling, sectioning, tessellating, folding, contouring, and forming are some of the digitally assisted form manipulations that join *braiding* as the tools needed to create the architectural blobs, folds and boxes of the twenty-first century. The language of architectural design is undergoing a revolution unlike any in the past. After all, we have been holding on to "commodity, firmness and delight" for the past 2,000 years.

See also: **Commodity, firmness and delight (Archispeak) • Digital architecture • Sustainability (Archispeak) • Tessellating • Topology (Archispeak) • Weaving**

▌Branding

Associated with appropriation and status, *branding* describes the identification of commercial products and corporate structures. Originally a sign of ownership burnt on to livestock, or earlier on prisoners, *branding* is also used to discriminate the existence of products or services in the market place and to communicate persuasive concepts about identity, quality, and associated lifestyles.

Marketers and ad people know that words and color associations used to describe an idea or object can strongly influence the way the idea or object being described will be viewed or dealt with. Known as "brand value," a product or a service can be differentiated: that is, imbued with an ethos and even made to transcend the very nature of its existence. Similarly, to brand a building design with a nickname can import a sense of identity to the form; in other words, it can idealize or "brand-mark" the design in a manner to suit the intention of the project. For promotional reasons, most major cities attract names, such as the "Big Apple" and the "City of Dreaming Spires." Similarly, the branding of buildings occurs when names, such as "Paddy's Wigwam" (Basil Spence's Liverpool Cathedral) and "Fred and Ginger" (Frank Gehry's Prague office building) are sometimes affectionately or cynically appropriated by users or designers who often invent such labels as a means of personalizing a "brand new" design idea or domesticating unusual architectural forms. Through such characterization, *branding* can be persuasive; labels often metaphorically and poetically capture the essence of a specific quality prominent in the design, while, as architect Will Alsop points out, helping others to accept and "buy into" the idea.

Global marketing has meant that a universal vocabulary of *branding* pervades cities across the world, causing them to create a "brandscape" – an invasion that, in eroding local identity and contextual formalism, appears to have created a new urban typology. McDonald's has invaded many sacred places with its brash brand. Not even the Pantheon in Rome is safe (Figure 27). It is one that has not gone unnoticed in those architectural programs conscious of the evolution of an urbanscape more concerned with global marketing than with socio-political issues or questions of context. Here, dedicated student projects study brands and *branding* techniques as a means of articulating aspects of our culture and to revitalize the city. To do so, brand values, image and the style of product are studied in the attempt to create an architectural response. TP

See also: **Brandmark (Archispeak) • Commoditization • Typology (Archispeak)**

Figure 27: Big Mac at the Pantheon, Rome

Caricature

A representation, especially pictorial or literary, in which the subject's distinctive features or peculiarities are deliberately exaggerated to produce a comic or grotesque effect. — *The Free Dictionary*

... this rush to take possession of the latest fashion, this productivistic superficiality, that makes it possible to say that the architecture of these times is not mannerism but caricature, and primarily self-caricature. — Vittorio Gregotti

As we become numbed by the onslaught of media, cultural critics are increasingly resorting to cryptic, hyped narratives, rather than the carefully crafted analysis. Criticism has become the production of sound bites that are no more than *caricatures*. Blogs and tweets are treated seriously. Architectural discourse has not been immune. In our need for a "quick fix" we embrace simplistic labels and extreme architecture at the expense of the full appreciation of the serious works of architecture that are occurring in the rest of the profession. Starchitects have become caricatures of themselves, caught up in their own media image. To help sort things out, critics such as Charles Jencks feel compelled to map the recent architectural discourse by applying labels to every star and their ideology. That map is also a *caricature*. In the popular twentieth-century media of television and "the movies," faux architects Mike Brady of *The Brady Bunch* and Wilbur Post, the owner and stable mate of *Mr. Ed, The Talking Horse*, have been replaced by the more noble and heroic architect caricatures of the architect/electrician Paul Newman in *The Towering Inferno* and Wesley Snipes in *Jungle Fever*.

Serious architecture with a depth of virtuosity is not immune to being caricatured. Caricaturization is mainly for the amusement of the media and the general consumer, and not for the serious connoisseur of architecture. Charles Jencks, in *The Language of Post-Modern Architecture* (1977), presents a number of characterizations of important architecture, including Le Corbusier's chapel at Ronchamp as a duck, and the Sydney Opera House as breeding turtles. Unfortunately this incessant need to reduce architecture to a sound bite devalues architecture in the eyes of the public. The perception that architecture is nothing more than frivolous exterior decoration is reinforced by cynical, consumer-oriented, buildings like the miniature white castles that house the American White Castle hamburger chain and their miniature hamburgers (Figure 28).

See also: **Branding • Branding (Archispeak) • Starchitect**

Further sources: Gregotti (1999: 19)

Figure 28: White Castle
"Eat like a little king"

Cartooning   ▮

Derived from the Italian word "cartone" and the Dutch "karton," meaning a large sheet of heavy-duty paper, the term *cartooning* originally described a process used by the old masters. It refers to the production of a full-sized, detailed compositional outline drawing executed on sturdy paper as a preparatory study, or "modello," and made in preparation for its trace-transfer to a surface intended for a painting. Typically, the cartoon was transferred by rubbing the back with chalk and redrawing the outline with a stylus, thus transferring its delineation to the canvas or panel. Cartoons were also used as a guide in the production of frescoes, to quickly and accurately transfer a compositional drawing before it was painted on damp plaster. To do so, cartoons received pinpricks along the contours of the design and, while held against the wall, a bag of powdered pigment was then dabbed or "pounced" over the cartoon to stencil dots directly on to the plaster. Surviving cartoons by Renaissance painters, such as Leonardo da Vinci and the famous Raphael cartoons, are highly prized in their own right. However, the latter, intended for tapestries, were colored and used in a different way: that is, as a visual register by weavers when working at the loom.

The modern meaning of the term "cartoon" was born in 1843 by association with the subject matter of a drawing by John Leech published in *Punch* magazine, which poked ironic fun at politicians by humorously satirizing the preparatory cartoons for frescoes in the then new Palace of Westminster. With its roots in the biting, satirical drawings of nineteenth-century caricaturists such as Honoré Daumier in France, and possibly even earlier in the eighteenth-century lampoons of British caricaturists such as Thomas Rowlandson, modern cartooning finds its heroes in the likes of Gerald Scarfe, Mel Calman, and Gary Larson. With offshoots in the subculture of comic books, comic strips, and graphic novels, cartooning also became animated.

When used in architectural currency, *cartooning* loosely describes the production of a preparatory sketch delineation. However, in this context the cartoon is usually devoid of any humor. An interesting development related to *cartooning* is the growing number of architectural textbooks illustrated with cartoons. It is a sign of the times, as is the book *Architecture for Dummies* (Dietsch, 2002). *Time Management for Architects and Designers* by Thorbjoern Mann is a case in point (Figure 29). Comic

Figure 29: Beware of isms

books are also written by, and for, architects. Often these are produced to introduce the beginning student to architecture. The architect and cartoonist Louis Hellman's prolific architectural and planning cartoon output, including the comic book *Architecture for Beginners* (1988), comes to mind. More recently, Rem Koolhaas and OMA produced a follow-up to the groundbreaking *SMLXL* (1995) with a serious comic book/magazine *Content* (2004). It is an example of architectural cartooning that is certain to be copied by other architects striving to be "hip." One wonders what clients think of this "dumbing down" of the profession. TP

See also: **Branding • Caricature • Starchitect**

Further sources: Gehry 28

▌Catastrophe theory

Catastrophe Theory is not primarily concerned with what we call catastrophes but, with the more prosaic "phase transitions" that are everywhere visible in nature: the dramatic transformation of water into ice at zero degrees centigrade, or the sudden transformation of corn kernel into popcorn. — Charles Jencks

It may seem that there is little relationship between *catastrophe theory* and architectural theory, but that is in the process of changing. Twenty-first-century architecture will be increasingly interested in the application of phase transitions as it embraces biomimicry. One of those applications is the process of folding. Folding creates a dramatic change in direction, moving suddenly from a two-dimensional plane to a complex three-dimensional shape in space (Figure 30). The catastrophic spatial transition is a happy one. Another phase transition sequence associated with the production of architecture is the move from the mind of the designer to the digital information and design model, to a CNC-produced physical architectural fabrication. Similar to the production of popcorn, the architectural element resides within the computer, waiting to burst forth in a metamorphosis that is a dramatic transformation – a catastrophe.

As architecture increasingly courts nature for its inspirations, architectural catastrophes of the best kind will become common. Architecture that is biomorphic, responsive, and dynamic (much like the sunflower) will become the goal. With the assistance of artificial intelligence, buildings will be able to initiate and execute a transformation

Figure 30: Catastrophic spatial transition

when required. This may be a future form of high-performance, yet low-carbon-footprint, architecture. Thus, buildings that can reconfigure themselves as the seasons change may be one of the first architectural applications of *catastrophe theory*. It will be a brave new world of dynamic architecture.

See also: **Biomimicry • Cosmogenic architecture • Fold • Responsive architecture**

Further sources: Jencks (1995: 53)

Cave

The cave represents the first spatial element.
— Christian Norberg-Schulz

As Laugier presents the system, the forest is allowed to triumph over the cave... — Karsten Harries

Western architecture has evolved from the *cave* to the forest to the cathedral, and now has returned to the *cave*. Obviously that statement is a gross oversimplification. The vertical, rectilinear, post, and lintel architecture that grew out of the forest has dominated architectural form for the past 5,000 years. Finally, it is starting to be replaced by non-Euclidean cave-like architecture. It may take a while, as relatively little *cave* architecture has been produced to date. Seattle's Experience Music Project (EMP) by Frank Gehry, a *cave*, is still controversial ten years after opening. It was voted one the five most ugly buildings in the world in a recent Internet-based poll. On a lighter note, the cave that Santiago Calatrava created in downtown Toronto is universally liked (Figure 31). Unlike the EMP, it avoids claustrophobic spaces and instead bathes the now enclosed street with light.

There is a chance that *cave*-form architecture may not become the norm until it has proven to be a sustainable and affordable form of architecture. It is still more economical to build boxes based upon the Euclidean geometry of readily available traditional building materials.

Are we returning to our beginnings in terms of spatial ordering systems? Louis Kahn would be pleased, as he was always most intrigued by "Volume Minus One." It may be inevitable that the cave, in a reversal of history, will eventually replace the primitive hut. After all, the curvature of the universe allows us to eventually loop back in space–time as an act of "back to the past as the future."

See also: **Primitive hut • Tabula rasa**

Further sources: Harries (1998: 96, 11)

Figure 31: The Allen Lambert "Cave" Galleria, Toronto

Character

> ... a distinctive trait, quality, or attribute.
> — *Webster's Unabridged Dictionary*

> **Character is a large word, full of significance; no metaphoric river can more than hint at its meaning.** — Louis Sullivan

> **... suspicious though architects and critics became of "character" in the modernist era, they never...found it possible to dispense with it altogether.** — Adrian Forty

The modern era in architecture succeeded in all but eliminating references to *character*. It was considered unprofessional to consider such a subjective, personal judgment about a work of architecture. The twentieth-century rational human did not engage in speculation about such unscientific matters. That was left to the poet.

The discussion of *character* was rediscovered with the emergence of post-modern architectural theory. Its project was the restoration of meaning in architecture, thus the question of *character* became relevant. Although architects and their professional critics still seldom use the term, everyone else likes to evaluate the *character* of a work of architecture. Some of the *character* descriptors that are used by cultural happenings critics and the public include cute, cold, fun, formal, imposing, amusing, and friendly. One can hardly imagine an architect, or serious architectural critic, describing a work of architecture as "cute." The descriptors may change as future buildings become more lifelike, or anthropomorphic. Once the buildings of the new reflexive architecture begin to have more of a personal relationship with their occupants, they are more likely to take on a personality. It may become an era of pet architecture. As a pet, architecture will become even more personified than the face buildings of yesterday and today. One wonders if they will also reflect the *character* of their owners?

See also: **Pet architecture • Responsive architecture**

Chatter

> **Chatter: communication, such as e-mail and cell phone calls, between people who are involved in terrorism or espionage, as monitored by a government agency.** — *The Free Dictionary*

Chatter is the informational deluge of the day for all of us, not just terrorists. Tweets, e-mails, blogs, texts, YouTube, Facebook, Bing, tabloid television, political criticism comedy, documentary movies, and so on provide today's informational orgy, which is analogous to drinking out of a fireman's hose. To prevent drowning, the privileged manage the *chatter* using artificial intelligence filters and sorters such as spam blockers and Google-type "search" tools.

In situations involving the production of architecture, the resulting refined intelligence becomes fodder for the cyber design machine. The goal is to be inclusive and democratic in the development of project parameters. The static, bounded architectural brief (program) is no longer a sufficient guidebook for designing. Those were simpler times. Once form that follows function was no longer the primary objective, the description of activities to be housed in the new building became only a small, and mostly irrelevant, part of the design challenge. Now each act of architecture is understood to be part of a much larger social, political, and environmental situation over time. The multidimensional design agenda is too diverse and complex for one member of the project delivery constituency to understand. As the arbitrator, the parametric digital model is expected to provide the answers that establish the questions. Design becomes the preparation of soup – many ingredients with a complexity that comes from the synergy of tastes. One only hopes that there is still a chef who knows what type of soup it was meant to be.

See also: **Algorithm • Artificial intelligence • Brief (Archispeak) • Parametric design**

Classicism   ▌

... a style which imposes purity of part, category, and order, via a set of rules which depend on the imposition of absolute boundary, in the firm delineation of architectural elements. — Katherine Shonfield

It is a mistake to define classicism. — John Summerson

Is *classicism* still relevant in the twenty-first century? Perhaps it is, as the classical in architecture extends beyond the simple assessment of the appearance of a building. When considering the spatial order of a work of architecture, the result may qualify it as classical, even though it is a contemporary building. The most discussed example is the work of Le Corbusier. His five points of a modern architecture described in *Towards An Architecture* (1923/1986) have more in common with classical rules than the rules of the modernism with which he is most associated (Figure 32). Peter Eisenman, in his seminal 1984 essay, "The end of the classical," takes the position that the classical lasted from the fifteenth century up to the last part of the twentieth century. In his assessment, the entire enterprise of Modernism was merely another manifestation of the classical.

With the late-twentieth-century incursion of post-structuralist theory, architectural ordering systems became anti-classical. The architecture of rules gave way to a "no rules" architecture – or so it seemed. Even the no-rules deconstructivist architecture that briefly made the scene fell victim to analysis and parsing. Rules for being a deconstructivist were invented by critics to make their jobs easier. Ironically, more recent advances in digital design technology have further reined in the freedom of the "no rules" architect. In order for integrated practice, using a shared parametric building information model, to be successful there needs to be careful agreement by all parties regarding the rules of the game. Canonic design is making a comeback.

... the lessons to be learned today from classicism are not found in classicism's stylistic wrinkles but in classicism's rationality.
— Demetri Porphytios

See also: **Building information modeling: BIM • Deconstructivism (Archispeak) • Integrated practice •Modernism (Archispeak) • Post-structuralism (Archispeak)**

Further sources: Antoniades (1990: 166); Eisenman (in Nesbitt 1996); Harries (1998: 228); Shonfield (in Borden 2000: 300)

Figure 32: Le Villa Savoye: Classical modernism

▌Cliché

A trite or overused expression or idea. — *The Free Dictionary*

Words, like images quickly become clichés, losing their original capacity to make someone listen and think. — Gwendolyn Wright

Architectural clichés abound. "Form follows function," "God is in the details," "Architecture is frozen music," and so on are well-worn clichés. The entire home design industry is based upon the use of decorative clichés. The Greek-columned portico, (Figure 33), the pseudo-Mediterranean tile roof, and the Tuscan villa of the American suburbs, are just a few of the *clichés* associated with the American house.

The architectural *cliché* is not always as bad as it sounds. It may be ironic, or it may be a deliberate strategy used to engender familiarity. Fast-food chains rely on architectural clichés, such as the golden arches, to assist their customers in finding them, regardless of which remote part of the world they are operating in. According to Enrique Walker, a received idea or *cliché*, plus an arbitrary self-imposed constraint, may be a valuable creative technique for the discovery of unexpected, and yet appropriate, architectural moves. Also, the *cliché* meeting another *cliché* may result in surprising and useful results. On the other hand, many clichés hound architects. Unfortunately one of those clichés – the architect as the exterior decorator of buildings – is becoming increasingly true. As the current preoccupation with the building skin grows, there is the danger that the primary design contributions expected from the architect will be confined to the aesthetics of the envelope. All other matters will be rationally

Figure 33: Cliché façade

derived from a process of inserting performance-based parameters and associated algorithms into a BIM – hardly the interest or current expertise of the architect.

See also: **Algorithm • Building information modeling: BIM • Branding • Facadism • Typology (Archispeak)**

Closure   ∎

Closure is the opposite of openness. *Closure* is a term found in several disciplines, from computer science (a function and its environment that can be passed into another function) to law (the closure of a trial) and legislative assembly (a procedure for ending a motion or a debate and taking a vote). However, while a dictionary will define *closure* as the drawing of lines of finality under events, or closing the door on the past, its use in architecture speaks more of an aspect of our bodily movement through sequences of space. The term is borrowed from psychology to describe the visual *closure* of space. In one sense it refers to the creation of a perceived break in a chain of connected spatial events that, while momentarily containing the eye, does not restrict nor eradicate the sense of progression beyond.

Closure occurs in both interior and urban space. For instance, to progress through Oxford's serpentine High Street, often described as the most beautiful high street in Europe, is to walk through a series of identifiable spatial pockets – each seemingly enclosed as we pass through them. However, due to the street's winding footprint, their closure is illusory as each is connected by the continuum of space – the result of this apparent "containment" increasing anticipation and arousing curiosity of what lies beyond. This kind of spatial experience chimes with the ideas of the architect, influential urban designer and pioneer of the concept of townscape, the late Gordon Cullen, who in his seminal book *The Concise Townscape* (1961/1995) wrote, "A long straight road has little impact because the initial view is soon digested and becomes monotonous."

Closure is also an important aspect of visual perception. In this context it refers to our capacity to close, or visually "paint-in," incomplete information in the stimulus. This is the law of *closure*, when, in order to complete its understanding of an incomplete image – that is, to increase its regularity – the brain may experience elements it does not directly perceive through sensation. The term derives from the Gestalt psychologists who, in 1912, studied visual perception as an interactive, dynamic, and creative process. Their theories stress that, in seeking harmony and unity in visual data, our perception first sees a "gestalt" (image) as a unified whole before an identification of its constituent parts, and therefore its meaning. Also, as part of this visual reconstruction process, our tendency to perceptually group like elements into simple units is governed by proximity (the relative nearness of elements to one another) and similarity (the relative sameness of elements).

There is also the term "premature *closure*," that, drawn from the world of creative writing, describes a form of mental constipation in problem solving. Those architects and students of architecture who avoid any extensive search for options before commitment, and thereby fail to push new ideas to the limit, appear to suffer from this condition. Conversely, the exhaustive design processes of architects like Louis Kahn, Charles Moore, and Carlo Scarpa seem to have the opposite problem, that is, frustrating their clients by continuing to explore different avenues of enquiry well beyond their deadlines. TP

See also: **Closure (Archispeak)**

▌Commoditization

Commodification (or commoditization) is the transformation of goods and services (or things that may not normally be regarded as goods or services) into a commodity. — *Wikipedia*

The twentieth century saw the developed world career into a consuming frenzy (Figure 34). Everything that could be bought became a commodity, including architecture. The unspoken goal in life became to "die with the most stuff." The standard of living, measured in GNP and personal wealth, ignored such meaningful measures as happiness and spiritual health. The negative effect was the devaluation of everything that was beyond value. As Warhol showed us, commodity became art and art became commodity. The slogan "everything has a price" became generally accepted as a truism. Integrity gave way to profit.

Even leading architects became commoditized as starchitects. Iconic buildings became brands, to be replicated and sold on the open market, much like shoes. Of course this is not really new, as it also happened with structures such as the Eiffel Tower, the Statue of Liberty and Big Ben. Every tourist gift shop has miniature versions of these symbols of the cities they represent. It is the icon in these cases that has been commoditized. The Bilbao effect meant that the goal of new public architecture became that of marketing the town, rather than providing the needed well-designed concert hall or museum.

The twenty-first century may restore the balance. As concern for conservation mounts, flash may be replaced by substance. The only threat to this return to architectural pragmatism might be the blobs and folds generated by a handful of avant-garde firms. If the environmentalists prevail, architecture may once again be restored to a higher level of value than that of a commodity.

See also: **American pragmatism • Avant-garde (Archispeak) • Bilbao effect • Branding • Starchitect**

Figure 34: Times Square, New York

Communitarianism   ▋

A model of political organization that stresses ties of affection, kinship, and a sense of common purpose and tradition.
— *Oxford Dictionary of Philosophy*

The thesis that the community, rather than the individual, the state, the nation, or any other entity, is and should be at the centre of our analysis and our value system. — *Oxford Dictionary of Philosophy*

With the recent viral spread of Internet-based virtual communities through social networks such as MySpace and Facebook, "community" has undergone a dramatic redefinition. As predicted by Martin Pawley 36 years ago in *The Private Future* (1974), individuals are staying home and building their communities from their armchairs, rather than at the country club. Under these circumstances, *communitarianism* takes on a different meaning. As an ethical posture, it remains a laudable goal – that of serving the entire community, rather than the wishes of individuals or organizations with power. The problem is one of dispersal. The online social-networking-based community is not place specific. It is deterritorialized. On the surface this seems to be a problem for the future of architecture, as issues that are architecturally related tend to be place bound, or at least within a limited geographical area. Has the importance of physical community faded away? Hardly. It turns out that the virtual community serves as a vehicle for increasing the incidence of physical gathering, as local events are efficiently cyber-broadcast to members of the local interest group. Due to the effectiveness of the tweeting, messaging, and posting associated with social networks, spontaneous community gatherings are well attended. Another benefit of "Facebooking" is the growth of a multitude of special interest communities that can exert influence over policies associated with architecture and the environment. We are living in an age of heightened *communitarianism*. It is a brave new virtual world. *Computer City*, the visionary proposal by Archigram's Dennis Crompton (1964; in Cook, 1967), has come to pass.

See also: **Archigram (Archispeak)** • **Atopia** • **Deterritorialization/ reterritorialization**

Further sources: Bess (in Nesbitt 1996: 372) Nesbitt (1996: 370)

Conservation   ▋

... the emergence of conservation has been greatly aided by the positive meaning that this word has recently assumed as a protector of architectural heritage, of nature, and of historical memory, in opposition to a modernization that demolishes and forgets.
— Vittorio Gregotti

The commonly understood definition of *conservation* is "the preservation and careful management of the environment and of natural resources." Due to the relatively recent worldwide campaign to raise awareness of the need for resource conservation, designers are now expected to incorporate conservation principles and practices into their work. This poses both a challenge and an opportunity for the twenty-first-century architect. Design freedom (a myth all along) appears to be even more curtailed. Accountability for the consequences of design decisions has expanded beyond the client and the immediate public to include the world's population and the health of the planet. At the same time, the introduction of the challenge of conservation has given a tired profession looking for relevancy a "shot in the arm." In the public's mind architecture has found a raison d'être beyond the decorative. After decades of alienation from public favor, architecture is being embraced once again as important to the community. Although in reality architecture is still largely "part of the problem," it is being heralded as "part of the solution." This iconic catchphrase of the nascent Woodstock revolution is heard once again, this time in the boardroom.

Architectural conservation takes many forms. It includes historic preservation, adaptive reuse, energy-efficient practices, and Buckminster Fuller's credo of doing the "most with the least" (Figure 35). The responsible use of non-renewable resources is now intimately related to the design of buildings. Thus, alternative building materials such as rammed earth, straw bales, and bamboo have become of great interest to clients and designers. Just as the twentieth century may be ultimately known as the century of consumption, it is hoped that the twenty-first century will become known as the century of *conservation*. As Al Gore would say, our future existence depends upon it. We are not off to a good start. The developed world is making a token effort that is being cancelled out by the rapidly developing Asian continent. Denmark is no match for China. The "tipping point" is rapidly approaching as we "fiddle."

See also: **Cradle to cradle • Green design (Archispeak) • Hannover principles • Sustainability (Archispeak) • ZEB – zero energy building**

Figure 35: Expo 67: Man and His World,

▌Constraints

The human race built most nobly when limitations were greatest and, therefore, when most was required of imagination in order to build at all. Limitations seem to have always been the best friend of architecture. — Frank L. Wright

... architecture that relies on autonomy and independence from purpose is merely wishful thinking. — Paul-Alan Johnson

The history of architecture is replete with constrained design. A hallmark of classical architecture is the imposition of a strict set of rules, or canons. Following the prescribed way to create architecture was the goal of achieving the perfect architecture with meaning and beauty. Vitruvius, and later, pattern books, provided the recipes.

With the emergence of modern architecture, the set of *constraints* shifted from established formal rules about aesthetics, to rules and procedures about form making. *Constraints* were redefined as "problems" and "opportunities" (Figure 36). Of particular interest was the acceptance of the *constraints* of honesty of materials, expression of structure, minimalism, absence of ornamentation, function as the authority for form, and a dedication to socio-political causes.

The *constraints* imposed on the post-modern architect shifted to a concern for ensuring that architecture had meaning, even if very few individuals could decipher the meaning.

In the current environment of parametric, digital, and green architecture, the term "constraint" has taken on a new meaning. While the "parameter" defines the values of the elements, a "constraint" defines the relation between them, thus dictating their behavior. Meeting design parameters for sensitivity to context, energy utilization levels, the use of healthy and sustainable materials, and the conservation of natural resources, has imposed an unprecedented level of constraint upon the designer. If Frank Lloyd Wright was correct, it may mean that we are moving into an era of great nobility in architecture.

See also: **Green design (Archispeak) • Modernism (Archispeak) • Parametric design**

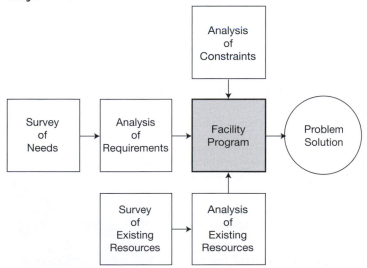

Figure 36: Role of constraints in the "problem-solving" design process

Contextualism

> ... contextualism has been used as an excuse for mediocrity, for a dumb servility to the familiar. — Philip Johnson

> Contextualism offers a middle-ground position between an unrealistic frozen past with no future development permitted, and urban renewal with the total loss of the urban fabric. — Kate Nesbitt

Contextualism was an anathema to the international style. In reaction to the placelessness of modern architecture, *contextualism* emerged in the 1960s, first in Colin Rowe's studio at Cornell, and soon after in almost every design studios in North America. The notion of responding to an immediate context remained a popular and simplistic recipe for restoring meaning and a sense of place to architecture. It only lasted for a short period of time, as post-modern architecture shifted the notion of context from the spatial to the temporal. In the twenty-first century the relationship between *contextualism* and design is more mixed. Contemporary digitally based architecture is once again forgoing *contextualism* in favor of the exploration of blobs, folds, and boxes. The design of the new Seattle Public Library caused a ruckus among those citizens concerned about preserving the undistinguished context that the 2004 Koolhaas building was to inhabit (Figure 37).

In contrast to the mannerist exercises in fetish blob and fold architecture, the environmental crisis has spawned a renewed concern for context. As good stewards of the environment, "green" architects are considering the found environment as a starting point when developing the basic fabric of their buildings. Passive design strategies, green roofs, green walls, and a greater interest in climate-responsive building are making an appearance in a growing number of award-winning architectural projects. But is this contexualism? Most green buildings are self-absorbed exercises in the sub-optimization of specific technical issues associated with energy conservation and sustainability. The results are often foreign to their immediate context. The green building is still an unwelcome element in its neighborhood.

Towns make the milieu for individual buildings, and one needs to understand the interdependence of buildings and milieu if one is to design a successful building – a building that sustains life, and that becomes a thriving organism.
— Ballantyne on Deleuze

See also: **Conservation • Critical regionalism • Fetishization • Green building (Archispeak) • Passive design**

Further sources: Agrest (1993: 150); Forty (2000: 132); Johnson (1994: 285); Nesbitt (1996: 32, 294) Stern (in Nesbitt (1996: 103)

Figure 37: Seattle Public Library: anti-contextualism?

Continental philosophy   █

Continental philosophy is an inaccurate term used to refer to the
writings of philosophers influenced by European political philosophers
such as Hegel, Marx, or Heidegger; by phenomenology and
existentialist schools, or by post-Structuralist French philosophy.
— *Oxford Dictionary of Philosophy*

Continental philosophy, as outlined above, is a semi-pejorative, not
particularly descriptive umbrella term. It describes a host of divergent
philosophical positions that mainly share their geographic locale and
interest in debunking analytical philosophy. The term was coined as
a term of convenience in British and American academic circles. It is
generally not used in Europe, where the notion of *"continental philosophy"*
is viewed with as much wariness as the idea of a "continental breakfast"
(Descombes 1983). The writings of nineteenth-century French and
German philosophers were of particular interest to the purveyors of the
more esoteric post-modern architectural theories of the second half of
the twentieth century. According to legend, when Colin Rowe brought
continental philosophy across the Atlantic, it was watered down to the
level of theory to suit the less scholarly North American architectural
academy.

Today, interest in *continental philosophy* has faded or moved to the
background. A few intelligentsia are still hanging on, but that generation
is rapidly being replaced by the young guns who are blazing the way with
their brazen, neo-baroque, digitally conceived constructions. Theory is
being presented as intelligence for the benefit of practice. *Continental
philosophy* paved the way for the break from the cold grasp of analytical
modernist dogma. For that we are grateful. But it would be wise to
contemplate what is filling the vacuum. The current mood appears
to be that of returning to the tyranny of environmental and economic
pragmatism and heartless logic. Despite the good work of continental
philosophers, it is analytical philosophy that may win the day, as the
struggle for survival on our depleted planet demands unfeeling rational
thought.

See also: **Intelligence** • **Phenomenology** • **Post-structuralism (Archispeak)** •
Baroque

Cosmogenic architecture   █

Cosmogenesis is the metaphorical web that penetrates every area of
life and matter, tying them together in a partly finished architecture.
— Charles Jencks

In *The Architecture of the Jumping Universe* (1995), and *Critical Modernism*
(2007), Charles Jencks devotes entire chapters to *cosmogenic
architecture*. He defines it as consisting of emergent "natural" forms
that are multivalent, complex, ecological, eclectic, and based on current
cosmic sciences. His prescription is that *cosmogenic architecture* is the
appropriate twenty-first-century architecture, at least for the start of

the century. Jencks also traces cosmic architecture as the precursor to *cosmogenic architecture*. One of the examples of cosmic architecture he cites is Arata Isozaki's Team Disney building in Orlando (1991) (Figure 38). It includes a large cone-shaped cosmic sundial with a Japanese garden as its floor.

The metaphor of cosmogenesis is generally acknowledged and embraced by the current generation of starchitects and their followers. Of particular interest are the non-Euclidean geometries found in natural forms when viewed through the lens of complexity science and chaos theory. Folds, fractals, and blobs emerge as viable architectural forms. Of less interest is the cosmogenic principle of sustainability. It is largely neglected in the pursuit of twenty-first-century cutting-edge magazine architecture. Magazine-worthy digitally generated forms tend to be about their cleverness and uniqueness, rather than about their environmental performance. One exception is the Greater London Authority building by Foster (2002). Its form was derived directly from the pragmatics of responding to climate. It is at "one with the cosmos." In the case of most other blobitecture the generous use of energy-intensive metal skins, combined with the complex steel armatures needed to produce the desired complex, non-linear forms, are certainly in violation of the basic environmental tenets of cosmogeneity. It seems that achieving the appearance of a *cosmogenic architecture* trumps following the environmental ethic of cosmogenesis.

See also: **Emergence • Starchitect**

Figure 38: Team Disney
Headquarters

▌Cosmopolitan architecture

Cosmopolitan: a citizen of the world. — *Webster's Unabridged Dictionary*

... architectures that match the fluidity, flux and complexity of contemporary existence, an existence that is epitomized by the cosmopolis; architecture that might therefore described as "cosmopolitan architectures." — Neil Leach

Due to omnipresent bombardment by electronic media, including social networks, the world has become our community. Citizens participating in this global world community are by definition cosmopolitan. Similarly, architecture that is increasingly globalized is also cosmopolitan, but only if it resists provincialism. The forces of regionalism and contextualism conspire against the new international style – cosmopolitanism. The earlier effort at cosmopolitization, namely the "international style" of the first half of the twentieth century, failed due to its dogmatic insistence upon simplicity, rather than complexity, the static, pure, and precious object, rather than a fluid, changing, and indeterminate organism. The new international style of the twenty-first century is not a style at all, but rather the expression of a new freedom, unfettered by locale. It is complex, rich, expressive, fluid, and indeterminate, as it is based upon an organic metaphor, rather than the machine metaphor of the earlier international style. Today, significant architecture is inescapably cosmopolitan. Once created, contemporary cutting-edge architectural images are broadcast worldwide to become part of the lexicon of twenty-first-century *cosmopolitan architecture*. After all, we are also cosmopolitan due to the power of the World Wide Web. Architecture can no longer escape to the safety of the provincial. In the words of Gilles Deleuze, we have been deterritorialized. Despite the loss of the possibility of provincialism in this increasingly globalized world, there is still a tendency in some quarters to attempt to retreat into provincialism in order to hang on to identity of place. (Heidegger certainly provides a model for this with his romantic musing about a farm in Bavaria.) The rest of us, including the princes, sheiks, and mullahs, have embraced the worldwide spread of American culture, including fast-food franchises, Wal-Mart, and the American-style skyscraper.

See also: **Atopia • Contextualism • Deterritorialization/reterritorialization • Globalization**

Further sources: Leach (in Ballantyne 2002: 100)

Cradle to cradle   ▮

Injustice anywhere is injustice everywhere. We are caught in an inescapable network of mutuality… tied to a single garment of destiny… whatever affects one directly affects all indirectly.
— Martin Luther King

The human race is challenged more than ever before to demonstrate our mastery … not over nature … but ourselves. — Rachel Carson

In the last half-century, our modern society has evolved into a throwaway economy, which is wasting our resources in materials acquisition as well as energy in the production, processing, and disposal of these materials. Every product we purchase is just the tip of a vast pyramid of extracted resources, burnt fossil fuels, and toxic wastes, and often produced with sweatshop labour. In the early 1990s in Germany, Friedrich Schmidt-Bleek and Ernest von Weizsacker first recognized the potential for reducing material use by proposing that modern industrial economies could function very effectively using only one-fourth of the virgin raw materials prevailing at the time. Later Schmidt-Bleek, who founded the Factor 10 Institute, argued that raising resource productivity by a factor of ten was within reach of existing technology given certain incentives.

Reducing materials use begins with recycling, which also creates tremendous energy savings, cuts carbon emissions, cuts air pollution, cuts water pollution, and reduces our growing landfills. The steel discarded each year in various forms is enough to meet the entire needs of the US auto industry. Steel made from recycled scrap metal takes only 26 percent as much energy as that from iron ore. Recycled aluminium needs only 4 percent, recycled plastic uses only 20 percent, and recycled paper uses 64 percent as much, and with far less chemicals for processing. Steel and aluminium can be recycled indefinitely.

Rather than designing products with limited reusability ("cradle to grave"), designers are called on to design systems that support reuse in regenerative products and services, much like the larger system of nature. This concept of "*cradle to cradle*" is explored by American architect William McDonough and German chemist Michael Braungart in their book, *Cradle to Cradle: Remaking the Way We Make Things* (2000). They conclude that waste and pollution are to be avoided entirely, and state, "pollution is a symbol of design failure." They call for "closed-loop" lifecycles that recycle outputs and byproducts of one process as inputs for another, such that "waste equals food," and promote the best manufacturing practices possible for the way things are made. Their *cradle to cradle* (C2C) protocol is a voluntary sustainable product certification, which uses guidelines to guarantee products are high performing, efficient, and harmless to the delicate balances of nature and the human body. This is all based on the notion that everything we own should be recycled, remade, or buried in the ground to compost. EL

See also: **Green design (Archispeak)** • **Sustainability**

Further sources: McDonough (in Mallgrave 2008: 597)

▌ Craft

Architecture is to masonry what poetry is to literature; it is the dramatic enthusiasm of the craft. — C.N. Ledoux (1804)

Craft is a techne as it takes raw nature and transforms it into useful utensils and tools by means of a carefully preconceived and reasoned intelligence. — Demetri Porphyrios

In the contemporary environment of experimentation with blobs and folds, the issue of *craft* has become relevant. A number of high-profile building failures have occurred due to a lack of *craft* in the detailing of the complex connections associated with the new non-Euclidean geometries. Frank Gehry and Daniel Libeskind are notable examples of architects who have over-reached their ability to control the *craft* associated with their complex form adventures. Gehry's problems with the new addition to the Art Gallery of Ontario (Figure 39), and the MIT Computer Sciences building (STATA), are well documented, as are Libeskind's problems with the Denver Museum of Art and its younger sister, the Royal Ontario Museum.

Figure 39: Art Gallery of
Ontario

Recent visitors to the newly reopened and much celebrated Toronto gallery have been shocked to find condensation fogging up and streaming down many of its outer windows, while buckets dot its famed Douglas fir central staircase, catching errant drips.
— Ames Bradshaw, *Toronto Globe and Mail*

The Massachusetts Institute of Technology has filed a negligence suit against world-renowned architect Frank Gehry, charging that flaws in his design of the $300 million STATA Center in Cambridge, one of the most celebrated works of architecture unveiled in years, caused leaks to spring, masonry to crack, mold to grow, and drainage to back up.
— Shelley Murphy, *Boston Globe*

Although there is nothing new about architect-designed buildings having leaking roofs, the problem has become more serious because of increasingly complex building geometries, experimentation with new materials, shortened project schedules, a shortage of constructors with an appreciation for *craft*, and the involvement of more members of the integrated team with responsibility for maintaining a high level of quality. Design by committee can cause things literally to fall between the cracks. The responsibility of the architect for detailing the building has also been distributed among the design architect, the architect of record, the project manager, the product representative, engineering consultants, and the constructors. As more projects fail, there may be a backlash against experimentation with non-Euclidean digital architecture. It will be a shame.

See also: **Blob architecture (Archispeak)** • **Blobitecture** • **Digital architecture** • **Fold** • **Integrated practice**

Creativity   ∎

... the bi-association of two previously unrelated ideas.
— Arthur Koestler

We typically say that there is *creativity* at work when somebody has produced an idea that is surprising, startling, unusual, new, and unconventional. However to be legitimate, it must also be a plausible answer to a worthwhile problem. It must be a real challenge. Just coming up with some weird, crazy answers to irrelevant questions does not cut it. Typically, *creativity* takes conscious effort, often using *creativity* techniques. Sometimes it happens in your sleep, but that is the exception. More often it happens when you "walk away" from the problem at hand.

Brainstorming is a popular technique that involves unfettered spewing forth of ideas without judgment or criticism. Bi-association of unrelated ideas or things is another *creativity* technique. Superimposition of unrelated drawings sometimes does this. Some architects (Will Alsop, Michael Graves, Max Scoggin) paint until a creative direction for the building design reveals itself. Even Le Corbusier liked to combine painting with architectural design. Frank Gehry uses the gesture sketch. Other *creativity* techniques include: taking apart, separating; distorting (squeezing, stretching); exaggerating, taking to extremes; inverting: inside out, upside down; reversing direction; questioning; asserting the negative; finding other ways of looking at it; using metaphor, analogy, symbolism; systematic analysis, and modeling.

Creativity is seldom taught in architecture school. It is perhaps considered to be an innate ability of anyone who selects design as a career choice. Ironically, it is taught in most other disciplines, most of which are not known for *creativity*.

See also: **Craft • Metaphor (Archispeak) • Superimpose (Archispeak)**

▌Critical humanism

Most architects would admit architecture is concerned with people, but as part of a broad-brush humanism based on their ad-hoc assimilation of social and behavioural research findings and their own experience rather than as the core of a finely tuned and critical humanism.
— Paul-Alan Johnson

The term *critical humanism* combines two words that are difficult to pin down. In order to provide a working definition of the term *critical humanism*, the following oversimplified definitions are provided. "Humanism" is the philosophy that believes in humans, rather than God, and reason over belief. The term "critical" implies the use of informal logical argumentation to find truth. Thus, based on the above, and for our purposes here, *critical humanism* can be understood to mean concern for the welfare of humans using a system of argumentation that is rational but not constrained by science or formal logic. It is concerned for the welfare of all sectors of humankind. Combining critical theory and the philosophy of humanism creates a useful paradigm for the architects of the twenty-first century as they face the human and environmental challenges to come.

However, as Johnson points out above, architects do not tend to function as critical humanists. They are "broad brush" humanists who practice their profession as conscientious servants. They subscribe to an unselfconscious ethic of good works that is based on their upbringing as citizens. Whenever possible, the architect attempts to design to the best interests of their larger constituency, as well as to their client's program or brief. The scope of that effort may be political, economic, aesthetic, cultural, or environmental.

With the growing concern for the welfare of the planet, even the architect who is captive to the selfish mandates of their paying client is being drawn into a concern for the welfare of the environment. The dilemma is that architecture, as a discipline, is not yet blessed with an organized and shared body of critical humanist knowledge. Only the most mundane and measurable design recipes are available to be shared. Unfortunately, critical theory is starting to lose its luster in this age of practical efforts at environmental salvage. There are still sporadic and isolated attempts at exploring *critical humanism* in architectural schools, but these efforts may be simply remnants from a past era of academic esotery.

See also: **Critical theory • Brief (Archispeak)**

Further sources: Johnson (1994: 355)

Critical modernism   ▌

... the continuous dialectic between modernisms as they criticize each other ... many modernisms forces a self-conscious criticality, a Modernism # 2. — Charles Jencks

Jencks identifies five modernisms: modernism, reactionary modernism, late modernism, post-modernism, and *critical modernism*. He regards *critical modernism* as the latest evolution of modernism. To quell the voices of the many critics of his pet term post-modernism, he appears to be joining the ranks of critical theorists. As his book *Critical Modernism* (2007) reveals, his interest in critical theory is as a panacea for doomsday fatigue. Critical theory is expected to arrive at alternative scenarios for the survival of humankind from the results of global warming. *Critical modernism* in architecture, on the other hand, is defined as a sort of meta-modernism that floats above the squabble between the other modernisms. Jencks remains the consummate cataloguer, a latter-day Aristotle. If *critical modernism* is to be our salvation, a second coming of modernism, then it carries with it the responsibility of doing even more with less. Unfortunately, the term "critical" has received so much use, and abuse, that it has lost its special meaning. Interestingly, *critical modernism* is almost an oxymoron, as the rational, mechanistic, positivistic basis of modernism runs counter to criticality, in its rejection of pure rationalism and its preference for the organic over the mechanistic. Can *critical modernism* be the answer to our future challenges? Given the extravagance of many of the current crop of digitally mastered architectural confections, it is hard to imagine that we will be spared.

See also: **Critical theory • Late modern architecture • Modernism (Archispeak) • Post-modernism (Archispeak)**

Critical regionalism

Critical regionalism – an investigation of "resolved difference."

How is a work local and universal at the same time? That is the paradox that *critical regionalism* attempts to resolve. The act of holding two disparate ideas simultaneously in the mind is the beginning of critical thinking. Kenneth Frampton's discourse on *critical regionalism* (1983) includes the benefits of embracing both the avant and arrière-garde points of view. Frampton proposes that the arrière-garde position will generate a "resistant, identity-giving culture ... having discreet recourse to universal technique." To maintain a critical edge, an architect needs to be aware of the idiosyncrasies of populism in addition to the canons of academic theory.

An application of Frampton's theory is Alex Tzonis and Liliane Lefaivre's "The grid and the pathway" (1981) – a "bridge over which any humanistic architecture of the future must pass" (P. Ricouer). Critical regionalism will mediate the spectrum between universal civilization and the particularities of place. Ricouer questions "how to become modern and to return to sources; how to revive an old, dormant civilization and take part in universal civilization." This question asserts the necessity of a historical model of continuous evolution whereby lessons of the past inform future moves. However there often exists, as Ricoeur states, the requirement to "abandon a whole cultural past in order to take part in modern civilization." If critical regionalism is a solution, then one would want to know how a region is to be defined or redefined under the circumstance of whole cultural abandonment and therefore its shifting boundaries.

Thoughtful applications of *critical regionalism* appear in Tadao Ando's work. There is a substantial shift away from the "tradition" of Japanese construction and context; however, the severe geometries of his work emerge from the continuous evolution of the minimalist art, spiritual practice, culture, and landscape of Japan. CH

See also: **Atopia • Contexualism • Globalization • Spirit of place**

Further sources: Frampton (in Foster 1983: 16); Frampton (in Jencks 1997: 97); Frampton (in Mallgrave 2008: 519); Frampton (in Nesbitt 1996: 470); Jameson (in Leach 1997: 247); Nesbitt (1996: 468); Tzonis and Lefaive (in Nesbitt 1996: 484)

Critical theory

A whole range of theories which take a critical view of society and the human sciences. — *Dictionary of Critical Theory*

Critical theory is any mental schema which abstracts a model, explanation, speculation, hypothesis or method of action for any aspect of social life. — Iain Borden and Jane Rendell

The umbrella of critical theory covers the work of disparate thinkers and groups whose work shares common threads, such as gender theorists, post-structuralists, post-colonialists, postmodernists, and deconstructionists. — Adam Sharr

Originally developed by the Institute for Social Research, founded in 1929, and known as the Frankfurt School, *critical theory* has evolved from its beginnings as a Marxist-influenced social philosophy into a broad umbrella of theories that have as their common agenda the development of a descriptive and normative basis for increasing the freedom of humankind. *Critical theory* is critical in that it accepts arguments that are based on informal logic – a logic that is accepting of information that has not been scientifically proven. *Critical theory*, on the other hand, is not a theory as such.

    Critical theory is of interest to architectural theorists due to its emphasis on interdisciplinary social research that is philosophical, yet embraces practical reason and rejects all forms of reductionism. Critical theorists generally believe that science and its related positivism are full of non-theoretical interests and are repressive due to their strict adherence to reason. In its focus on the emancipation of all humankind in a democratic global society, *critical theory* includes previously practical and neglected areas of architectural theory such as feminism, race, and the concerns of other marginalized constituencies.

    The co-founder of *critical theory*, Max Horkheimer, stipulated that a critical theory is adequate only if it meets three criteria: it must be explanatory, practical, and normative – all at the same time. (Normative in this context means "what ought to be" – Macey, 2000) Being released from the grip of strict rationalism and positivism is a relief for architects who survived the dogmatic modernism of the first half of the twentieth century.

The central insight of critical theory is that meaning itself-the way we explain what happens around us and thus how we act in response – is a constructed thing. — William Hubbard

See also: **Deconstructivism (Archispeak)** • **Frankfurt School** • **Globalization** • **Normative theory** •**Postmodernism (Archispeak)** • **Post-structuralism (Archispeak)** • **Structuralism**

Further sources: Sharr (2007: 112)

Criticism

While the word "critic" entered the English language in the middle of the sixteenth century, it derives from the Greek *krites* meaning "judge." — Paul-Alan Johnson

Criticism, by most accounts, is ineffectual, disappearing, and on the retreat. — Bernard Tschumi

Everyone is a critic. As the general public is increasingly asked to vote on the winner of *American Idol,* or its equivalent around the world, the role of critic is becoming dangerously egalitarian. Blogs and personal websites contain endless opinions on every topic. Many are inane. Social networks apps poll their membership relentlessly. This popularization of amateur *criticism* has led to a broad, shallow, and generally ill-informed public discourse about the arts, including architecture. Blog postings often degenerate into vulgarities when the author runs out of things to say. Thus, critical discourse has been devalued to the level of the uninformed, unwashed masses. The din from the hordes drowns out the few brave souls who are actually qualified to provide a critique.

Academic criticism involving the theory and philosophy of architecture is increasingly marginalized, as interest moves towards concern for practice and the pragmatic. Most of the architectural intelligentsia who have been critics in the past have retreated into practice. Eisenman, Koolhaas, Libeskind, and Tschumi are on that list. Few newspapers in North America still employ a professional architectural critic. Paul Goldberger and a handful of others are the exceptions. More and more of the criticism by the professional community is now self-generated and thus self-serving. Offices such as Reiser and Umemoto and OMA produce promotional publications disguised as a critique of their acquired intelligence and production. In the future, how will we know what to think about architecture? Professional criticism is becoming a lost art, as public opinion polling has removed the need for critical analysis and reflection.

Daniel Libeskind's angular new addition to the Royal Ontario Museum in Toronto, called "the Crystal," [see Figure 40] was placed at No. 8 on a list of the world's ten ugliest buildings assembled by VirtualTourist. com. The rationale mentions its stark incongruity with the original museum's Romanesque architecture.
— *Toronto Star*, November 20, 2009

See also: **American Pragmatism**

Further sources: Ghirardo (in Ballantyne 2002: 68); Johnson (1994: 43)

Figure 40: The Crystal Invasion

Cryptodeleuzian materialism   ▌

Michael Speaks (2010) uses this term as a label of our current preoccupation with the metaphorical and obtuse writings of Gilles Deleuze and the homespun materialism that he espouses. Hefted sheep, machines, rhizomes, film, the milieu, reterritorialization, the fold, and a preoccupation with the body – including its baser functions – disguise a disdain for the entire effete enterprise of academic post-structuralism. It is seen as the hallmark of our age.

There are two unrelated meanings for the term "materialism." The first is the commonly understood, and somewhat base, meaning of materialism that involves the excess desire for goods and wealth. The other meaning is the one that Speaks talks about. It is the view that the world is entirely composed of matter, with no place for hypothetical abstractions such as universals. Immaterialities are not accepted within this definition of materialism.

To reduce Deleuzian philosophy to a cryptic version of itself is perhaps a disservice to the many interesting and somewhat folksy musings of the man and his collaborator Felix Guattari. The worlds of popular culture and high culture have merged, as have the intellectual and guttural worlds. Particularly important contributions to architectural thought have been his writings on the fold, rhizomes, and film and architecture. It leaves one with the sense that anything goes.

See also: **Deleuzianism** • **Deterritorialization/reterritorialization** • **Film and architecture** • **Fold** • **Post-structuralism (Archispeak)** • **Rhizomatic**

Cultural theory   ▌

This term has been applied to diverse attempts to conceptualize and understand the dynamics of culture. Historically these have involved arguments about the relationship between culture and nature, culture and society, the split between high and low culture, and the interplay between cultural tradition and cultural difference and diversity.
— *Oxford Dictionary of Sociology*

Cultural theory proposes, without reservation, that existing conceptions of architecture need to be replaced by broader and more inclusive issues such as race, gender, space, image and the unequal distribution of resources and opportunities.
— Murray Fraser and Joe Kerr

The above "existing conceptions" are of a male-oriented architecture for the elite. Women, minorities, the poor, are the architecturally disenfranchised. The feminist movement in architecture is still perceived as the responsibility of a few female critics, practitioners, and teachers. Serving the underclasses is still a fringe movement that everyone agrees with, but few make the commitment to participate in. Fortunately, there is a growing counter-culture movement in architecture. As it was with the Woodstock generation of the 1960s, the idea is to once again be "part of the solution," rather than "part of the problem." Programs such as the

Rural Studio at Auburn University in the United States are leading the way in providing a model for an egalitarian, inclusive architecture. Their $20,000 house is a visible demonstration that it can be done. Longstanding programs at Harvard, MIT, and other schools are also preparing the next generation of architects to be more service oriented. It is a sign of our hard times. The "me" generation is being replaced by the "us" generation. The effort is not new. Worker housing programs of the early modernists were a concerted effort at social justice through architecture. Unfortunately Marxism fueled that effort, which made it untenable in North America, particularly during the McCarthy era. This time around the sociopolitical barriers have come down, or have they?

See also: **Critical theory • Feminism**

Further sources: Deleuze (in Leach 1997: 3); Fraser (in Borden 2000: 125)

Datascapes

External programmatic, sociological, or technical facts are what designers call datascapes. — K. Michael Hays

Form becomes the result of such an extrapolation or assumption as a "datascape" of the demands behind it. It shows the demands and norms, balancing between ridicule and critique, sublimizing pragmatics. — Winy Maas

A *datascape* is a type of architectural landscape that reflects external demands placed on it. The Dutch firm MVRDV developed the notion of *datascapes* as pragmatic, yet unconventional, form responses to the myriad of data (chatter) and constraints that are imposed from without. As a reaction to the abstract and theoretical concerns of many contemporary practices, MVRDV focuses on the down-to-earth realities of a project, and in particular, the rules and regulations that supposedly limit it. It is clear that regulations impose unintended uniformities in the urbanscape. One can guess the governing development rule by observing the datascape that it has generated. The simplest is the height restriction. Because of the law that restricts the height of buildings to the width of the adjacent street plus 20 feet, Washington D.C. has no tall buildings, yet land is limited and costly, resulting in a uniform building datum, a "datascape." The artificially precious town of Seaside in North Florida has a number of buildings that follow the strict rules intended to promulgate a version of a nineteenth-century New England seaside town, yet manage to subvert the intended conceit. The cottage designed by Leon Krier (Figure 42) is a good example of bucking the intended datascape (Figure 41).

The challenge for designers is to embrace, but subvert, the restrictions and constraints that comprise the existing datascape. The task becomes that of reinventing the possibilities afforded by those external constraints beyond those envisioned by the regulators.

See also: **Constraints • Pragmatism**

Further sources: Mallgrave (2008: 568)

Figure 41: The intended Seaside datascape: The Truman Cottage

Figure 42: Seaside cottage by Leon Krier: going against the datascape

▌De-architecture

De-architecture suggests a rejection of Modernist role models, an expanded definition of architecture as a concept, and a use of buildings as a means of providing information and commentary rather than expressing form and symbols. — James Wines

In a thinly veiled reference to Marcus Vitruvius Pollio's *De architectura*, Wines provides his 1987 "manifesto to mania" critique of the modern movement. It was visionary in terms of the recipes it provided for a consummated marriage between art and architecture, and landscape and architecture. The work of SITE, Wines' design firm, reflects his rejection of the formalism and functionalism of the modern movement. For him, architecture is practiced as an environmental art. In the 23 years since *De-Architecture*, the work of his firm SITE has evolved into a commitment to "green" environmental architecture. The 2000 publication of his coffee-table book *Green Architecture* established him as a spokesperson for the movement.

Although it received some attention in 1985, the term *de-architecture* never caught on and is now largely forgotten. However, the critique it presented became mainstream. It was 20 years ahead of its time.

See also: **Green building (Archispeak) • Modernism (Archispeak)**

Further sources: Wines (1987: 32)

▌Decentering

The idea of a loss of the conscious self-control exercised by a rational subject is implicit in all theories of decentering.
— *Dictionary of Critical Theory*

Decentering involves moving away from the center. It manifests itself in architecture as the phenomenon of the architect losing their mythical status as the "master builder." Just as humanity was decentered by the discovery that the sun did not rotate around the earth, so the architect is discovering that the architectural project does not revolve around the architect. As the reliance upon cyber designed, and managed, projects increases, the decentering of the architect increases. Other aspects of contemporary decentering include the realization that explicitly rational and "scientific" methods of design are illusionary. The messy truth is that there is no center. The model of a cloud, as described by Charles Jencks (1995), may be an appropriate metaphor for the innate thought process associated with designing.

However, because of the binary needs of the computer tools being used, the design process may finally need to dissipate the cloud and become solid and centered. That center may be the digital model itself. Only the architect remains decentered.

See also: **Deterritorialization/reterritorialization • Digital architecture**

Further sources: Hale (2000: 221)

Decomposition

Decomposition suggests a process whereby one takes a given whole apart in order to find new ways to combine the parts and to evolve possibilities of new wholes and new orders under different structural and compositional strategies. — Anthony Antoniades

A great building must begin with the un-measurable, must go through measurable means when it is being designed and in the end must be un-measurable. — Louis Kahn

Architectural *decomposition* is going to be more prevalent in the future. As the need to salvage components and materials from buildings that are being dismantled increases, the need for buildings to be designed as decomposable will increase. Designing buildings from recycled parts will require a rethinking of the design process. It will more resemble the process of designing and building the informal dwellings found around the world in slum settlements. The result may be more industrialized panel and box technologies, rather than bricks and sticks. There will be an ad hoc element to the design process in cases where the architect must utilize the materials and assembles that have just been salvaged from a building in the process of being disassembled. Much of this already occurs in a modest way in flea markets that recycle old doors, windows, fireplace mantles, and so on. Eventually all buildings will be designed to be easily decomposed and reused. They will tend to be made up of prefabricated assembles, even entire boxes. The Montreal Habitat 67 housing project by Moshe Safdie was an early experiment in stacking boxes, much like shipping container architecture that has become popular recently (Figure 43). Unlike Habitat, the containers can be relocated and reassigned. Shipping containers appear to be at the vanguard of decompositional architecture.

See also: **Ad hocism**

Further sources: Antoniades (1990: 66); Vidler (2008: 60)

Figure 43:
Habitat 67

Decoration

There are three arts: painting, music and ornamental pastry making –
of which architecture is a sub-division. — unknown pastry chef

When Modern architects righteously abandoned ornament on
buildings, they consciously designed buildings that were ornaments.
They substituted for the innocent and inexpensive practice of applied
decoration on a conventional shed ... to promote a duck.
— Robert Venturi in *Learning From Las Vegas* (1977)

Decoration is a word that is not accepted by the architectural community.
It has the connotation of cake decoration, where the icing is added after
the cake has been baked. Architecture that is "baked" (built), and then
"iced" (decorated) by adding superfluous materials is considered poor
design practice. It is the decorated shed at its worst. *Decoration*, in the
form of ornament, has a long history in architecture. Since the infamous
"ornament is crime" pronouncement by Adolf Loos, decoration has been
controversial. Post-modern architects delighted in decorating the sheds
they produced. Robert Venturi was perhaps its greatest proponent, as
can be seen in the Children's Museum in Houston (Figure 44). Since the
passing of post-modern architecture, the task of decorating architecture
has fallen on the technology of the building. Solar control glazing, brises-
soleil, green walls, and even wind turbines now decorate our buildings.
Color is also reappearing, as can be seen in buildings like the EMP by
Frank Gehry. It is a relief to the consuming public that the consideration
of decoration is once again an aspect of architectural design, even if most
architects are still reluctant to admit it.

See also: **Decorated shed (Archispeak) • Ornament (Archispeak) • Post-
modernism (Archispeak)**

Further sources: Gadamer (in Leach 1997: 135, 157); Shonfield (in Borden 2000:
300)

Figure 44: Houston
Children's Museum

Deep structure ▮

The elements of spatial syntax that reside at the most basic level of language. — Donald Palmer

The linguist Noam Chomsky first used the term as part of a theory of grammar that identified levels of structure in language from deep to surface. As part of structuralism and its linguistic theory, it claims that we all possess an innate capacity for creating sentences. That capacity resides at the level of deep structures that represent certain fundamental understandings of the world. Those deep structures of language underlie every sentence it is possible to utter. The mechanism for creating meaning involves raising deep structures to the surface to form surface structures using prescribed generative rules.

The specific adoption of Chomsky's model of language allows Eisenman to clearly distinguish between deep (conceptual) and a surface (perceptual) structure.
— Mario Gandelsonas

The transformative process in moving from deep to surface structure in language is the key to the interest in *deep structures* by some architects, Peter Eisenman being the most visible. In generating his House 11 he started with the *deep structure* of a cube, which he subsequently put through a series of transformations, including the introduction of a grid with resulting negative spaces to be occupied. He regarded this process as analogous to the process of transforming *deep structure* to surface structure in language. The resulting architecture was intended to reveal the *deep structure* of the cube as a basic type – an "architecture of architecture" (Jacques Derrida). Architectural interest in *deep structure* has faded since its popularity in the 1980s. Perhaps its lasting contribution has been that of establishing "type" as a legitimate basis for approaching the architecture of architecture.

See also: **Semiology (Archispeak)** • **Structuralism** • **Typology (Archispeak)**

Defamiliarization ▮

Defamiliarization is the process of strange making or ostranenie. Rendering something that is familiar unfamiliar is a technique for lateral thinking and creativity. Betty Edwards used the technique of drawing upside down to promote seeing something for the first time, rather than seeing what one expects to see. Sometimes just repeating a word over and over, or staring at an image for a long time renders it strange. Placing an everyday object in a gallery makes the audience see it differently. Marcel Duchamp's 1917 urinal as fountain is the most famous example. Architecture can make a familiar element appear strange by placing it outside its milieu. The post-modernists delighted in placing familiar historic building elements out of context. Even popular cultural icons can become fodder for the post-modernist architect, as is evidenced by Robert Stern's treatment of the Disney Casting Building (1989) (Figure 45). Mickey has become a scupper.

Cinderella's castle is defamiliarized as a banal two-storey office building – very strange.

Digital design provides many opportunities for strange making. The ability to deform shapes, change colors and textures with ease makes the game of *defamiliarization* possible and often desirable. By shifting the familiar into the unfamiliar, one can begin to see opportunities that were previously hidden by their familiarity. You see it for the first time again. Eventually refamiliarization takes over and the moment is lost.

See also: **Abstraction • Allusionism • Associative design • Cartooning • Mask**

Figure 45: Disney Casting Office Building

Deleuzianisms

It is difficult, if not impossible, to find in the writing of Deleuze and Guattari a coherent "rational theory" in the classical sense. In other words, there is not a theory consisting of basic ideas, connected by basic rules of reasoning, into a consistent set of mutually supporting statements of clearly distinguished descriptive, explanatory, or normative nature that can be "tested" like a scientific hypothesis. This is the very message from Deleuze. The message is in the message. It is about focusing on the chaotic, demoniacal, Dionysian, emergent, shapeless, provisional, shape-shifting aspects of life, rather than the orderly. The changing, emerging patterns that result are due to many local decisions, rather than overall grand form ideas. Inconsistencies, rather than answers, bring the resulting experience of self closer to the experience of life, thus preventing theory-driven design from becoming an obstacle, a prison, and a barrier to life.

Deleuzian thought relates to critical theory, in the sense that it challenges traditional assumptions and therefore constraints of conventional "rational" norms – aiming for emancipation, freeing the individual to explore opportunities, possibilities and experiences – a fuller, more Dionysian, chaotic life.

Applied to architectural design, Deleuzian thought rejects traditional preconceptions about "good form." It abandons composition rules in favor of experiments resulting in forms that challenge preconceptions about form. The results, including le pli (the fold), open up new possibilities for life in these environments. Other interesting terms and concepts associated with Deleuze are: se rabat sur, abstract machine, cottage orné, déconner, delirious flight, desiring machines, deterritorialization, emergent form, haecceities, hefted sheep, hermit crab, immanence, machines, body w/o organs, nomadic thought, provisionality, rhizome (vs. tree), schizophrenia, self-organizing systems, singularities, solar anus, sonority, the tick, wasp and orchid, and Uexküll. As can be seen from the above list, there are a lot of *Deleuzianisms*.

See also: **Critical theory • Cryptodeleuzian materialism • Deterritorialization/ reterritorialization • Emergence • Film and architecture • Fold • Hefted sheep • Machines • Rhizomatic**

Further sources: Ballantyne (2007)

Dematerialization   ∎

The vast glass walls of the Dessau building, in Gropius's words "dematerialized" the line between inside and outside ...
— Mark Wigley

Today we are covered in two different natural bodies: the primitive physical being and the virtual being. The attempts to create a "dematerialized" space – a gravitational space that is perceived as a space of null gravity – and a real space founded on virtual images, are, for me, the only endeavors that can supply us with a new reality.
— Toyo Ito

Dematerialization has become an option for the expression of architectural space. Venturi and Rauch's 1976 Franklin Court project in Philadelphia dematerialized Benjamin Franklin's house by erecting only the outline of it. It became a wire-frame diagram of the house. Since then, there have been other notable examples of dematerialized architecture. Herzog and de Meuron's Blur building again redefined the necessary materiality of architecture. Santiago Calatrava has produced several buildings that seem to dematerialize into a lacework of structure (Figure 46). A less successful example of *dematerialization* is the mirrored glass building. Popular a few years ago, it created problems for birds and drivers hit with the glare of the sun. Fortunately mirrored glass facades fell out of fashion quickly.

Dematerialization has another meaning in architecture. As one constructs a digital model of a building, the constituent building assembly layers can be isolated in a process of disassembly. In the case of the building information model (BIM), the model is constructed based upon objects, rather than vectors, making it ideal for disassembly and *dematerialization*.

William Mitchell (1999) points out that cities are also undergoing a minor *dematerialization* as increasingly sticks and mortar places are being replaced by virtual workplaces. As Toyo Ito points out, the virtual world is our new dematerialized reality. Our avatars inhabit that world as our representatives. As the boundary between the material and dematerialized worlds becomes violated, as we have begun to see with the Sony Wii, our daily lives may move from materialized to dematerialized and back at will.

See also: **Abstraction** • **Building information modeling: BIM**

Further sources: Gausa (2003: 154); Mitchell (in Mallgrave 2008: 580)

Figure 46: Oriente Train Station, Lisbon

Deontic

Deontology: the theory of duty or moral obligation.
— *Webster's Unabridged Dictionary*

The *deontic* question of what "morally ought to be" is the most fundamental question that needs to be addressed when starting a design, yet it is the most difficult question in the sequence of intelligence gathering prior to and during designing. It raises issues of fairness and equity that require client and design team agreement at a fundamental level of values. Often the *deontic* questions are difficult to isolate, or even articulate. In many cases the project proceeds with the unspoken assumption that everyone shares the same ethical foundation. If the basic *deontic* questions are not fully answered, the entire enterprise might be a house of cards, propped up by a seemingly rational process of development. Answers to the wrong questions, developed by a process that has ignored the fundamental moral questions, are often persuasive, particularly if the results are presented in fully rendered animation. The situation is further complicated if the *deontic* parameters of a project are deeply embedding in a complex and comprehensive building information model (BIM).

In an all too common scenario, the designer is trying to provide an environmentally responsible design solution that benefits the entire community for a long period of time, whereas the client may be most interested in the short-term profitability of the development. What becomes the focus of the project may be the result of a negotiation between the two. However, the responsible answer in our current state of the planet is the position taken by the moral designer. Fortunately clients are increasingly sharing the designer's concern that buildings be environmentally and socially responsible. This may be happening because green architecture has become good business.

See also: **Alethia** • **Building information modeling: BIM** • **Green design (Archispeak)** • **Intelligence**

Design   ▮

All of the ambiguities surrounding the word "design" are contained in the present-day "designer sunglasses," or "designer T-shirt."
— Adrian Forty

The general public refer to a number of objects and activities as *design*. As a result, the word has become watered down to the point where it has lost its specialized meaning in the design professions. Even within current architectural usage, the meaning of the term is not as obvious as it may seem. In *Words and Buildings* (2000), Forty devotes six pages to the history and explanation of the term within the architectural lexicon. Forty notes that the use of the term did not appear until the seventeenth century, or relatively recently in the history of architectural discourse. At first it simply meant "drawing," or "composition." It was a controversial appearance, as it marked a split between the "work of the mind" and the "work of the hands." The architect was no longer the "Master Builder." Design became a separate intellectual and liberal pursuit. Interestingly, the earlier conjoining of design and construction may be making a comeback with the increasing use of CAD/CAM and integrated design practice. What is old is new again. What we now understand as the activity of architectural "design" may need to be reevaluated as architectural design once again becomes merged with engineering and construction design. We are returning to a pre-seventeenth-century state where it is difficult to draw a distinction between the "work of the mind" and the "work of the hands." The difference this time around is that the hands are robotic.

See also: **Design criteria (Archispeak) • Design genesis (Archispeak) • Design integrity (Archispeak) •Design intent (Archispeak) • Design rationale (Archispeak) • Integrated practice**

Further sources: Forty (2000: 136); Lang (1987: 57); Scruton (1979: 23)

Detail   ▮

Le bon Dieu est dans le détail. — Gustave Flaubert (1821–1880)

God is in the details. — Mies van der Rohe

The architectural detail is typically the place where two materials meet, creating a problem of seams or boundaries. The conventions for dealing with details have changed – from the use of molding to cover seams to the design of reveals that leave a gap between materials, literally "revealing" the joint, and more recently to the creation of curved surfaces that appear seamless.
— Bernard Tschumi and Irene Cheng

The architectural *detail* holds a special place in the heart of the designer. It is often credited with being the seed that generated the building. Modern architecture in particular paid a great deal of attention to the detail as a metaphor for the design ethic brought to the building. Mies van der Rohe exemplified this with his famous corner *detail*. Ironically, the simplicity of the detail was a ruse. The problem of differential expansion of steel and glass, as it passes from inside to outside in a climate like Chicago or Toronto, made it impossible to accomplish the detail without resorting to visual trickery. The minimalism is an illusion. Other architects have also made their reputation with the *detail*. Carlos Scarpa, Alvar Aalto, and Louis Kahn come to mind. In the design of the Kimbel Art Museum (1972), the detail Kahn used to introduce indirect natural light into the galleries became the generating idea for the form of the building. He also made a point of expressing the process of building construction through the use of the *detail* (Figure 47).

Since the end of Kahn style modernism, the *detail* has been transformed from a form-generating device to an algorithmically driven script for a surface with repetitively morphing surface characteristics. With the quick fabrication capability of CNC tools, alternative building skin details can be the object of comprehensive study using physical mockups. The modernist's search for "form for form's sake" has been replaced by the search for "surface details for form's sake."

See also: **Abstraction • Aesthetics • Decoration • Self-similarity**

Figure 47: – Kahn's "honest" concrete detail: Kimbel Art Museum

Deterritorialization/reterritorialization

It refers to the increasing loss of literal and figurative borders between nation-states. — collaborative.curriculum.ca

All life is deterritorializing. — Gilles Deleuze

Deleuze and Guattari use *deterritorialization* as an important aspect of their economic philosophy. Money, labor, and production are all involved. Capitalism is seen as a radical *deterritorialization*. Along with the multinational banking system and the degree to which all economies are linked, the *deterritorialization* of the developed world is almost complete. The system has reterritorialized at a global level. Much of the world is functioning as a common market. The European Union was an important *reterritorialization*, the first to be overtly formed. Along with economic *deterritorialization*, there has been cultural *deterritorialization*. For example, when a new area of the world gains access to the Internet, the community also gains access to every other community that has access to the Internet. At that moment the deterritorializing process begins as the global community envelops the local culture. Here, *deterritorialization* and *reterritorialization* are seamlessly conjoined; *reterritorialization* occurring immediately afterwards, as the local community becomes a part of the global culture. This relates to the idea of a globalization of culture, including architecture (Figure 48). In this process, culture is simultaneously deterritorialized and reterritorialized in different parts of the world as it moves. As cultures are uprooted from certain territories, they gain a special meaning in the new territory into which they are taken. American skyscraper architecture is an example of an export that has caused *deterritorialization* in various parts of the Middle and Far East. The locus of skyscraper construction has shifted from Chicago and New York to Hong Kong, Dubai, and so on. The influence of western architecture on the world is more extensive than tall buildings. Starchitects practice globally. Their brands are spreading like McDonald's.

Post-modern hyperspace has finally succeeded in transcending the capacities of the individual human body to locate itself, to organize its immediate surroundings perceptually, and to cognitively to map its position in a mappable external world. — Fredric Jameson

See also: **Globalization • Starchitect**

Further sources: Ballantyne (2007: 13); Colebrook (2006: 89); Leach (in Ballantyne 2002: 99)

Figure 48:
Deterritorializing office buildings in Paris

Diachronic architectural theory

di·a·chron·ic adj: involving, or relating to the study of, the development of something, especially a language, through time.
— *World English Dictionary*

An architectural theory may be considered diachronic if it is about sustaining traditional architectural language and its evolution. It is based on universals which result in work that can be considered to be organic over time. This evolutionary quality implies that architectural theory is slowly and constantly changing from the bottom up by consensus. Diachronic architecture seeks visual continuity with what exists, possibly using the same materials, window shapes, roof geometries, building organization and orientation. The architectural symbols employed tend to be literal, identifying their purpose. If we see a building with a steeple we will understand it as a church. Thus, diachronic architecture describes or comments on the status quo or "state of the art" of its location. Diachronic architecture is conventional and thus everyone understands it. Societal beliefs and traditions are presented in the work.

It celebrates place making through the recognition of cultural bias by creating continuity in the urban fabric, and societal identity.

Since *diachronic architectural theory* is about what already exists, it tends to be prescriptive. It focuses on the putting together of elements in a prescribed manner. Thus, creating diachronic architecture involves learning the rules, why they are important, and how to apply them.

Architects whose work might be considered diachronic in nature are Christopher Alexander, Robert Stern, Charles Moore, and Robert Venturi. The twenty-first-century generation of digital architects seems much less interested in diachronic architecture in favor of the synchronic. MA

See also: **Contextualism • Diachronic (Archispeak) • Place (Archispeak) • Synchronic**

▌Difficult whole

Since nature has designed the human body so that its members are duly proportioned to the frame as a whole ... in perfect buildings the different members must be in exact symmetrical relations to the whole scheme. — Vitruvius

The difficult whole in an architecture of complexity and contradiction includes multiplicity and diversity of elements in relationships that are inconsistent or among the weaker kinds perceptually.
— Robert Venturi (1966)

Venturi is committed to the idea of the difficult whole, and this seems to follow from his feeling about the Zeitgeist. — Robert Maxwell

In Venturi's view, it is an obligation of the architect to acknowledge the messiness of his projects and the programs that he is executing. It also includes the potential satisfaction of achieving a difficult, rather than a simple, legible whole. Unfortunately, the *"difficult whole"* is a phrase that has been largely forgotten since Venturi coined it in 1966. The relevance of the *difficult whole* to the current architectural idiom is clear. As parametric design grows in the profession, there is the danger that the obligation to consider "the whole" can be forgotten. Even though the utilization of a "parti," or overall form concept, is old fashioned, it is an important obligation of the architect to be the steward of the whole. One can envision an architecture of sub-optimized parts without a "big idea" to pull it together, to give it coherence and thus meaning. An even greater disaster would be if each actor in the integrated team insisted upon the project being driven by his or her "big idea." A single project with many *difficult wholes* under consideration would be impossible to bring to clarity. The role of the architect in this situation could be that of arbitrator, but preferably she should just pull rank as the generalist. After all, the *difficult whole* is difficult because it is more than the sum of its parts. But what does that difference consist of? Perhaps the difference is the intangible poetics of the whole.

See also: **Elementarism • Parametric design • Parti (Archispeak) • Poetic (Archispeak)**

Digital architecture

I think there are very interesting times ahead for digital practices, and eventually it will just be the only way. — Winka Dubbeldam

Digital tools to assist architectural design extend back to the late 1960s, when IBM's CRAFT program for topological juggling was developed. One of the applications involved room adjacency assignments in complex buildings. An early version of an architectural digital design assistant that employed CRAFT was the PDP 15 system by the now defunct DEC Company. The program was limited to two-dimensional manipulations of proximity and spatial geometry. I used the system in the mid-1970s to plan room adjacencies and geometries for a new university in Saudi Arabia. The exercise took only one weekend, whereas the manual version would have taken several weeks. Ten years later, AutoCAD emerged as the breakthrough digitally based drafting tool. It became the industry standard for a decade. Since then, digital tools for architectural representation have evolved into three-dimensional rendering and animation tools. Programs such as Sketchup and ArchiCad also began to be used as visualization tools in the early stages of design development (Figure 49). Currently building information modeling systems (BIM) such as Revit are becoming the office standard for design, design analysis, production of construction drawings, and project management. Clearly, *digital architecture* is now the standard practice in architectural firms. It is on the verge of radically redefining the very nature of architectural production itself through the parametric integrated team design process and the ability to produce and evaluate complex design schemes rapidly and repetitively. Rapid prototyping, using in-house CAD/CAM capability, is adding to the profound impact that digital practice is having on the architectural enterprise. Interesting times are ahead as the technology moves from its current early beta stage to a fully developed and mature technology. By then we may be discussing holographic architecture.

See also: **Building information modeling: BIM • Integrated practice • Rapid prototyping • Topology (Archispeak)**

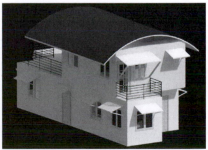

Figure 49: Student digital model

Digital materiality

Digital materiality: design using computer programs directly, resulting in finished building elements.

The architect provides the program for the CNC machines and takes responsibility for the manufacturing of the building elements .... Mockups can be used in the design office more readily to explore and refine architectural ideas in the flesh.
— Fabio Gramazio and Matthias Kohler

The implications of the above development for the role of the architect are profound. To resume control over the material assemblies that are used in a design is a significant step towards re-establishing the direct involvement of the architect in the materiality of the building. For too long, that involvement has been at arms' length, as product suppliers and various contractors have assumed responsibility for the development and detailing of building products and assemblies. The traditional "mock-up" was a step in the right direction, but it was typically a one-time simulation for the purpose of demonstrating to the client an element of the proposed facility, and not a series of "prototypes" produced in order to refine the design and production process of a building assembly. Many schools of architecture have invested in rapid prototyping capability. In my recent design/build studio at Florida A&M University, student Thomas Yohe assembled a working three-dimensional printer for rapid prototyping

of his design projects (Figure 50). Programs such as the Yale studio of John Eberhard have for nine years given students the hands-on opportunity to explore the potential of *digital materiality* by having CNC milling machining capability. It is a hopeful sign that eventually the design of entire building skins may benefit from the digitally supported manipulation of materials and their configurations. The architect has resumed the role of master builder with the help of his robot friends.

Figure 50: Tom Yohe's rapid prototyper

... a digitally controlled robot called R-O-B has been laying 7,000 bricks in a 22-meter-long looping wall along patterns specified by a computer. The project is the brainchild of two architects, Fabio Gramazio and Matthias Kohler. They're out to prove that "digital characteristics can enrich a material and thus influence its architectural expression." They've even coined a term for this notion: digital materiality. — *ARCHITECT digital Newswire* (October 27, 2009)

See also: **Digital architecture • Prototyping**

Further sources: Iwamoto (2009)

Disneyfication

Disneyfication is the deliberate packaging of places wherein culture and heritage inauthenticity are actively promoted and impose an enormous distance between inheritance and lived reality.
— Kelly Shannon

It is in Disney that the worlds of architecture and entertainment, which have been moving closer to each other for years, ... becoming so intimately intertwined that it is sometime impossible to tell which is which. — Paul Goldberger

EPCOT is the ultimate example of *Disneyfication*. Ironically it was originally intended as a prototype community of tomorrow (Figure 51). Instead, it has become an embarrassing showcase for stereotyping each country that has the dubious honor of being parodied. The inauthentic nature of this orgy of *Disneyfication* is appropriate as it is a Disney production. The audacity of EPCOT is only exceeded by the current version of Las Vegas. Las Vegas is EPCOT on steroids. Where else can you experience Paris, Venice, New York, and a mammoth "Egyptian" glass pyramid within walking distance of each other? Theme cities are another version of this phenomenon. The Old West, New Orleans, Key West, and the medieval European town (the new urbanism) have been recreated throughout North America. Often the recreation is achieved by the use of stucco to represent stone and fiberglass or plastics to represent everything else, including tile roofs.

Disneyfication is part of the current commoditization of architecture. In fact it is the most honest and direct form of commoditization. It does not hide behind the aura of a starchitect. The stamping out of Gehry buildings that reference the Guggenheim at Bilbao is no less an act of commoditization than the New York, New York casino.

In a more subtle fashion, almost every city has become victim to *Disneyfication*. The fantasy of traveling to a place that is authentic without leaving town is appealing to consumers. These inauthentic places become pathetic substitutes for the real thing. Regardless of how many cocktails have been consumed at the bar while waiting for a table, people do not really believe that they are in Italy as they dine in the plastic splendor of "The Olive Garden."

See also: **Bilbao effect • Commoditization • Globalization • Hyperrealism (Archispeak)**

Further sources: Shannon (in Gausa 2003: 173)

Figure 51: Disneyland

▍Eco-tech

Today, technology destabilizes and transforms the modern age.
— Sir Richard Rogers

Technology causes problems as well as solves problems. Nobody has figured out a way to ensure that, as of tomorrow, technology won't create problems. — Jared Diamond

The only way to make change is to make that which you hope to change obsolete. — Buckminster Fuller

Innovations in design occur when a need or opportunity arises, hence the old adage that "necessity is the mother of invention." The "high tech" school of architecture in the 1970s, personified by such influential buildings as Renzo Piano and Richard Roger's Pompidou Center in Paris (1977) and Roger's Lloyds Building in London (1984), was briefly challenged in the 1980s by the emergence of post-modernism. The subsequent rejection of the objectivity and mechanical instrumentality that had informed the practice of modern architecture through much of the twentieth century gave way to picturesque and historical interpretation. The tectonics and systematic organization of services then received little attention. Later the growing awareness of the limited resources of fossil fuels and their irreversible destruction of the Earth's climate created a new perspective on the methods of environmental controls in buildings. In Victor Olgyay's influential book, *Design with Climate* (1963/1973), he constructs a framework for the interconnected balance between the environmental functions of architecture and technology, and explains working with nature rather than against it.

Currently a new generation of buildings and architects have begun to again expand the vocabulary of architectonic language articulated in buildings but with different objectives, the most significant of which is the view of sustainability in architecture. The expression of clear functional relationships between space, construction, and environmental systems is expressed again. Brise-soleil, glass facades, independent framework, roof gardens, and other elements of the external envelope are again becoming more intricate in the service of environmental control. The tectonic begins to favor the sophistication and diversity of the modern environmental envelope. High-tech forms and materials in innovative approaches for environmentally intelligent methods are brought together. The term *"eco-tech"* is used for these designs that are organizationally efficient, energy conscious, and technologically appropriate in addressing the broad spectrum of ecological and cultural issues while suggesting ways to enhance life on this planet. EL

Most people are more comfortable with old problems than with new solutions. — Charles Browe

See also: **Cradle to cradle • Green design (Archispeak) • Sustainability (Archispeak)**

Elementarism

■

The advance of modern science has been dominated by elementarism and reductionism. Every phenomenon considered is divided into its basic elements and relations and is viewed as the sum of these elements. The elementarism view has been dominant in the theory, and practice of art and architecture. — Juhani Pallasmaa

"West meets east" could be the slogan for the post-Newtonian, relativistic, universe of the second half of the twentieth century. Modern scientific method was replaced by phenomenology and eastern philosophy as the theoretical foundation for architectural practice and design. The validity of Cartesian dualism was challenged and holism took command. It was an age of restoring unity between philosophy and science.

However, in the twenty-first century the *elementarism* associated with classical modern science may be returning to architectural production. The popularity of digitally based parametric design is overtaking the design arts. Parametric design, by definition, involves the reduction of a design challenge, or "problem," into its constituent elements (Figure 52). Each element is then isolated and suboptimized or "solved," as though designing is analogous to working through a mathematical problem. It is the second coming of twentieth-century reductionism. The making of architecture becomes a process of programming a computer model using algorithms, or scripts, developed to meet the performance specifications for suboptimizing the specific parameter under consideration. The computer model does the rest, as the architect sits back and waits for the results to spit out. Green architecture parameter lists such as LEED further promote *elementarism*, and thus frustrate the ability of the architect to treat the design as a whole. Team design practices also create an agenda of concern for the constituent parts, rather than a poetic and elegantly resolved whole.

See also: **Algorithm • Emergence • Holism • Parametric design • Phenomenology (Archispeak)**

Further sources: Pallasmaa (in Nesbitt 1996: 449)

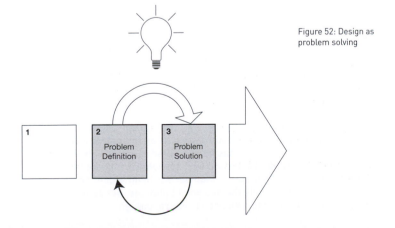

Figure 52: Design as problem solving

▌Emergence

Emergence requires the recognition of buildings not as singular and fixed bodies, but as complex energy and material systems that have a life span, and exist as part of the environment of other buildings, and as an iteration of a long series that proceeds by evolutionary development towards an intelligent ecosystem. — Michael Hensel

Emergence is generally described as a process of arising, emerging, coming to attention or gaining shape or pattern not from an overall plan or concept, but out of the self-organizing arrangement of smaller elements guided by simple rules of combination or cooperation, the properties of those elements, and information about the immediate context of each element.

The concept of *emergence* and emergent properties dates back to antiquity, but has been the object of increasing attention for the past 150 years or so. It is used and discussed in many disciplines, but more recently in architecture and urban planning. The phenomenon of emergence is present in nature – both in living and in non-living, physical systems. The patterns and designs resulting from emergent processes are often of surprising beauty, fluidity, and efficiency, for example structural strength and economy. They are "unexpected" – the variety and forms cannot immediately be reduced to the component, and exhibit a sense of coherence and wholeness. Techniques and programs using emergence principles can lead to innovative and surprising results. "Emergent Technologies and Design" is a Master of Architecture program at the AA Graduate School started in 2003. It is the beginning of a promising avenue of architectural research.

The possibility of programming computers to simulate emergent processes has given rise to building information modeling (BIM) software that supports the development and representation of designs for structures and buildings. It not only generates the designed model, but also supports implementation by keeping track of the dimensions, materials, costs, specifications, and so on. The programs can then be used to digitally control production and assembly. CNC milling tools for cutting, extrusion, connection, and assembly make the construction of designs more feasible and economical than was possible with earlier design and construction methods. The technology is rapidly developing and changing. Possibilities of "growing" buildings using digitally controlled emergent processes are being envisioned, for example using nanotechnology: components at nanoscale fed with materials to "grow" structures.

In urban planning, the concept is more widely used to describe urban growth and organization patterns that are based on relationships between small neighboring elements (for example, houses) as opposed to overall formal concepts or large-scale patterns such as the Manhattan street grid or radial street patterns.

Emergence, or evolutionary optimization, is an important new concept that in recent years has been applied to artificial intelligence, information theory, digital technology, economics, climate studies, material science and biometric engineering. In an architectural context it involves not only the design of buildings, but also the composition of new materials and structural design. — Helen Castle

See also: **Artificial intelligence • Building information modeling: BIM • Chaos theory (Archispeak) •Morphogenetic design**

Further sources: *Architectural Design*, 74(3); Jencks (1995: 143)

Emptiness   ▌

Emptiness is more akin to the idea of space, or interval. The Japanese have the word *ma* which comes close to the meaning of emptiness ... the gap between the stones ... the silence between the notes ... when a child's swing reaches the point of neither rising or falling.
— Michael Benedikt

Emptiness is the space of absence. If we look on architecture as a complex system of information that can not only express itself in buildings but is also represented by everything that characterizes the space between buildings, and between the people who experience the buildings, and on a broader scale, the city and the urban environment, *emptiness* can be an absence of objects or built elements; it can be an absence of quality or an absence of emotions and identity.

The first case, the absence of built objects and elements, finds its greatest expression in the Japanese concept of *emptiness*: minimalism as an extreme feature, a space enclosed by boundaries thinned down and dematerialized as something qualitatively sought after, so as to have minimal influence and enhance the power of *emptiness*. This, however, is a consciously created *emptiness*, an *emptiness* designed to represent and reinforce the value of absence. This is an *emptiness* arising from the contrast with the quality of what contains it and surrounds it.

The second case concerns spaces without quality, urban and suburban spaces not occupied by buildings or occupied by inhabited or industrial container buildings, where the design contribution is so qualitatively poor, if not non-existent, that it represents not only an architectural void, but a vacuum in life. Sprawl, characterized by an uncontrolled and disorderly spread of containers devoid of identity and of unifying elements such as car parks and shopping centers or open spaces, is to be considered as qualitative *emptiness*.

It is more difficult, especially in architectural terms, to define *emptiness* as an absence of emotions. Emotion in architecture is given by the balance or imbalance of the composition/aggregation of elements, which, on different scales, make the space appealing, dense with inspiration, dynamic, and emotionally attractive. A space that does not arouse emotion or inspiration can amount to an empty void. A building that does not stimulate and is lacking in architectural quality is synonymous with a vacuum.

In spite of what we have said, the notion of space today is no longer closely connected with real space. Thanks to new technologies, the perception of space has become fluid, boundless, and infinitely extendable. Reality can even be augmented through flows of information and images visible only on the screen, which are superimposed on real images. Thus *emptiness* can be customized and transformed into a parallel reality, a different space, thick with information. In this way empty surfaces and spaces within material reality, through the use of digital interfaces, become virtual venues and spaces for sharing events, information and emotions, as well as useful tools for changing the perception of reality. AO

See also: **Absence/presence • Minimalism (Archispeak)**

Further sources: Benedikt (1987: 32); Heidegger (in Leach 1997: 124)

Envelope-driven design

The new envelopes are integrally tied to contemporary digital design technologies and specific kinds of software that coordinate and synthesize multiple parameters and all sorts of data into a smooth, frictionless flow. — K. Michael Hays

The history of architecture has been dominated by *envelope-driven design*. For at least the first 2,000 years it was the correct design of the façade that occupied the Western architect. In the first half of the twentieth century there was a very short period of time when modern architecture shifted the design emphasis to form, rather than surface. After less than 50 years of modern architecture, post-modern architects returned the attention back to the envelope. It was the envelope that was to reveal the meaning of the building. Since then, the new digital architecture has taken the design of the building envelope much further. The emphasis has now shifted to the technology of the skin. High-performance metal and glass skins have replaced the modern and post-modern rectilinear curtain walls hung on Euclidean structural grids. Walls and roof can now form a continuous blobular or folded envelope. The contemporary envelope is considered to be the most important component of a sustainable, environmentally sensitive, building.

Lord Norman Foster's Swiss Re building (2004) demonstrates the process of allowing the design of the building envelope to determine the form of the building (Figure 53). Unfortunately, it is the most expensive building in London, based upon its recent sale.

Architecture is increasingly becoming lifelike. As the investigation of biomimicry continues, reactive skins may become common. It is a much more sophisticated version of opening a window when the weather is nice.

See also: **Biomimicry • Digital materiality • Facadism • Post-modernism (Archispeak) • Vitalism**

Figure 53: Swiss Re Building

Eroticism   ▮

Eroticism is not the excess of pleasure, but the pleasure of excess.
— Bernard Tschumi

**Architecture is the ultimate erotic object, because an architectural act,
brought to the level of excess, is the only way to reveal both the traces
of history and its own immediate experiential truth. Neither space nor
concepts are erotic, but the junction between the two is.**
— Bernard Tschumi

Eroticism today is not necessarily linked to explicit forms portraying
the sexual attributes of the body or to the representation of erotic acts:
eroticism in architecture, as in art and music, is a subliminal, sensual
message engendered by the wish to create spaces that interact with
human bodies and their senses. It can be communicated by the use of
soft organic shapes that are not directly associable with the body but
suggest a fluidity of forms similar to that of the body, or by assonances
or dissonances between the interior, the exterior, and the arrangement
of various features, by apparent contrasts which stimulate our sense of
perception to provoke a shiver in us and envelop us, making us feel an
active part of the space in which we move.

The main characteristic of *eroticism* is to arouse desire and attraction,
so in buildings and spaces *eroticism* is expressed by the capacity for
attraction and fascination that they are able to provoke, by the desire
for both visual and physical penetration that is awakened in people. The
tension between transparency and mass, between voids and volumes,
the intensity of light and shade, the altering of surfaces caused by
the incidence of light or by the passage of people, the capability for
transformation and "movement" that a building can express through
the use of sensitive materials or changing surfaces: all this gives erotic
characteristics to spaces and volumes. Also the relationship with the
surroundings is a factor contributing to the *eroticism* of a building or
space and to its "emotional intensity," whether based on strong contrasts
or on a more minimal and enveloping inclusion that becomes evident in a
less obvious manner but is none the less communicative. AO

See also: **Allusionism • Architectural psychology • Fetishization • Morphogenetic
design • Phallocentrism •Psychological needs • Soft architecture**

Further sources: Tschumi (in Ballantyne 2002: 44); Tschumi (1994: 70, 89)

Essentialism   ▮

**The metaphysical view that in reality there exists not only individual
objects, but also essences.** — Donald Palmer

**Essentialism is a belief in the priority of essences. An essence would
be something like a Platonic Form – a definition, a formula, and a set
of characteristics that stabilizes objects in the world. The essence of
humans is that which they all have in common, "humanity."**
— Roland Barthes

Essence is part of the Platonic schema that describes reality as existing at two levels, the "particular" and the "idea." It has been a part of the architectural tradition of all but the brief period of deconstructivism, when all previous constructs about essences were abandoned. Essences were seen as fictions, arbitrarily invented by man and not the product of a divine hand. The new paradigm was to be a new start for architecture, free of any encumbrances from the past. The deconstruction of essentialism posed a dilemma for the designer, as all traditions were forsaken, leaving a vacuum – a tabula rasa. Gone were the primacy of Euclidean geometry, aesthetic norms, contextualism, concern for constructability, and even structural limitations. The architect could no longer rely on an innate understanding of the essence of the thing to be designed, its *essentialism*. What emerged was mostly an orgy of personal mannerist forms, presented in illegible superimposed graphics. Little deconstructivist architecture was actually built. The critics and the architectural media eagerly received the few buildings that were constructed. They made good copy.

Once the novelty wore off, the way was clear for recognition of a new architectural essence. *Essentialism* returned in the form of critical theory. Outdated constructs regarding platonic form, purism, and the pre-eminence of the functional imperative, were replaced by an understanding of the universal condition of humanity and its interdependence with the natural world and Gaia, or our earth essence. Twenty-first-century architecture contains the promise of becoming more inclusive, less preoccupied with itself, and more interested in the larger role it plays in the community of man and her earth.

... how to make architecture that ... would refuse to acknowledge the stability of the concept of architecture which is buttressed by a grounding metaphysics of essentiality and which in turn allows for the appearance of the timeless self-evidence of architecture's "essential" features. — David Goldblatt

See also: **Critical theory • Deconstructivism (Archispeak) • Gaia architecture • Green design (Archispeak) • Tabula rasa**

Further sources: Goldblatt (in Ballantyne 2002: 159); Palmer (1997: 143)

▌Ethics

An architect must choose between fortune and virtue.
— Leon Battista Alberti

Contemporary architecture's main task is to interpret a way of life valid for our time. — Sigfried Gideon

The discussion regarding *ethics* in architecture can occur at two levels. The first comes under the label "professional ethics." It is concerned with the behavior of the architect. The second aspect of *ethics* in architecture is more philosophical. It asks the question "What is the appropriate role of architecture in society?" This aspect of architectural ethics is much more difficult to pin down.

Professional *ethics* are bound up in the outdated notion that architecture is a gentleman's profession, bound by unwritten rules of conduct and decorum. The "rules" were the same standards of conduct that were expected of any Victorian gentleman from the upper classes. Fair play, service to country and the less fortunate, honesty, loyalty, and reserve were valued. Eventually as the profession opened up to the less privileged masses it became necessary to codify and enforce the rules of professional *ethics*. Professional organizations such as the American Institute of Architects and the Royal Institute of British Architects now provide a "Code of Conduct" that prescribes and enforces the appropriate ethical behavior of its members.

The history of *ethics* in architectural design reaches back at least as far as Vitruvius in the first century AD. He prescribed that architecture ought to provide durability, convenience, and beauty. Andrea Palladio took the ethical challenge further with the stipulation "that work (architecture) cannot be called perfect, which should be useful and not durable, nor durable and not useful, or having both of these should be without beauty" (1739). Nikolaus Pevsner restated the same sentiment when he famously made the observation that "a bicycle shed is a building; Lincoln Cathedral is a piece of architecture" (1958/2005). Ethically a work of architecture must therefore serve a higher purpose than mere shelter. That higher purpose has been described as "poetically dwelling" (Heidegger, 1977). In the first half of the twentieth century architectural ethics were intertwined with social/political agendas, in particular Marxism. The concern for architecture in the service of the worker class and humanity in general was subsequently put on hold as architects delved into archi-philosophy for a couple of decades.

Since the decline in interest in structuralist theory in architecture, the focus has shifted to that of being accountable for the consequences of a built work of architecture. Thus an ethical architecture of the twenty-first century is green, sustainable, inclusive, and it is hoped, affordable.

See also: **Archi-philosophy • Green design (Archispeak)**

Further sources: Ballantyne (2007: 32); Harries (1998: 4)

Event space   ▌

Event space refers to architecture as a catalyst and promoter of social activities, and is closely linked to the contemporary view of public space and the public value of buildings. It does not refer in this case to spaces dedicated to specific, planned events, such as theaters, stadiums, and churches, but rather to the design approach to the space conceived as an *event space*. The event is what happens when various needs, desires, and actions meet and intersect, creating a dynamic tension between the space and the human activities correlated to them.

When we design a building or a place, thinking of it as *event space* and therefore as a catalyst and propagator of energy, we imagine the space in its multidirectional and interchangeable qualities, both functional and visual; we design, not according to a strictly functional logic, but rather according to an emotional, interactive logic, which leaves room for opportunities and the unforeseen, and which reinterprets the function in the light of the will to initiate events.

The *event space* is a conceptually dynamic space, fragmented and fluid at the same time, tangential to the function, created to favor the occurrence of events without planning them beforehand. It is a loose space. If we want to give the event space a concrete connotation, we can say that in it the use of color, from the surprise aspect in the use of the materials and the visual and functional dynamism of the surfaces, acquires a communicative and not just a decorative value. Having said this, such choices do not automatically generate an *event space*, because the manner of use of these elements is fundamental; it is the interaction with the context and the destabilizing and surprising effect of the space or building in relation to it that generate the *event space*. AO

See also: **Absence/presence • Communitarianism**

Further sources: Colebrook (2006: 102); Hale (2000: 126); Kipnis (in Mallgrave 2008: 546); Tschumi (1994: 157, 255)

Evidence-based design

Evidence-based design (EBD) is the process of basing decisions about the built environment on credible research to achieve the best possible outcomes.

EBD has emerged out of the healthcare design industry in the United States. It is part of a larger trend towards accountability in architecture. Healthcare architects can now earn the EBD credential to place after their names. It certifies that they have taken additional coursework and passed a certification test. The emphasis is upon the use of legitimate research as the basis for making design decisions. It sounds like a laudable goal. The problem is that relevant hard scientific research findings related to architectural design decisions are almost nonexistent. The research that has been conducted tends to be social science research whose findings are difficult or inappropriate to generalize as recipes for "best practices." Environmental psychology, man–environment relations (MER), and environment/behavior studies (EBS) have been some of the labels that have been given to efforts at the development of a research-based design practice. It is significant that most of this work was done in the 1970s, with little impact on architectural practice, then or now. This is best demonstrated by the work of the Environmental Design Research Association (EDRA). It is in its forty-second year as an organization that promotes environmental design research, yet the research findings of its members are not part of the mainstream architectural knowledge base. The problem is that EBD must rely on answers to only those questions for which findings can be generalized beyond the specific circumstance that the research encounters. Even a simple question such as the effects of different colors on mood and behavior has no solid answers, despite a number of studies. Even the often-claimed calming effect of pink on prison inmates has been refuted.

Perhaps one day architects will have a reliable body of research findings on which to base design decisions. That day seems very far off. At best, the questions that will be answered by research will be the least important ones that the architect faces. Research will tell us what to do about some technical or functional aspect of the building, but not why to do it, or if the result is beautiful.

See also: **Architectural determinism • Architectural psychology • Behavior and environment • Intelligence •Performance-based design • Psychological needs**

Existentialism   ▮

Man is nothing else but that which he makes of himself.
— Jean-Paul Sartre

Existentialism – like phenomenology, to which it is closely related – is one of the major schools of twentieth-century philosophy. It has had a significant influence in architecture and many other fields concerned with the relations between ideas and things. The term itself was probably coined by the French Catholic philosopher Gabriel Marcel around 1945, but it was popularized by his compatriot Jean-Paul Sartre, initially through the 1946 lecture and book entitled *Existentialism and Humanism* (Sartre 1948). The sources of existentialist ideas can also be traced back to a number of significant thinkers from the nineteenth century, including Karl Marx, Søren Kierkegaard, and perhaps most importantly for Sartre, the iconoclastic work of the German philosopher Friedrich Nietzsche.

Seen by many as a branch of phenomenology, a key source for existentialist ideas is the early work of Martin Heidegger, particularly his magnum opus *Being and Time*, first published in 1927, which influenced Sartre's own major philosophical work *Being and Nothingness* which appeared in French in 1945. True to one of the basic principles of the existentialist approach that philosophy should develop from the "bottom up" (as in the famous slogan "existence precedes essence"), Sartre sought to make his ideas accessible at all levels of society, creating works in a number of literary genres such as novels, plays, and political magazines, and going on to become a major public figure in the post-war French intellectual scene.

The crux of the existentialist approach is that each individual must take responsibility for his or her own actions and decisions, and that – in Heidegger's terms – authentic being involves acknowledging the finiteness of life (or "being-towards-death") and celebrating the possibilities offered by dwelling within the Fourfold (Heidegger, 1971). Often accused of encouraging unnecessary angst and despair at the futility and apparent meaninglessness of life, Sartre claimed his seemingly nihilistic philosophy was actually profoundly optimistic. He emphasized both the freedom and the obligation for each individual to create a fulfilling and satisfying life by transcending whatever humble and unpromising circumstances they might originally find themselves in. Rather than blaming "outside" forces such as social conditions or genetic inheritance, it is up to each of us to take responsibility for our own successes and failings.

In architecture these ideas have had a profound – although diffuse – influence, including in the work of broadly phenomenological writers such as Christian Norberg-Schulz (1971, 1975, 1985) and Juhani Pallasmaa (2001). On a more directly political level these ideas have also fed into the area of professional and environmental ethics, where many architects have been motivated to engage directly with building users in the task of improving their everyday living conditions, such as Christopher Alexander, Lucien Kroll, and Alvaro Siza. JH

Man is nothing else but what he purposes, he exists only insofar as he realizes himself, he is therefore nothing else but the sum of his actions, nothing else but what his life is. — Jean-Paul Sartre

See also: **Phenomenology**

▌Existential space

Existentialism believes that existence precedes essence. It asserts that there is no such thing as "human nature," rather the determinant of our behavior is our freedom. — Donald Palmer

Lived existential space resembles the reality of the dream and unconsciousness that are both structured experientially and mentally, independently of the boundaries and characteristics of physical space and time. — Juhani Pallasmaa

Post-modern hyperspace has finally succeeded in transcending the capacities of the individual human body to locate itself, to organize its immediate surroundings perceptually, and to cognitively map its position in a mappable external world. — Fredric Jameson

The existence of *existential space* is not universally acknowledged. It is dependent upon a belief in phenomenology and the denial of essentialism. It could even be argued that *existential space* is not architectural, as it exists beyond the realm of an objective and evident reality that can be shared. The case that can be made for it involves the fact that for too long our total experience, physical and metal, rational and irrational, has been denied by the tyranny of the measurable. In Cartesian dualistic terms, the mind and body are separated. In *existential space* they are reunited into one integrated touching, feeling, and dreaming experience. The reductionism favored by science denies that experience as unreliable. It is however our reality in the world.

The design of existential architectural space is perhaps impossible, as it must violate the basic laws of space and time. *Existential space* has been attempted, however in post-modern cinema with a mix of dream sequences, flashbacks, animation, and nonlinear timelines. Although it may not be possible to design it as such, architecture becomes existential once it is personally encountered and felt spiritually, emotionally, as well as haptically.

See also: **Existential (Archispeak)** • **Existentialism** • **Phenomenology**

Expert systems

An expert system is software that attempts to reproduce the performance of one or more human experts, most commonly in a specific problem domain, and is a traditional application and/or subfield of artificial intelligence. — *Wikipedia*

As we move through this period of a return to a focus on the pragmatic design concerns associated with sustainability and performance, architectural expert systems will increasingly come into their own. Building information models (BIMs) already incorporate *expert systems* designed to perform routine problem-solving duties. They draw upon an acquired knowledge base, and "knowledge engineering" routines that have been proven in real world head to machine situations. More advanced *expert systems* will incorporate learning systems that will cause the system to evolve as it is used. These more advanced *expert systems* will quickly leave their human teammates behind in acquired knowledge and the wisdom of what to do with it.

Despite the ominous sound of the above, *expert systems* could provide a welcome opportunity for the architect. As expert software outperforms the human designer in the systematic resolution of "problems," she will be freed up to focus on those aspects of the project that go beyond the measurable – that is, the poetic. Socio-cultural relevancy, meaning, and aesthetics are difficult for the current generation of *expert systems* to comprehend. However, it is only a matter of time before architectural expert systems will assume even those subjective designing tasks. Artificial intelligence software will personalize design decisions to match the preferences and choice tendencies of the host architect, thus freeing him or her up to focus on the generation of the initial design concept and interacting with the client on behalf of the designing machine.

See also: **Artificial Intelligence • Building information modeling: BIM • Sustainability (Archispeak)**

Extrusion

Extrusion: The act or process of pushing or thrusting out.
— *The Free Dictionary*

The Autocad command – extrude – had been literally transposed to the production of hyper-dense, high-rise structures. Form follows finance.
— Kelly Shannon and Laura Vescina

"Extrusion Start" and "Extrusion End" will allow you to adjust the placement and size of the mass relative to the view plane from which it is constructed. — Revit instructions

Extrusion is a basic shape manipulation in the creation of digital architecture. It is in the toolbox of most CAD software, including Revit. Other Revit terms such as "align," "split," "trim," and "offset" are used to create and manipulate walls. Massing terms include "reference plane," "work plane," "extrusion properties," "place mass," "solid form," "void form," and "simplify surface." The data entered to define each of the above manipulations is called a parameter, for which explicit values are entered. The categories of parameters include "constraints," "graphics," "materials and finishes," and "identity data," as well as "color." Materials and finishes are further described by attributes such as "transparency," "smoothness," and "shininess." As designing becomes increasingly cyber bound, the above terms will become the language of design.

As described above, the ease of duplicating and extruding digital forms has encouraged the production of repetitive high-rise buildings in rapidly urbanizing cities. Traditional international style modernist skyscrapers evolved as extrusions of their standard floor plate. The same could not be said of many of the current crop of skyscraper hyper-buildings. Contemporary tall buildings attempt to avoid the boring repetition of the same floor plate. Tall buildings that twist and even rotate are emerging.

See also: **Hyperbuilding**

Further sources: Arroyo (in Gausa 2003: 212)

Fabric architecture

Fabric architecture has three connotations. The first deals with the role of the architecture in the urban landscape. Fabric buildings provide the connective tissue of the city, thus allowing the non-fabric building to shine as a landmark. *Fabric architecture* is the architecture that you don't notice.

The second type of *fabric architecture* is the architecture that uses fabric as its main enclosure material. The tent is the basic fabric building. With the development of new, high-tech fabrics, permanent buildings can now be made from fabric. Fabric has become an increasingly common adjunct material. The German Pavilion at Expo 67 is an example of fabric in architecture. (Figure 54)

The third type of *fabric architecture* is the architecture of folds, weaves, and braids. It is the architecture that has emerged with the help of digital design and representation tools. Fabric is a metaphor for the supple, plastic forms now possible. Architecture is beginning to resemble clothing more than the architecture of previous centuries, which resembled a cigar box. Gilles Deleuze and Felix Guattari invoke sewing, and the difference between cotton felt and woven fabric, as metaphorically equivalent to the shift in architectural tectonics. The more recent development of woven nano-fabric, with its endless possibilities for dynamic shape generation, may be the architectural material of the next decade. It may mean that architecture will morph into mega-garment.

Finess breaks down the gross fabric of building into finer and finer parts such that it can register small differences while remaining an overall coherence. — Reiser +Umemoto

Fabric with seams and folds is a metaphor for the new formalism.
— Gevork Hartoonian

See also: **Blobitecture • Digital materiality • Envelope-driven design • Fold • Tectonic form**

Further sources:
Mallgrave (2008: 550)

Figure 54: German pavilion, Expo 67

Façadism

Writing in *Vancouver Review* (2004), Gudrun Will takes stock of the widespread incidence of *façadism* in that city. She refers to the common sight encountered in many cities of those wafer-thin elevational shells, propped up by hefty steel I-beams, of what were once three-dimensional heritage buildings. In this context *façadism* is another term for selective demolition, often conducted in the name of heritage conservation, when a building is razed while retaining only one or two of its street-facing walls for purely aesthetic or decorative purposes. Looking for all the world like a stage set, the intact, paste-on frontage that remains then awaits its turn to be "façadomized," that is, to be surgically rear-ended with a transplanted replacement structure that may or may not bear any relation to its style or scale (Figure 55).

Will's article reviews the debate surrounding the practice of *façadism*. On the one hand, there is the question concerning the complete demolition of historically important city landmarks – their disappearance being wasteful and destabilizing any sense of place. On the other hand, *façadism* does ensure, albeit as a paper-thin presence, a veneer of heritage. Will concludes by quoting an entry on *façadism* in a UK conservation glossary

Figure 55: Toronto Stock Exchange as a front

that states: "while it is a practice much condemned by conservationists, in fact there can be arguments in its favor, but it needs careful handling."

Façadism on an epic scale was practiced during the Age of Enlightenment by one of Catherine the Great's regional administrators. Following the peasant's revolt in 1773, Catherine, in her effort to reform and "westernize" Russia, had divided the country into fifty manageable provinces, planning new settlements for each of the regions. On learning that Catherine and her entourage planned to pass through his province, one administrator, anxious to show building progress, erected a cardboard cutout "collage city" of the unbuilt settlement so that, seen from a distance, an illusion of its completed existence would be perceived.

Another meaning of the term refers to a design preoccupation with "skin-deep" elevational treatments. In this usage, *façadism* disparagingly describes a two-dimensional architectural approach in which the appearance of the public "face" of a building takes precedence over its three-dimensional existence. Historical examples of this approach can be found along Bath's Georgian terraces, crescents, and circuses, where beautifully proportioned and unifying façades often disguise a hotchpotch of accommodation that sometimes exist along the rear elevation. This aggrandizing approach can also be found in Virginia City in the United States – a preserved "cowboy" town dating from Montana's Gold Rush in 1862. Here, typical of all those gunslinging frontier towns seen in Western movies, tall, elegant, and occasionally ornate wooden façades, cosmetize and put a brave face on the humbler, rather ordinary and smaller-scale structures built immediately behind them. TP

See also: **Envelope-driven design**

Fashion █

Architecture aims at eternity; and therefore is the only thing incapable of modes and fashions in its principles. — Sir Christopher Wren

... just as fashion is a system with three parts – a material product, images, and words – so architecture is a three part system constituted out of the building, its image and its accompanying critical discourse. — Adrian Forty

Fortunately, architecture is less constrained as a field than, say, certain of the sciences, though this means that it is perhaps more susceptible to the vagaries of fashion than some might wish. — Paul-Alan Johnson

How naïve Wren's eighteenth-century words sound in today's world obsessed with *fashion*. First the modern, then the post-modern project, succeeded in revealing that Wren's "eternal" classical principles are fictions, just another set of human inventions available for challenge and replacement with whatever is the current intellectual or aesthetic *fashion*. The more recent emergence of the starchitect is further evidence of the power of the media to create and promote fashion. The Bilbao effect has shown that a single, ground-breaking, well-published work of architecture can sway client taste, and subsequently cause their architects to follow the current fashion. The commoditization of almost all aspect of twenty-first-century life makes architecture just another commodity. It poses a dilemma, as popular fashion changes faster than it takes to complete an architectural project. This is not to say that architecture as practiced by the bulk of the profession is as susceptible to *fashion*, as that produced by the few individuals who go out of their way to promote their brand.

A significant change in this dynamic may be now in the works. The sustainability movement may be a return to "eternal principles," not vulnerable to the whims of the latest "thing."

... because the vagaries of fashion so permeate architectural culture, many architects seek something more substantial to hold on to as their authority ... — Paul-Alan Johnson

See also: **Bilbao effect • Branding • Starchitect**

Feminism █

... the approach to social life, philosophy, and ethics that commits itself to correcting biases leading to the subordination of women or the disparagement of women's particular experience and of the voices women bring to discussion. — *Oxford Dictionary of Philosophy*

Belief in the social, political, and economic equality of the sexes. The movement organized around this belief. — *The Free Dictionary*

Feminism in architecture can be defined as women's aspiration not only to work within the space designed by others, in the capacity of decorators or interior designers, but to be architects in their own right and accordingly take part, as designers, in the creation of the space itself. In other words, they have an aspiration to acquire equal professional rights in the design of the container rather than limiting themselves to defining its content.

The professional role of women was always complementary to the design, relegated to determining the details and the arrangement of the furnishings, and not the primary one of establishing the planning and concept of space. This was because the space known to the woman was limited primarily to the domestic environment. The system of architecture, always linked to the complex system of building, a reflection of male socio-economic models, has always excluded the woman from a primary role in architectural design as also in the theorization of architecture. The enjoyment and utilization of the space outside the home was always a male prerogative, so that women lacked the necessary acquaintance with the problems relating to social life, movement, work activities, and exchange, an awareness essential for the design of space and buildings.

As a result the design and planning of towns, from the arrangement of public spaces to the buildings themselves, was not part of a woman's professional activity, as it concerned spaces that did not belong to her culturally. The social conquests achieved over the last few decades, the greater freedom of cultural expression, as with greater freedom of movement, autonomously and independently of the family context, have enabled women to interact with the urban space and absorb its features so that they are then able to manipulate them in a critical, designing sense. Today women architects have the necessary tools for the meta-design and the "concept" of buildings and urban space on a level with male colleagues, as they too have the chance to interact daily with these spaces, although they are not yet allowed equal opportunities in the field of design, as the system of architecture remains a prevalently male territory. AO

See also: **Critical theory**

Further sources: Forty (2000: 42); Johnson (1994: 116, 168); Nesbitt (1996: 38); Owen (in Foster 1983: 60); Rendell (in Borden 2000: 247)

▎Fetishization

Derived from the French word fétiche, *fetishization* refers to an idea or thing abnormally stimulating or attracting sexual desire. It is the act of attributing inherent value, such as supernatural power, to an inanimate object. Another earlier root of the term is feitiço – a Portuguese word used to describe the voodoo practices of religious cults by the natives of their West African territories who saw objects as embodying magical powers or being inhabited by spirits. Theoretically, various degrees of fetishism are present in many religions, traditions, and cultures around the world, and are exemplified in manic obsessions with "blood," "cross," "bones," and so on.

In Freudian terms, a fetish object is often associated with sexual desire. *Fetishization* denotes a cultural, psychological, and social technique of fetishizing things by making them appear larger than life, animate, or sexually desirable (Figure 56). For instance, the erotic interest in particular items of clothing, as in shoe fetishism, is a typically male obsession – usually for high-heeled shoes. This is one such fetish, like the obsession with underwear, where their real or fantasized presence is deemed a necessary aid or substitute for sexual gratification.

In the nineteenth century Karl Marx appropriated the term to describe "commodity fetishization," that is, the symbolic importance attached to commodities, as a key component of capitalism. Nowadays, fetishism is a central concept of Marxism. Indeed, *fetishization* is a useful concept for analyzing communication processes – as it illuminates important aspects of consumers' relationships with media, as well as how a popular communication culture creates objects of desire. It is noteworthy that recent car commercials in the United States are using buildings such as Los Angeles' Walt Disney Concert Hall by Frank Gehry (2003) and the Mercedes-Benz Museum building in Stuttgart by UN Studio (2006), as shooting locations that increase the sex appeal of the featured automobiles. It now appears that certain sensuous, blobular, buildings have joined the ranks of cars as fetishized consumer objects. TP

See also: **Beauty • Blob architecture (Archispeak) • Blobitecture**

Further sources: Lefebvre (in Leach 1997: 144)

Figure 56: Fetish Florida roadside attraction

Fictional architecture

It's entirely possible to write "architecture fiction" instead of "science fiction." Like, say, Archigram did in the 60s. "Plug-in City," "Living Pod," "Instant City" ... and the "Walking City. — Bruce Sterling

So let's dump the idea of reworking performance architecture into green building and turn to architecture fiction instead. Let's find creative ways to live in what we already have. — Kazys Varnelis

The volume of *fictional architecture* is increasing due to the enhanced design and representation capabilities of the digital tools available today. It is now easier to produce visionary schemes than it was for twentieth-century groups such as Archigram and the Metabolists. Today's unbuilt work forms a substantial portion of twenty-first century published architecture. It is fictional in the sense that it is utopian and typically unbuildable. Often a commentary on the state of the art in architectural practice and society, *fictional architecture* holds up a mirror to the future.

Fictional architecture is also present in film. From the grim near-future Los Angeles architecture of *Blade Runner* and *Batman*'s New York, to the optimistic architecture portrayed in *The Jetsons*, fictional architecture is part of our collective consciousness. Science fiction and architectural fiction are inseparable in our cultural memory.

Another current and growing fictional architecture is the architecture produced for the video gaming industry. Many of the urban warfare games such as Sony's *Modern Warfare 2* include elaborate fictional architecture that can be occupied and exploited by the avatars representing the players in the game. A gentler architecture appears in the popular SIM series. *Second Life* has already been recognized by architecture students as an important architectural representation tool.

As we move closer to the prospect of architectural representation that is holographic with three-dimensional photo-realism, fiction will become ever more important as a substitute for the real thing. Eventually the fictional and the non-fictional may become difficult to parse. In the end it may not matter, as reality and hyper-reality merge, and we forget that there was a difference.

See also: **Archigram (Archispeak)** • **Film and architecture** • **Metabolism (Archispeak)** • **Visionary architecture**

Further sources: Deleuze (in Ballantyne 2002: 54); Shonfield (in Borden 2000: 301)

▌Film and architecture

During the first decades of this century [the twentieth], when architectural and urban theories with their corresponding images were developed, the art system that served as a reference was still painting – a two dimensional reality, an abstraction. Despite the fact that film was being developed at that time with extraordinary vigour, it was not acknowledged in architecture. — Diana Agrest

In its interaction with the city, film carries a multiplicity of means through which to reveal elements of corporeal, cultural, architectural, historical and social forms, as well as to project the preoccupations with memory, death and the origins of the image that crucially interlock cinema with urban space. — Stephen Barber

Architecture and film are both media that rely upon collaborative teamwork as well as technical and economic know-how, in order to achieve realization. As such, they are considered close cultural bedfellows. Both are also concerned with the articulation of space, structure, aesthetics, time, and identity, and albeit they have been appropriated from movie-making by architects, they share a common terminology that includes terms such as "montage," "narrative," "serial vision," and "storyboarding.," Furthermore, while influential movie directors like Fritz Lang (*Metropolis*, 1927), Jacques Tati (*Playtime*, 1967), and Ridley Scott (*Blade Runner*, 1982), have made their cinematic visions of the condition, often dystrophic, of the contemporary and future built environment, some architects work with a filmic eye.

A direct link between architectural design and film making is found in the practice of Rem Koolhaas. He sees his role as being more like a scriptwriter or movie director who conceives architectural episodic sequences as being suspenseful over time – as building up to a climax of spatial experience. Indeed, the route through his Rotterdam Kunsthal is structured like a movie plot: that is, with a beginning, a middle sequence, and a powerful climax. Movement through this museum is celebrated by bombarding the visitor with a montage of conflicting and changing impressions, a cinematic shock tactic first pioneered by Sergei Eistenstein in movies such as *Battleship Potemkin* (1925). Deliberate juxtapositions include the deployment of commonplace and exotic materials, surprise encounters, contrasting functions, and the blurring of interior and exterior views. These are "cut" and "edited" to heighten sensory awareness and create the potential for a new architectural expression. It comes as no surprise that, before embarking on his architectural career, Koolhaas had, like Eisenstein, studied, directed, and acted in movies.

In echoing Le Corbusier's use of the unfolding serial experience of the architectural promenade, many of the buildings of Steven Holl also reflect a filmic spatial sequencing as if in a progression of cinematic stills. He suggests that our perambulatory spatial navigation is made up of an infinite number of perspectives projected from an infinite number of viewpoints. This implies a need to create architecture that not only gives priority to the bodily experience, but also serves to bind the intention of the architecture to the perception of the viewer.

Movie making itself has also found a design and marketing role in architectural design. For example, one architect who adopts sophisticated "Pixar-style" animation techniques as a powerful master-planning tool is Will Alsop. By showing how gradual changes to the urban context can cause a dreamlike metamorphosis into a totally different built landscape, his movies transform town planning into a cinematic discipline. It is one in which the spectator follows a visionary process that depicts in real time and in a CGI realism how urban development is more a question of movement, light, composition, mass, and the needs of people than policy decisions.

Movies and architecture may share a common future. As movies become three-dimensional, multi-sensory, brave new world "feelies," and architecture becomes increasingly ethereal and dynamic, they might merge as one art form. TP

See also: **Abstraction • Allusionism • Deleuzianism • Representation**

Further sources: Agrest (1993: 129)

Flexibility   ▮

Flexibility is the ability to adjust to change.
— *Webster's Unabridged Dictionary*

We must be aware of the glove that fits all hands, and therefore becomes no hand. — Aldo van Eyck

Flexibility is a modern architecture issue. It became a concern when it was realized that the goal of precisely fitting a building form to function fails to recognize the inevitable growth and change that occurs over time. In response, a number of strategies were proposed for achieving the needed *flexibility*. They included "universal space," "multipurpose space," "loose fit space," "convertible space," "transformable space," and more recently "responsive space." Each of these approaches had pros and cons.

Universal space, or space that can theoretically accommodate any demands placed on it, was promoted by Mies van der Rohe with his elegant empty glass and steel boxes. Crown Hall (1956), the architecture building at the Illinois Institute of Technology, and his swan song, the New National Gallery in Berlin (1968), are notable examples of universal space architecture. Famously the gallery does a poor job of housing art, as few concessions were made to the particular needs of the collection. Only large-scale sculpture that won't be harmed by natural light coming in from the glass walls can be housed on the main floor. The bulk of the collection is relegated to the basement.

Multipurpose space is designed to meet the needs of a limited range of uses. The ubiquitous auditorium/cafeteria, or "cafatorium," found in many American schools, is an example of multipurpose space. It generally serves both uses poorly, as compromises are made to arbitrate between conflicting needs.

The *flexibility* achieved through loose-fit design mainly accommodated growth. Buildings are initially built too large, with the expectation that as the occupying organization grows, it reaches an optimum fit until it becomes overcrowded (Figure 57). This approach is inefficient.

Multi-strategic space is designed to accommodate a fixed range of current and expected future uses. It anticipates a limited number of likely changes and provides built-in potential for those changes to occur with a minimum of fuss and cost. Providing conduits for additional communications and electrical services is an example of providing for future change. Multi-strategic space provisions tend to involve providing potential for potential technology upgrades.

Convertible and transformable space relies upon technology to quickly change the characteristics of space with a minimum of effort. Hotel ballrooms that that can be converted from one large space into several smaller meeting rooms by closing movable walls are an example of convertible space.

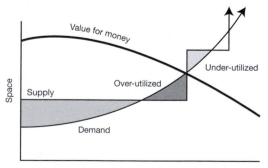

Figure 57: Overbuild strategy

There are now experiments in achieving flexibility through the use of responsive or dynamic architecture. It's an exciting new frontier that involves architecture that moves, as it responds to changing demands and our minute-to-minute needs and fancies.

Flexibility – on the one hand it has served to extend functionalism and make it viable, but on the other hand it has been employed to resist functionalism. — Adrian Forty

See also: **Functionalism • Indeterminate architecture • Responsive architecture • Universal design**

Further sources: Forty (2000: 142); Lidwell (2003: 86)

Fold

A fold is always folded within a fold, like a cavern in a cavern. — Gilles Deleuze

"if a very small insect were to move from the section of skirt in Mrs Who's hand to that in her left hand it would be quite a long walk for him if he had to walk straight across." Swiftly Mrs Who brought her hands, still holding the skirt together. "now you see," Mrs Whatsit said, "he would be there, without that long trip." — Madeleine L'Engle

Thoughts unfold over reality. Spaces unfold over volume. Composition is substituted for a pendulous process between unfolding and doubling. Folding is a generative process of form. Forms unfold their possibilities being part of the program, on site, according to budget, etc. — Federico Soriano

Rene Descartes's system of x,y,z coordinates and resulting flat spatial grids has from the beginning been challenged as the way to carve up Euclidean space. For example, Gottfried Leibniz, a contemporary of Descartes, postulating that all straight lines are curves and that the smallest element in space is not the point, but the *fold*. However, the notion that a flat, grid space is the space we inhabit is so ingrained in our psyche that the alternatives seem bizarre, even impossible. Thus, despite competing schema, the Cartesian method of confronting Euclidean space has remained the de facto conception of architectural space – until recently. Architectural theory began to embrace non-Cartesian space towards the end of the twentieth century. In particular Gilles Deleuze, taking his cue from Leibniz, has promoted the "fold" as "the new conception of space and time," thus garnering the interest of his admirers, including Peter Eisenman, and a whole generation of younger architects. The architecture that has resulted from this new freedom is topologically complex, smooth, supple, and ironically form conscious. It appears to be a new mannerism, perhaps a baroque modernism.

Space and time when no longer defined by the grid but rather by the fold, will still exist, but not as place and time in its former context, that is static, figural space. — Peter Eisenman

Despite its recent entry into architectural theory lexicon, folded space is an established concept in Astrophysics. As demonstrated by Mrs Who's skirt, space can be warped or folded in the time/space continuum (Figure 58). Space is now understood by the physicist to be curved, as Leibniz stated 300 years ago.

The fold as a technique in architecture ... can represent a sudden change of direction ... it can resolve differences in a way which is distinct from the other architectural methods .... This is by enfolding, by connecting that which is different in a smooth transition.
— Charles Jencks

Thus, at the end of the century a sea change was occurring in the design of architectural space, as experimentation with folds and blobs, bolstered by new digital tools, became the order of the day. Whether the momentum can be sustained in the new environment of pragmatic design remains to be seen. If it can be demonstrated that architecture resulting from "folding in time" is an economical and effective utilization of scarce resources, it may have a chance of enduring. Its downfall may become the same as that of modern architecture – it lacks a history, and thus a meaningful connection with its constituency.

... we need more ground and permanence in architecture instead of "folds."... blobs and folds take the city as an additive texture without any coherence; they consume too much space since they want to stand on their own imagined pedestals. — Arie Graafland

See also: **Baroque • Blob architecture (Archispeak) • Blobitecture • Mannerism • Topology (Archispeak)**

Further sources: Ballantyne (2007: 92); Borden (2000: 240); Colebrook (2006: 136); Deleuze (in Mallgrave 2008: 541); Iwamoto (2009: 60); Jencks (1995: 139); Jeremy (in Bortden 2000: 284); Kipnis (in Jencks 1997: 121); Leach (1997: 308); Lynn (in Jencks 1997: 125); Lynn (in Mallgrave 2008: 543); Mallgrave (2008: 477, 536); Morales (in Gausa 2003: 232, 644); Rosa (2003: 32)

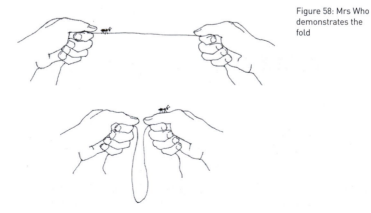

Figure 58: Mrs Who demonstrates the fold

Form

Form as a goal always ends in formalism. — Mies van der Rohe

That it is not a permanent or timeless category of architecture is clear. In a sense, "form" is a concept that has outlived its usefulness.
— Adrian Forty

The creation of *form* was the primary design goal of modern architects up to the 1980s. Although not acknowledged as such, it was the primary decorative element. Despite being invoked each time modern architecture is described, the meaning of the term remained unspecified. Was it merely another word for "shape"? If it was more than "shape," what did that more consist of? Other than shape, the other common understanding of *form* comes from the Platonic notion of "essence" or "idea." *Form*, in the Platonic sense, implies that there are two levels of *form*, the "particular" and the "ideal." The *form* we confront through our senses is the "particular." The "ideal" is the idea of the *form* in its unattainable perfection. Our minds merge the perceived particular *form* with our mental construct of the ideal *form*. By that action we can label the encountered *form* by its type, or essence. If the particular *form* has a cube-like appearance, it is understood and labeled as having an essence of "cubeness." Modern architects were seldom explicit about which meaning of form was being used. For the architect it was implicitly the Platonic version, for everyone else it was shape.

Once the public's rejection of modern architecture was acknowledged, architects began to shift their attention from *form* to surface. "Ducks" were replaced by "decorated sheds" (Figure 59). The development of cultural meaning through semiotic surface treatments was the preoccupation of the post-modernists, as they tried to win back the favor of their public.

In the twenty-first century, the designer of parametric green architecture regards *form* as the pragmatic building shape that results from resolving environmental issues such as enclosure to volume ratios and solar exposure. Surface remains the primary preoccupation of the design architect. This time around it is not the meaning, but rather the technology of the building skin, that receives the attention. *Form* is no longer recognized as a design goal. "Form follows function," the naïve mantra of the modernists, has been replaced by "shape follows LEED."

See also: **Decorated shed (Archispeak)** • **Decoration** • **Green design** • **Post-modernism (Archispeak)**

Further sources: Antoniades (1990: 67); Deleuze (in Ballantyne 2002: 88); Soriano (in Gausa 2003: 236)

Figure 59: Decorated shed – Barcelona Forum

▌Formal analysis

Formal is regularly used with the intention of giving emphasis to the specifically "architectural" properties in works of architecture; but as the nouns which it is generally linked – "order," "design," "structure," "vocabulary" – are themselves so ambiguous, the confusion is compounded. — Adrian Forty

Formal elements – style, harmony of parts, call them what you will – are sufficiently trivial to be awarded top billing in architectural discourse. — Diane Ghirardo

There are four levels of formal analysis of architecture. They are: descriptive, analytical, interpretive, and judgmental. Descriptive analysis simply develops a description of the building(s). It can include a description of *form*, materials, size, and relationship to *context*. Descriptive analysis makes no value judgments. It is informative but it can hardly be called analysis.

An analytical analysis answers questions about why and how the architect achieved the described result. The analysis may be typological, iconographic, compositional, historical, or thematic. The bulk of formal analysis falls into this category. Each form of analytical analysis listed above deserves far more elaboration than is possible here.

Interpretive *formal analysis* involves extracting the meaning of the work. Post-modern critics, and in particular critical theory academics, have an interest in interpretive analysis. Unfortunately, most works of architecture are devoid of deeper meaning. Typically post-modern architecture is shallow and derivative. The exception is perhaps the abstract, rather than literal, monument and the commemorative museum. The work of Peter Eisenman and Daniel Libeskind comes to mind.

Judgmental analysis employs a formal system of assessment to give it a rank in relation to other works of architecture. It asks the question: "is it good architecture?" Judgmental analysis determines the value of the thing being analyzed. In this age of the Internet blog, judgmental analysis is a common recreation for the masses. It has been co-opted as entertainment and thus been downgraded to informal analysis.

In summary, the ultimate goal of *formal analysis* is to determine the deeper merits of a work of architecture according to an explicit and critical prescription for "good architecture." Since it tends to be an academic pursuit, few pay attention to the *formal analysis* of architecture. For most, it seems to be a case of trying hard to artificially make objective something that is essentially subjective.

See also: **Bracketing • Critical modernism • Critical theory • Criticism • Form • Meaning • Post-modernism (Archispeak)**

Further sources: Ghirado (in Ballantyne 2002: 64)

Formalism

The doctrine that it is the arrangement or structure of its elements rather than their representational content that gives value to a work of art. — *Oxford Dictionary of Philosophy*

... the formalist position looks to certain autonomous qualities such as composition, language, meaning, and morphology, and is primarily self-referential. — Colin Rowe

Formalism is typically defined in opposition to realism. — Victor Burgin

The history of architecture is largely the history of formalism in architecture. For a short time in the early part of the twentieth century *formalism* was rejected as unsuitable for a modern architecture, Bauhaus style. Le Corbusier, with his "five points for a new architecture" (1927/2007), was the exception – a unique example of formalism in early modern architecture. In response to the limitations of raw functionalism, a "new formalism" emerged in the 1950s. It tried to reassert abandoned classical aesthetic devices, such as proportion and symmetry. The formal rules for an appropriate and beautiful architectural expression became of interest because of the poverty of *form* as the only modernist aesthetic device. Bruno Zevi, in *The Modern Language of Architecture* (1978), documented the new formalism. Zevi sets forth seven principles, to codify the new language of architecture created by Le Corbusier, Walter Gropius, Mies van der Rohe, and Frank Lloyd Wright. In place of the formal classical language of the Beaux Arts School, with its focus on abstract principles of order, proportion, and symmetry, he presented a formalism based upon an organic marriage of engineering and design, a concept of living spaces that are designed for use, and an integration of buildings into their surroundings.

Architectural *formalism* was re-engineered again in the 1980s. It was guided by a preoccupation with the structure of language as a means for achieving meaning in architecture. Eventually the structuralist project deconstructed itself and was abandoned, leaving a void. Architecture became a "no rules" enterprise at the end of the century.

In the twenty-first century we are faced with few formal rules to guide architectural design. At this point in our history an agreed-upon architectural *formalism* seems almost incomprehensible, if not irresponsible. The closest thing we have is the potential development of standardized parameters for the achievement of sustainable digital architecture. Pragmatics will shape whatever *formalism* does emerge. We are in an age that is confronting harsh realities. Aesthetic *formalism* is a luxury that will have to wait.

See also: **Beauty** • **Digital architecture** • **Modernism** • **Structuralism**

Further sources: Ghirado (in Ballantyne 2002: 70); Jencks (2007: 81); Knights (in Borden 2000: 71); Kruft (1994: 438); Vidler (2008: 11, 71)

Frankfurt School

In the early part of this century, a loose aggregation of intellectuals
known as the "Frankfurt School" produced a body of work ... in such
abstruse phenomena as avant-garde art, psychoanalysis, dialectical
philosophy, and a messianic religious faith. Their studies – which go
under the general name of "Critical Theory" – were among the first
which can be properly labeled interdisciplinary. — Rolf Wiggershaus

... a regime of planned work on the juxtaposition of philosophical
construct and empiricism in social theory.... To organize inquiries, on
the basis of current philosophical questions, in which philosophers,
sociologists, economists, historians and psychologists can unite in
lasting co-operation. — Max Horkheimer

The *Frankfurt School* is regarded as the birthplace of the larger movement
labeled "critical theory." As Horkheimer mentions in his 1930 inaugural
lecture above, the primary feature of the *Frankfurt School* was the
interdisciplinary examination of the utility of theory. Early members of
the *Frankfurt School* included Theodor Adorno, Max Horkheimer, Herbert
Marcuse, Walter Benjamin, and Erich Fromm. The essential project of
the *Frankfurt School* was to resist the notion that science and positivism
are value free. In the process of stating what was a sacrilege at the time,
the goal was to grant greater freedom to individuals in their pursuit of
knowledge. Neil Leach, in *Rethinking Architecture* (1997), has reintroduced
the critical architectural writings of Adorno, Benjamin, and Habermas
to a wider audience. The message is clear. An architecture of justice for
all must embrace the full complement of our community of man. That
embrace must go far beyond the physical act.
   We must hope it won't be too late, as we are subsumed by the growing
digitally driven green movement and its impatience with anything not
involving the technology of sustainability.

See also: **Critical humanism • Critical theory**

Further sources: Colquhoun (1991: 251) Frampton (in Borden: 4, 7); Gregotti (1996:
xiii, 96); Jencks (2007: 216); Sharr (2007: 112)

Frozen music

Architecture is music in space, as it were frozen music.
— Friedrich Von Schelling (1802)

I call architecture "petrified music." Really there is something in this;
the tone of mind produced by architecture approaches the effect of
music. — Goethe (1829)

Good architecture is like a piece of beautifully composed music
crystallized in space that elevates our spirits beyond the limitation of
time. — Tao Ho (1980)

Rudolf Wittkower, in *Architectural Principles in the Age of Humanism* (1962), outlines the genesis of the relationship between architecture and music. He describes musical concepts of harmonic proportions and balance derived by Pythagoras and subsequently applied to architecture. Alberti is quoted as writing: "The numbers by means of which the agreement of sounds affects our ears with delight, are the very same which pleases our eyes and our minds."

As one can see from the various statements above, architecture has been described as analogous to music since the beginning of architecture. Unfortunately, the comparison has now become trivial. Our current environment of a digital architecture pays little attention to the subtleties of aesthetics that relate to music. The musical devices of rhythm, cadence, harmony, balance, tempo, and theme no longer apply. Only the atonal music of Schoenberg favored by the partially deaf Adolf Loos may still have a chance at relevance. The only remaining valid comparison between music and architecture might be the way they both make us feel. Perhaps the musical analogy that is more appropriate to our times is that of the symphony orchestra. With the adoption of building information modeling (BIM) and integrated practice, with its multiple players and scores, the notion of the architect as the conductor of the "symphony" may be useful. Unfortunately, the originator of the symphony may no longer be the composer, but rather the players in the orchestra (or the BIM itself). It will probably not be the conductor/architect, who won't know the script.

Ultimately, rap might be the music that architecture emulates as it moves from the subtleties of musicality to narrative, from the poetic to prose.

See also: **Building information modeling: BIM • Integrated practice**

Functionalism   I

The principle of excluding everything that serves no practical purpose.
— *Brockhampton Dictionary of Ideas*

It would seem that the functionalist theories used by the designers were wrong, but that failure confirmed the central importance of the form-function relationship. There could after all, be no functional failure if the relation between form and function were not powerful.
— Bill Hillier

Functionalism turned out to be yet another stylistic conclusion, this one based on a scientific and technical positivism ... — Peter Eisenman

The label "*functionalism*" was applied as a convenient way to summarize what appeared to be the central tenet of the modern movement in architecture. The functionalist ethic developed as a reaction against the nineteenth-century practice of imitating and combining earlier styles. The primary sound bite associated with *functionalism* was the cliché "form follows function," typically attributed to Louis Sullivan. In reality the slogan is a variation on an earlier statement by the American artist

Horatio Greenough. Both men were referring to something different than the utilitarianism of shaping buildings to the activities and equipment of its users. The term *functionalism*, which was not coined until the 1960s, became much misunderstood and misused. As explained in detail in *Words and Buildings* by Forty (2000), function had many connotations, including the romantic, organic one favored by Greenough and Sullivan. With the onset of post-modernism, functionalist became a convenient slur invoked by critics who wished to dismiss anyone still hanging on to the last threads of the notion of function as the primary form determinant.

In the academic architectural discourse today, function is not mentioned. It has been discredited as the cause of the dehumanizing aspects of the modern architectural style. When it does come up, function is dismissed as a lower-level aspiration of a building, and not an aspect of the building's status as architecture. Unfortunately, clients still expect to use their buildings. The blobs and folds buildings that have emerged over the past 20 years serve their functions notoriously poorly. Many starchitects have in common an unhappy building manager struggling to hang art on walls that are not vertical while the rain falls on them. The "greening" of architecture may be part of the answer, as it is realized that the efficient use of space is environmentally sound practice. Unfortunately, it may mean the end of architecture.

Architecture is the art of how to waste space. — Philip Johnson

See also: **Blob architecture (Archispeak)** • **Blobitecture** • **Fold** • **Functionalism** • **Starchitect**

Gaia architecture

> The idea that the earth is alive and is a super organism with a will of its own is common to many ancient cultures. Giving this personification a women's name, mother Earth, or the pre-Greek "Gaia."
> — Charles Jencks

> Confronted with the inaccessibility of our physical frontiers, my generation has turned inward and discovered two new immanent and infinite frontiers. These new frontiers of the next millennium are the uncensored, distributed self, and cyberspace – the location of the virtual self/community – Electric Gaia. — Michael Strangelove

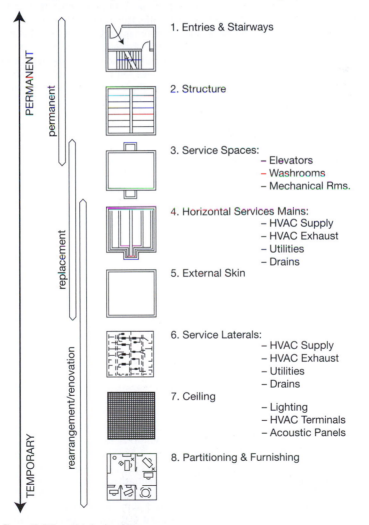

Figure 60: Differential obsolescence

The twentieth-century slogan "Spaceship Earth" is being replaced by the metaphor of Earth as a living mother, or Gaia. The metaphor is still not universally accepted, as the Earth lacks many of the characteristics of all living organisms, the most significant being that it does not reproduce. Despite the discrepancy, scientific community support for the hypothesis continues to grow. The metaphor has direct relevance to architecture. *Gaia architecture* is architecture treated as a living thing. It is an example of vitalism. As in all living organisms, architecture is conceived, is born, exists, and then eventually dies. During its lifespan architecture nourishes and supports its inhabitants, just as the Gaia Earth does. As buildings live for a long time, they must accommodate a changing world around them, as well the gradual aging of their systems and constituent materials. How well buildings respond to this aging process is largely dependent upon the design decisions made at the start of life. Buildings that are regarded as *Gaia architecture* will have built-in mechanisms for re-establishing homeostasis. For example, the differential obsolescence of parts of the building will have been anticipated so that the short-lived elements can be easily replaced (Figure 60). Just as leaves fall off of the tree, building cladding systems might respond to changing seasons by undergoing a metamorphosis. Biomimicry, and the resulting nano-technological bio-engineering, will become the standard practice of *Gaia architecture* as it evolves.

See also: **Biomimicry • Cosmogenic architecture • Cradle to cradle • Eco-tech • Green design (Archispeak) • Vitalism**

Further sources: Jencks (2007: 146)

▌Genealogy of ideas

Ideas rarely emerge out of whole cloth. The same is true of architectural theory. The genealogy of ideas in architecture reaches back to Vitruvius (first century BC). As our first known cataloguer of Western architectural "best practices," he is our architectural ideas ancestor. Thus, the genealogy of many of the current ideas about architecture can be mapped through 2,000 years of history. Such an exercise would consume an entire thick volume, as we can see from Hanno-Walter Kruft's *A History of Architectural Theory* (1994). In order to simplify the map, it is prudent to reduce the complex web of ideas down to two paradigms – rationalism and empiricism.

Rationalists believe that knowledge of the world is mediated through ideas and constructs that are present at birth. The mind, rather than the body, becomes the most important access to a reality that exists at two levels – the particular and the "idea." The rationalist tradition began with the ancient Greeks, and in particular Plato (427–347 BC). It came into its own in Western thought with philosophers such as Descartes (1596–1650), Spinoza (1632–1677), Leibniz (1646–1716), and Kant (1724–1804). The rationalist tradition was evident in twentieth-century architecture in the form of post-modern structuralism. The dragon eventually devoured its own tail when structuralism evolved into deconstructivism. The existence of innate structures was argued by Jacques Derrida (1930–

2004) and others to be an illusion, a myth. Reality, as the deconstructivist rationalists regarded it, was de-constructed.

Empiricists, on the other hand, contend that knowledge of the world is immediate and purely a product of sense data. This tradition, which began with Epicurus (341–270 BC), counts such important philosophers as Bacon, Hobbes, Locke, Berkeley, Hume, and Mill among its genealogy. It formed the genesis for twentieth-century ideas about architectural phenomenology. Despite being marginalized in the twenty-first century, phenomenology still remains the poetic ingredient of the architectural design process. Unfortunately it may be eventually subsumed by man/cyber architecture machines that churn out parametric, digital, green architecture. The intrusion of digital tools has once again raised the specter of architecture based entirely on the rational. The last time this occurred was during the early twentieth-century failed stark modernism of Gropius, Mies, Loos, and company. As mathematical models are the lifeblood of rationalism and the digital environment, the paradigm shift is unavoidable. In order to fit into architectural cyber practice, twenty-first-century architecture must be reduced to a binary, rational approximation of its true and total self.

See also: **Deconstructivism (Archispeak)** • **Phenomenology** • **Phenomenology (Archispeak)** • **Structuralism**

Globalization   ▮

Globalization variously signifies the hegemony of a worldwide capitalist system on the economic plane; the superseding of the primacy of the nation-state by transnational arrangements, both formal and informal, on the political one; the emergence of new, networked information and communication instrumentalities on the technological one; and the advent of an increasingly homogeneous, consumer oriented lifestyle and mentality on the cultural one.
— Joan Ockman

Post-modernism … the omnipresent reality, particularly in the West, of networking, social leveling, moral relativism, multiculturalism, global migration and media hype. — Charles Jencks

Although economic, political, and technological *globalizations* have received the most attention, *globalization* has taken many other forms. The global spread of western architectural iconography is one. With the rise of the starchitect, supported by token local architects integrated into a global architectural network practice, every developing city now boasts buildings by big-name architects. The situation is rapidly changing, however. The American starchitect has become unpopular in China. Home-grown architects are on the ascent, particularly in the Far East, even if their training is from the West. Whereas the common notion is that *globalization* is moving the world into a monoculture, there is evidence that the next generation of *globalization* will emphasize the local, supported by the global. Once the juggernaut of American cultural and commercial media has exhausted its expansionary project, and the growing environmental crisis begins to dramatically impact the ability to continue expanding, the forces of local institutions will begin to obtain the upper hand. The anti-globalization movement will transition from a fringe protest effort to a mainstream political, social, and economic fact of life. Ironically, the anti-globalization establishment will continue to benefit from the *globalization* of communications and social networks in particular.

Globalization makes possible the rise of new forms of empowerment among those who lack everything; it unsettles the status quo and other formalized arrangements. — Saskia Sassen

Anyone who has CNN or Al Jazeera beaming into their bedroom right now can attest to the fact that everything local is thoroughly permeated by the global, and everything global ultimately becomes inflected by the local. — Joan Ockman

See also: **Starchitect**

Further sources: Deleuze (in Ballantyne 2002: 84, 99); Fraser (in Borden 2000: 129); Gausa (2003: 264); Jencks (2007: 10)

▌Greenscaping

The recent popularity of green architecture raises the question of whether such projects are simply window dressing to cover up persistent corporate and governmental misdeeds...
— Victoria Meyers

A thing is right when it begins to preserve the integrity, stability and beauty of the biotic community. It is wrong when it tends otherwise.
— Aldo Leopold, *A Sand County Almanac* (1949)

Can we not create, from a beautiful natural landscape, an environment inhabited by man in which natural beauty is retained, man housed in community? — Ian McHarg

Place is a word to describe the complex interplay of climatological, biological, geological, and topographical features that create the differences we see around us and inspire our diverse aspects of culture. In the "place" of our landscapes across America we fervently strive to emulate a landscape from eighteenth-century England, where broad, open pastoral vistas were maintained by wealthy landowners. Frederick Law Olmstead, the father of landscape architecture in America, who designed New York City's Central Park, set the tone for suburban landscape development with his Riverside development outside Chicago, which mandated broad open lawns with scattered trees and houses set far back from the sidewalk.

Today suburbs are planted with the same monoculture of Kentucky bluegrass all across the country, despite very different climates and soils, and require tremendous inputs of water and energy while causing the negative impacts of air, water, and noise pollution. Lawn maintenance (mowing, blowing, trimming) accounts for approximately 5 per cent of the nation's air pollution, and watering lawns consumes 30 per cent of municipal freshwater in the United States (60 per cent in the West). Along with the resource and environmental burdens of maintaining lush lawns with fertilizers and pesticides, a large portion of these chemicals end up in stormwater runoff and in groundwater. Stormwater runoff from turf is one of our largest sources of water pollution. Extensive urban growth and sprawl over the last few decades have also significantly damaged the biodiversity of native bird and wildlife habitats.

In a move toward a more sustainable landscape design and a reconnection with the diversity of "place" and nature, "ecological design" has arisen as an integrative, ecologically responsive design discipline by placing ecology in the foreground of design. In minimizing energy, water, and material use, reducing pollution, restoring ecosystems and biodiversity, preserving habitat, and fostering community, health, and beauty, this new way of thinking attempts to improve natural conditions or reverse environmentally destructive impacts. By using the mandates of reduce, reuse, and recycle, *greenscaping* or natural habitat landscaping is a form of ecological design attempting to create balanced, self-sustaining ecosystems. The underlying goal of *greenscaping* is to create landscapes that exist in greater harmony with the natural environment. EL

See also: **Conservation • Eco tech • Passive design • Place (Archispeak)**

Hannover Principles

Developed by William McDonough Architects in 1992 for the city of Hannover, Germany, the following principles have served as a roadmap for the green movement, as well as the conscience of the design community:

1. Insist on rights of humanity and nature to co-exist.
2. Recognize interdependence.
3. Respect relationships between spirit and matter.
4. Accept responsibility for the consequences of design.
5. Create safe objects of long-term value.
6. Eliminate the concept of waste.
7. Rely on natural energy flows.
8. Understand the limitations of design.
9. Seek constant improvement by the sharing of knowledge.

The first principle seems self-evident to most designers, yet this has not always been the case. For most of the history of the development of the city, and its architecture, the objective has been to separate humankind from nature, to tame the wilderness. The result has been that nature has been exploited to the point of endangerment.

The second principle suggests that all things are connected and thus decisions should not be made in isolation. The positive and negative synergetic effects created by a collection of design decisions must be taken into account.

The third principle suggests that the Hannover planners should not neglect the whole person in favor of considering only the rational and measurable aspects of design. It is a plea for a holistic, phenomenological approach to design.

The fourth principle seems to be unnecessary, except that the design professions have not established an environment of trust with the public. In the United States construction projects often result in all parties being sued, but with no one taking responsibility.

The fifth principle is asking the designers to consider the long-term sustainability of the buildings that are designed. This has become one of the cornerstones of the green movement, along with principles six and seven.

Principle number eight is a reminder that design decisions are not the most influential decisions affecting humankind.

The last *Hannover principle* may be the hardest to achieve, as the design professions still jealously hold on to the acquired knowledge that gives them their competitive edge in the marketplace. Even so, design is becoming more diffused among the community. The do-it-yourself phenomena, assisted by access to an ever-growing amount of technical information on the Web, plus the spread of virtual communities, is threatening the exclusivity of the architect's knowledge base. To offset this trend, globalization, team design, and the webpage publication of best practices by firms may also eventually create an environment of information sharing that results in the dramatic advancement of the state of the art of architecture. It seems to already be under way.

See also: **Cosmogenic architecture • Cradle to cradle • Ethics • Gaia architecture • Globalization • Green design (Archispeak) • Integral design • Nature • Passive design • Universal design**

Further sources: Mallgrave (2008: 584); McDonough (in Nesbitt 1996: 409); Nesbitt (1996: 409)

Hefted sheep

The phenomenon of *hefted sheep* illustrates for Gilles Deleuze an extreme example of territorialization. The sheep are instinctively at home in the mountains that they, and their ancestors, have grazed for 1,000 years. They are so genetically programmed to their territory that they have a profound understanding of the place and their place in it. Were they to be deterritoralized, they would perish. The plight of *hefted sheep* is a metaphor for the growing dislocation of modern humankind from its ancestral place. The most extreme cases are the refugees herded into camps in neighboring countries because of civil war or famine. Somalia experienced a prolonged drought in the 1970s, causing traditionally nomadic tribes to abandon their herding lifestyle and move into permanent coastal settlements. The switch from a livestock-based economy to a fishing economy deterritorialized the tribes. As would happen with *hefted sheep*, they lost their instinctive surefootedness, sense of orientation, and survival ability. Today, many of the offspring of the former cattle and goat herders are pirates.

Architecture also has a version of *hefted sheep*. As populations migrate from a rural to an urban life, they risk losing their ancestral footing. To make matters worse, the selected urban places are losing their identity to globalized chain stores and fast-food franchises. This causes further alienation. Cities are becoming atopias, or places that are no-places. Recent migrants lack the necessary imprinting to navigate. Like the sheep, they may fall off the mountain. To combat "displaced *hefted sheep* syndrome," urban environments need to remind the displaced of their rural home.

See also: **Atopia • Deterritorialization/reterritorialization • Globalization**

Hermeneutics

Named after the Greek messenger god Hermes, *hermeneutics* refers to the study of understanding and interpretation. It was originally applied to the reading of texts, in particular scriptures and philosophical writings. Later it became connected to a more basic ontological question dealing with our understanding of our being and who we are.

The term, and related concerns, go back to Plato and Aristotle and continue throughout the history of philosophy, gaining renewed interest especially with Heidegger and his followers in the twentieth century. It is part of a general critique of enlightenment scientific traditions, including critical theory, which is self-referentially focused on the structure of its elements. Thus, *hermeneutics* emphasizes the importance of context, especially cultural context.

The hermeneutic circle, the movement back and forth between the parts and the whole of the text, is an important hermeneutical theme. It states that the understanding of the parts hinges on our understanding of a larger whole, which, again can only be understood on the basis of the parts.

Applied to architecture, *hermeneutics* deals with how architecture is received, and how that reception changes over time and according to context. Special attention has been given to sacred architecture. It is concerned with how a building is interpreted by critics, users, historians, and so on. *Hermeneutics* provides a critique of the application of overly scientific thinking to architecture; including systematic design studio teaching methods. In summary, *hermeneutics* involves historical study and the study of cultures. It treats design as a process of interpretation.

See also: **Contextualism • Critical theory • Phenomenology**

▌Heterogeneity

Consisting of dissimilar elements or parts; not homogeneous.
— *The Free Dictionary*

With the curious privilege of discriminating independent coherences, while sustaining a cohesion between the parts only by default and through spatial adjacency. — Demetri Porphyrios describing Alvar Aalto

Classical architecture was built on the principles of harmony, order, balance, symmetry, rhythm, proportion, and so on. With perhaps the exception of symmetry, modern architecture, as practiced by Mies van der Rohe, Le Corbusier, and their followers, shared a belief in many of the same classical principles. One of the exceptions was Alvar Aalto, as demonstrated by his Finlandia Hall project in Helsinki (1971) (Figure 61). It consists of disparate parts, visually held together only by the thin Carrera marble panels. The struggle to be homogeneous was abandoned. According to the post-structuralist Andrew Benjamin, origins are heterogeneous and only become homogenous with the imposition of traditions like the above classical canons. Since the break with modernist dogma, architecture has become increasingly heterogeneous. The homogeneous that had been valued was revealed to be artificial and arbitrary. With the freedom accorded the architectural world after the nihilism of deconstruction, a "no rules" architecture emerged for a brief time. Buildings started to become a collection of disparate parts, various blobs, or folds squashed together. The Experience Music Project building comes to mind. As we move ever further into the confines of pragmatic, parametric, green architecture, that freedom will dissolve. With this return to following the principles found in nature there will be an even greater tendency towards *heterogeneity*.

Figure 61: Finlandia Hall

See also: **Ad hocism • Classicism • Decomposition • Difficult whole •
Indeterminate architecture • Principle of consistency • Purism**

Further sources: Benjamin (in Leach 1997: 293)

Heterotopia   █

**... in every culture ... are something like counter-sites, a kind of
effectively enacted utopia in which all the other real sites that
can be found within the culture are simultaneously represented,
contested, and inverted. I shall call them, by way of contrast to utopias,
heterotopias.** — Michel Foucault

Thus, heterotopias are an unwieldy collection of "other," or atopic, places.
They are the spaces that are not quite "real" and certainly are not utopian.
Umberto Eco has described these places as hyperreality. Heterotopias
include amusement parks, Las Vegas, Disneyland, gated communities,
museums, military camps, colonies, libraries, and cemeteries (Figure
62). They are outside of the normal place of dwelling.

Foucault has outlined six principles of *heterotopia* (in Leach, 1977:
350):

1. All cultures have heterotopias and they are all different. There is no
   universal form of heterotopia.
2. Each heterotopia has a precise and determined function within a
   society, yet the same heterotopia can, according to the synchrony of
   the culture in which it occurs, change its function.
3. The heterotopia is capable of juxtaposing in a single real place several
   spaces, several sites that are in themselves incompatible.
4. Heterotopias are most often linked to slices in time – which is to say
   that they open onto what might be termed heterochronies.
5. Heterotopias always presuppose a system of opening and closing
   that both isolates them and makes them penetrable. In general, the
   heterotopic site is not freely accessible like a public place.
6. The last trait of heterotopias is that they have a function in relation to
   all the space that remains. This function unfolds between two extreme
   poles. Either their role is to create a space of illusion that exposes
   every real space, all the sites inside of which human life is partitioned,
   as still more illusory.

Figure 62: Las Vegas
heterotopia

Modern life seems to spawn heterotopic places. They are increasingly encroaching on those places that we have always believed to be real. As the amusement of cyberspace wears off, the heterotopic places in our midst will be our free time diversion. The architecture associated with *heterotopia* is consistent with the "otherness" of the current crop of digitally produced blobs and folds.

See also: **Atopia • Betweenness • Deterritorialization/reterritorialization • Disneyfication • Hyperreality (Archispeak) • Utopia (Archispeak)**

Further sources: Agrest (1993: 124); Chaplin (in Borden 2000: 206); Foucault (in Leach 1997: 348) Leach (1997: 348); Maxwell (1993: 151); Soriano (in Gausa: 293)

Historicism

The claim that the nature of any phenomena can only be adequately comprehended by considering its place within a process of historical development. — *Oxford Guide Philosophy*

In architecture, "historicism" is sometimes used to describe the introduction of stylistic or decorative features that "quote from" the styles of the past. — *Dictionary of Critical Theory*

Neo-historicism ... transforms department stores into mediaeval rows of houses. — Jurgen Habermas

Historicism as an architectural style is a variant on postmodernism. It involves the literal transfer of a past style into the present. Philip Johnson demonstrates this approach with the design of the Gerald Hines Building for the School of Architecture at the University of

Figure 63: University of Houston

Houston (Figure 63). It is a classical building based literally on an unbuilt design by the French visionary architect Étienne-Louis Boullée. A populist version of *historicism* is the new Victorian-style Mac mansion of the gated communities of America's wealthy suburbs. In the less wealthy suburb, the style of choice has become the craftsman style of the beginning of the twentieth century. Entire "theme cities" are developed to be instantly historical. New Orleans, Key West, and the Mediterranean village have become popular themes. The new urbanism movement attempted to restore the historic New England small town to new suburban developments. Despite the scorn that most architects feel for historicist design, it appeals to the consuming public. As architecture moves ever more into becoming just another consumer product, the protest by architectural purists might fade away.

See also: **Allusionism • Branding • Classicism • Facadism • Fashion • Hyperrealism (Archispeak) • Image**

Further sources: Antoniades (1990: 147); Colquhoun (1989: 12); Forty (2000: 196); Habermas (in Leach 1997: 230); Johnson (1994: 273); Nesbitt (1996: 200); Vidler (2008: 114); Vitamo (in Leach 1997: 149)

Holism   **❙**

Any doctrine emphasizing the priority of a whole over its parts.
— *Oxford Dictionary of Philosophy*

Since the Ecole des Beaux-Arts use of the parti in the nineteenth century, the need for a holistic architectural form concept has been generally accepted as one of the early steps in the modern designing process. In fact, the presence of a design concept is regarded as one of the characteristics that separate architecture from mere building. Architects such as Santiago Calatrava and Renzo Piano arrive at their holistic form concepts using inspiration from natural form; others depend upon gesture sketches (Gehry), daily watercolor exercises (Steven Holl), or abstract painting (Brian Alsop, Le Corbusier, Michael Graves). Architectural concept seeking is still in wide use today, but perhaps not for long. With the increasing use of parametric design methods, the "whole" is becoming lost in the flurry of "parts" that must be addressed by a hungry digital model. The sub-optimization of each parameter leaves little room for consideration of the whole. The "General Systems Theory" dictum that "the whole is greater that the sum of the parts" is forgotten in the process. Aggregating the product of each parameter's algorithm is not the same as a creative designer drawing upon the totality of their experience and creativity to make an educated, yet subjective, leap of faith to arrive at an initial form concept. As designing reverts back to "problem solving," something precious will be lost – the sublime elegance of the poetic vision of a single genius. *Holism* is the doctrine of the artist, reductionism the scientist.

See also: **Algorithm • Concept (Archispeak) • Elementarism • Gesture (Archispeak) • Parametric design •Parti (Archispeak) • Problem solving (Archispeak)**

Further sources: Gausa (2003: 276)

Hybridity   **❙**

Postcolonial theory has used strategies of "mimicry" and "hybridity" as motifs to provide a vocabulary that shifts colonial relations out of the dialectic of oppressor and oppressed. — Nishat Awan

It is crucial to stress that hybrid buildings stand differentiated from other multiple function buildings by scale and form. The scale is determined by the dimension of a city block. — Joseph Fenton

Hybrid buildings are commonly called multi-use or mixed-use buildings. At Seaside (Florida), Steven Holl has chosen to name his small multi-use building the Hybrid Building (1988) (Figure 64). It consists of retail on the bottom floor, offices on the second, and hotel suites on the top two floors. There is also a community hall in the back of the building. Twenty years later, Holl produced another "hybrid" building. This time it is the much larger "Linked Hybrid" multi-building, mixed-use, apartment complex in Beijing. There are many buildings in urban centers that can be considered to be hybrids. The John Hancock Center in Chicago is a prominent example. It houses stores, a gallery, parking garage, restaurants, apartments, and a television studio. The Hancock also qualifies as a hyperbuilding.

Buildings that are constructed from a combination of steel and concrete are also described as hybrid structures. As the mania for larger and larger buildings grows, there will be an increasing number of hybrid buildings until they evolve into hyperbuildings as hybrid cities. Single-purpose urban buildings might become a thing of the past.

See also: **Hyperbuilding**

Figure 64: The Seaside Hybrid Building

Hyperbuilding

The Hyperbuilding is a city-in-a-building, a self-sustaining indoor metropolis. — Rem Koolhaas

The Hyperbuilding may be less credible in the almost "completed" urban conditions of, for instance Japan or America, where strictly speaking it would have little significant qualities to add, than in a developing condition where the virtues of the hyperbuilding, the provision of an enormous controllable critical mass, could be a demonstrable advantage.
— OMA description of their Bangkok Hyperbuilding

The *hyperbuilding* has a history that goes back to the fable of the Tower of Babel. The contemporary *hyperbuilding* dates from Santa Elia's 1914 City of the Future, which incorporated a multimodal transportation hub, residential, retail, and commercial facilities. In the early part of the twentieth century the provocative drawings of the Russian Constructivists and paper projects such as Le Corbusier's 1930 Algiers Linear City continued the tradition of visionary *hyperbuildings*. In the 1960s the visionary architectural schemes of the Metabolists such as Kikutake and Isozaki's 1959 Floating City, and Archigram's Peter Cook's 1964 Plugin City, added to the collection of historic, hypothetical *hyperbuildings*. Some of the hyperbuilding proposals in the 1960s were imaginative. Ron Herron's Walking City was one of the most memorable. Yona Friedman, Paolo Soleri, Buckminister Fuller, Archizoom, and Frei Otto, among others, proposed visionary *hyperbuilding* schemes in the twentieth century.

The Place Bonaventure complex is an early *hyperbuilding* built in Montreal, Canada. When completed in 1967, it was the world's largest building with over 3 million square feet. It is an office, exhibition, and hotel complex perched over 18 rail tracks. The John Hancock Tower in Chicago (1970) by SOM is another early *hyperbuilding* in North America (Figure 65). It is a 100-storey tapering tower housing 700 condominiums, offices, restaurants, parking, a television studio, and a gallery. The forty-fourth floor sky lobby features America's highest indoor swimming pool.

Today, *hyperbuildings* are being proposed in the boom cities of the East. Japan leads the way with a multitude of unbuilt *hyperbuilding* proposals such as the 4,000 meter high X-Seed 4000, the 2,004 meter high Try 2004, and the Aeropolis at 2,001 meters. There is even a 1,000 meter tall proposal called the Hyperbuilding. OMA's 1996 Hyperbuilding proposal for Bangkok became a landmark unbuilt project. Dubai's Burj Kalifa, designed by SOM and completed in 2010, is one of the first twenty-first-century *hyperbuildings*. It houses 35,000 residents, along with hotel and office space.

The EcoTower *hyperbuilding* proposal by Ken Yeang points the way for future *hyperbuildings*. The promise of new cities that are carbon neutral, zero energy, and self-sufficient food producers, may reside in the *hyperbuildings* of the future.

See also: **Archigram (Archispeak)** • **Babel tower** • **Visionary architecture**

Further sources: Koolhaas (2004: 423)

Figure 65: John Hancock hyperbuilding

Hyper-modernism   **I**

In hypermodern ideology the notion of the project's aspects of possession, announcement, and the foundation of difference seem to be a prisoner of the present. — Vittorio Gregotti

Second-generation, mid-century, modern architects hyped modernism to the general public. It resulted in a devaluation of modernism, as it was representation without a commitment to principles. The bland, inhumane architecture that was produced contributed to the rejection of modern architecture by the critics and everyone else. Even the names coined for it predicted that it was going to be all over in a few short years. "Brutalism" and "minimalism" were not labels that appealed to a general consuming public, which preferred architectural styles that provided humane continuity with the past. The Boston City Hall by Kallman, McKinnell and Knowles (1968) is an iconic example of the brutalism wrought on the cityscape (Figure 66).

Hyper-modernism has reemerged in the twenty-first century with third-generation hyper-modernists insisting that this time around they will get it right. Architects that can be identified with the new *hyper-modernism* include Zaha Hadid, Steven Holl, and Renzo Piano. They share a common goal of subscribing to conventional modernist principles, but with a flair that should endear them to the general public. Common principles shared by this group include; the aggressive expression of structure, an emphasis on horizontal and vertical lines, a rejection of applied ornament, and an aesthetic exploiting industrialized materials. This time around, an effort is being made to create a modern architecture that is meaningful to place and people. The *hyper-modernism* of the twenty-first century is also environmentally conscious, digitally generated, and based upon a balance of individual creative genius and team design.

See also: **Banal • Modernism (Archispeak) • Post-modernism (Archispeak)**

Further sources: Wong (in Gregotti 1996: xxi, 24)

Figure 66: Boston City Hall – brutalism (1968)

█ Hyperspace

Post-modern hyperspace has finally succeeded in transcending the capacities of the individual human body to locate itself, to organize its immediate surroundings perceptually, and cognitively to map its position in a mappable external world. — Fredric Jameson

Hyperspace is space that has more than three dimensions. *Hyperspace* has emerged as a popular post-modern spatial conception largely due to modern advances in mathematics and theoretical physics. String theory in particular, with its multiple spatial dimensions, raises interesting questions about the future of architectural space. Three-dimensional space has been with us for such a long time that it is hard to imagine four or more spatial dimensions. It is one of the sea changes about our understanding about "reality" that has occurred with post-modern thought. Cyberspace is a newly familiar extra spatial dimension that is post-Newtonian. Science fiction revels in stories about parallel dimensions that violate our intuitive and experiential understanding of space and time. Einstein's space–time continuum started the whole thing. Television shows such as *Quantum Leap*, movies like *Avatar*, and video games like *Time Splitters* and *Braid* fuel our fascination with hyperspace as a method for travel faster than the speed of light, and thus into the past or future.

Architectural *hyperspace* may take the form of virtual reality experiences of multidimensional space utilizing advanced holographic technologies. *Star Trek*'s Holodeck may be our destiny as we travel to where no man has traveled.

The virtual reality world of Star Trek's Holodeck has been brought a step closer to reality by the development of a Cybersphere (a collaboration between University of Warwick's Warwick Manufacturing Group and virtual reality company VR Systems UK).
— *Science Daily* (October 23, 2000)

See also: **Cyberspace (Archispeak)** • **Hyperrealism (Archispeak)**

Iconography

Modern architects abandoned a tradition of iconology in which painting, sculpture, and graphics were combined with architecture. The diminutive signs in most Modern buildings contain only the most necessary messages, like LADIES ... — Robert Venturi

Iconography literally means "image writing" – the term originally denoting those religious images painted on to small portable wooden panels that, from at least the seventh century onwards, were used as devotional icons by followers of the Greek Orthodox Church. In this context, *iconography* refers to a system of symbolic meaning adapted from one, albeit pagan, already formulated in classical mythology and used by icon artists to communicate concepts such as "Christ" and the "Holy Spirit" – often depicted as a lamb with a flag and a dove respectively. Over time, the term became attached to any object or image that embodies some special meaning. It is mainly associated with academic art research and the interpretation of the meaning attached to pictorial representation. For example, much has been written about the meaning of the distorted human skull anamorphically depicted across the lower foreground of "The Ambassadors" by Hans Holbein the Younger – an enigmatic double portrait painted in 1533 and riddled with symbolism. More recently, the fascination with deciphering such symbols is the key to Dan Brown's success – the forerunner of his best-selling books including theories, largely shunned by the art historian fraternity, on the iconography of works by Leonardo da Vinci.

However, the term *iconography* (or iconology) has now infiltrated many different fields, including semiotics, media studies, and architecture. Art historian and specialist on early medieval churches Richard Krautheimer (1897–1994) was an early exponent of architectural iconography. His seminal article, "Introduction to an iconography of Medieval Architecture" (1942), did much to extend iconographical analysis to architectural forms.

Post-modern architecture attempted to reintroduce *iconography* as a device for helping the public to "read" a building. Robert Venturi, in the Houston Children's Science Center and the Seattle Art Museum, blatantly applied images on the exterior of the building to announce their purpose. An interesting folk art version of architectural iconography can be found in the Mitchell, South Dakota, Corn Palace (Figure 67). Each year the decorative facade made entirely of corn is replaced. The iconography is ironic and double coded. TP

See also: **Post-modernism (Archispeak)**

Figure 67: Corn Palace corn-ography

Ideogram   I

Communication is not only the essence of being human, but also a vital property of life. — John A. Piece

An *ideogram*, or ideograph, is a graphic symbol that diagrams an idea or concept. However, some *ideograms* are comprehensible only by prior knowledge of their convention; others convey their meaning through pictorial resemblance to a physical object, and therefore may also be described as pictograms, or pictographs. While pictograms are pictures that represent the phonetics of a word or phrase – pictography being the oldest form of writing, which dates from before 3000 BC – *ideograms* are characters or symbols that represent an idea or a thing without expressing the speech sound of the meaning of a particular word or word sequence.

Examples of *ideograms* are found at the world's crossroads, such as international airports, and in public buildings and road signs where, in order to convey meaning, the graphics of signage transcend the spoken language of different tongues. The classic example of the *ideogram* in the literature is the "no parking" or "parking prohibited" sign that uses symbols to express its meaning.

Occasionally, the term strays into architectural parlance, and here *ideogram* describes a diagram of an idea in flux – usually used during the birth pangs of a design to describe the graphic externalization of thoughts when they become too complex to be retained mentally. Often involving a language of abstraction in which hieroglyphs and annotation combine to chart the potential relationships between mental concept and reality, such drawings are more concerned with the essence of an idea than any premonition of appearance. Consequently *ideogram*, in the architectural sense of the term, functions as an alternative to "concept drawing" to describe constructive doodles with attitude.

The *ideogram* has also been referred to as an architectural meta-sketch – the direct product of a creative search. Architects as diverse as Louis Kahn, Le Corbusier, Steven Holl, and Helmut Jahn have employed ideograms in their search for a form inspiration. TP

See also: **Abstraction • Conceptual drawing (Archispeak) • Diagram (Archispeak)**

Further sources: Gausa (2003: 299)

Ideology   I

A term from the philosophy of Karl Marx, naming a kind of political propaganda that is presented as fact while at the same time masking contradictions within the political system it touts. — Donald Palmer

Based upon the above definition, *ideology* is a kind of deception of the masses. Its purpose is to win over the hearts and minds of a specific population. It has an agenda. Architectural ideologies are no exception. Modernism came with perhaps the most blatant *ideology* in the long history of architecture. Since the demise of early dogmatic modernism, there has been a confusion of architectural ideologies to fill the vacuum.

Michael Speaks, in a 2009 presentation at the Berlage Institute, has described five ideologies that shaped the architectural discourse at the end of the twentieth century. They are: crypodeleuzean materialism, post-modernism, folding, critical regionalism, and the superdutch. It could be argued that of that group, post-modernism is more of a meta ideology than the rest. After all, taken at face value, post-modernism implies that everything that has come after the end of modernism qualifies. As an *ideology* it seems too diffuse. Crypodeleuzean materialism, on the other hand, seems very specific to the still popular notions of Gilles Deleuze. Cryptic versions of Deleuzian philosophy, those that focus on those aspects of a wide-ranging and perhaps rambling ideology that bolster a return to guttural architectural manifestations, including materialism, as distinct from spiritualism, are perhaps also the hallmark of the twenty-first century. Each *ideology* continues to have a devoted following, perhaps beyond the legitimate tenure of the particular *ideology*.

See also: **Critical regionalism • Cryptodeleuzian materialism • Fold • Modernism (Archispeak) • Post-modernism (Archispeak) • Superdutch**

▌Image

Today the word "image" commonly refers to that part of a thing, person, or action that appears to others, rather than the subject that the image constructs or the method of its construction.
— Vittorio Gregotti

A representative of any person or thing; and idol, embodiment; a picture drawn by fancy; the appearance of any object formed by the refraction of the rays of light.
— *Webster's Universal Unabridged Dictionary*

The extent to which issues of form, aesthetics, and *image* must be addressed in a work of architecture varies with each project. *Image* is often used in the sense of bold, striking, innovative forms or shapes, and increasingly colors. These image clues can be representational or abstract, with the main consideration being the visual impact as a memorable whole. If the chosen architectural forms come from a distinct historical vocabulary, they become representational. The significance of the precedent buildings becomes part of the image message of the new design. Thus, *image* is sometimes used in the sense of such historical reference.

Especially in the corporate world, it may be important for a firm or organization to establish a coherent, instantly recognizable identity or "brand" in consumers' minds. This can involve anything from the styling of the firm's products to its logos, stationery, dress code, and the design of its facilities: in short, the firm wishes to establish a corporate *image*. Since this is often done predominantly through advertising, it has led many to use image in the sense of a shallow advertising device or "gimmick."

The image question is "What is this place like"? What other buildings or places do its design features call to mind? "Name-calling" and caricature representations are often helpful (exaggerated) reminders of the images evoked.

In discussions about architecture, people sometimes say that "function isn't everything" or that by focusing on functional or economic issues only we are missing something essential. If they manage to explain to others at least to some extent what that something is, most of the time, it is likely to be related to what we have called "image" above.

See also: **Branding • Caricature • Cliché • Fashion • Fictional architecture • Form • Historicism • Meaning • Myth • Representation • Romanticism • Scenographic**

Further sources: Agrest (1993: 139); Gregotti (1996: 95)

Immateriality in architecture   I

"Immaterial" has several disparate meanings, "spiritual," not pertinent to the matter at hand," and "of no essential consequence." These extreme variations cast a shadow over the significance of immateriality in architecture. — George Dodds

Architectural immateriality describes the subjective experience of place; the embodiment of culture, symbolism, and ritual; the uncountable ways that architecture articulates existential meanings. — Thomas Barrie

Immaterial architecture is the architecture of our subconscious and spiritual worlds. It is embodied in our memories, feelings, and "gut reactions." It is purely subjective and holistically experiential. Existentialism and phenomenology provide the philosophical basis for immaterial architecture. It is a powerful underlying dimension of architecture within which deeper meaning dwells. An architecture that combines its material and immaterial existence is architecture worthy of being a venue for worship of spirituality. The task of designing immaterial qualities into a work of architecture is an unconscious undertaking. Sensitive architects, with a concern for deeper meaning in their work, will instinctively strive to instill immaterial qualities into their architecture. Louis Kahn, in all of his obtuse declarations, was mostly struggling to articulate the immaterial. His statement that "order is intangible, a level of creative consciousness" showed his appreciation of the role that the immaterial plays in the search for architecture. Of even greater power as immaterial, existential architecture is Stockholm's Woodland Cemetery Holy Cross Chapel by Gunnar Asplund and Sigurd Lewerentz (1930) (Figure 68).

It must be remembered in our rush to be pragmatic and environmentally responsible that the human spirit also needs to be fed and sustained.

Leave it loose until it feels right. — Will Alsop

See also: **Existential (Archispeak) • Existentialism • Existential space • Phenomenology**

Figure 68: Woodland
Cemetery

Inclusive architecture

One of the persistent criticisms of architecture is that it is too exclusionary. Many regard architecture as a privileged service for the rich and powerful, and not available to the average citizen. Its popular image is that of an expensive and unnecessary luxury. That buildings only need a builder and someone to draw up the blueprints is the opinion shared by most of the American public. One of the factors that led to this situation has been the exclusivity of architecture as practiced historically, and even today. Governmental, religious, and commercial institutions are mostly associated with patronizing architects. A few rich individuals will hire an architect to design their personal home, but that number is very small. If architecture had succeeded in being more inclusive, as it tried to do with the Marxist-inspired worker housing movement in the early years of modern architecture, then perhaps the situation would be different today. As our environmental issues become increasingly challenging, architects must step forward and become "part of the solution." That will entail finding ways to be more inclusionary. It will not be enough to simply make their exclusive traditional client group green. Energy-saving devices on a megahome is feelgood "greenwashing."

Critical theory attempts to address this issue by focusing attention on the architecturally disenfranchised members of society. Women, the homeless, refugees, the disabled, the elderly, and the very young, are some of the constituency that is of interest to those promoting a more inclusive architecture. The emerging trend towards "universal design" is a promising development. Egalitarian architecture that doesn't discriminate should be the goal of even the most modest architectural endeavor.

See also: **Critical theory • Feminism • Integral design • Universal design**

Indeterminate architecture

A work may be considered determinate if there is usually a clearly defined hierarchical order in its organization and an importance expressed architecturally by size, position, and/or materiality of its architectural elements. A determinate work has a preconceived understanding of the value or importance of the various architectural elements.

A work that is indeterminate is unclear as to its organization. The reasoning for placement is often not hierarchical in nature but heteroarchical expressing of a series of architectural elements that vie for importance in the organization of the work. There is an importance placed on the process to define order in its order of expressing architectural elements, thus the developed work is one that "falls to hand." This seemingly undefined architectural quality is a reflection of the use of a process that does not have a preconceived concept, but is the amalgamation and synthesis of different, often external elements and/ or intentions.

While a work of architecture that may be considered determinant is a closed system of spatial order in that its perceived ability to grow is limited in manner, an indeterminate work has the perceived ability to expand in an unlimited way.

An example of indeterminacy in a series of historical architectural works is Piranesi's "Prison Series." The late Manfredo Tafuri in his book *The Sphere and the Labyrinth* (1992) illustrates Piranesi's synthesis of space structured by integrating three different perspectives to form spaces that at first glance seems to be the ruins of a single space, but upon an in-depth examination reveals their true origins.

A more contemporary work that might be considered indeterminate is Peter Eisenman's School of Architecture at the University of Cincinnati. This work is derived from a process that incorporates the manipulation and overlaying of shapes derived from the existing contextual fabric, building elements that are torqued, painterly use of color, and an attitude that "function follows form" to develop a work of architecture that is an example of indeterminate architecture.

The concept of being indeterminate is also expressed in the arts, most notably in music and in painting. The work of the composer John Cage is an early near-historical example of the concept reflected in music. In painting the work of the abstract expressionist Jackson Pollock is an example of the term as applied to painting. MA

See also: **Flexibility**

Further sources: Gausa (2003: 337)

Integral design   I

Building systems have traditionally been designed sequentially and separately. This has resulted in each individual building assembly being suboptimized to perform according to the parameters set for it, and it alone. Integral design, on the other hand, treats all building systems as part of a larger, integrated system. This means that the synergetic effect of combining systems is exploited. The result is a reduction in the duplication of effort to keep a building comfortable. The exterior cladding system is coordinated with mechanical and passive heating and cooling systems.

The Greater London Authority building (2002) by Norman Foster (Figure 69) incorporates many integrated design features. Its form, orientation, cladding, and glazed surface treatments all work together synergistically to maximize the efficiency of each system. Designed using building information modeling (BIM) software, its shape achieves optimum energy performance. A range of active and passive shading devices have also been employed: to the south the building leans back so that its floor plates step inwards to provide shading for the naturally ventilated offices; and the building's cooling systems utilize ground water pumped up via boreholes from the water table. These energy-saving techniques mean that chillers are not always required and that for most of the year the building can function with no additional heating. Overall, it has the capacity to use only a quarter of the energy consumed by a typical air-conditioned office building, even though the building maximizes natural daylight by using glass cladding for the entire façade. Each glass surface is designed to recognize its relationship to the path of the sun. For example, the north façade allows large amounts of natural light to enter the office spaces, while the atrium is to the south where heat gain is higher and the warm air is free to rise away from the occupied spaces. There are vents at the top of the windows to allow warm air to exit, and below there are intake vents as well. The atrium is located south in the building to create a buffer against the southern exposure and the interior spaces. This also allows more natural light into the building without excess heat gain. Each triple glazed low-e glass panel was laser cut and incorporates shading devices.

Integrated design will become standard practice as computer-based BIM is used in the design process.

See also: **Building information modeling: BIM • Cosmogenic architecture • Green design (Archispeak)**

Further sources: Jencks (1997); Sim Van Der Ryn (in Jencks 1997: 136)

Figure 69: Greater London Authority building

▌ Integrated practice

Integrated practice is a holistic approach to building in which all project stakeholders and participants – architects, engineers, construction managers, contractors and owners – work together in highly collaborative relationships throughout the facility life cycle.
— George Elvin

Born from the design/build movement, *integrated practice* involves interdisciplinary team efforts to plan, design, and construct architecture. The impetus for team practice is the use of the building information model (BIM) as the mechanism for bringing together all aspects of a project. Thus, *integrated practice* involves a fundamental realignment of the participants in the architecture-making industry. No longer is the architect automatically in an advantaged position as the lead project designer. That responsibility is now delegated, with a project manager as the head of the team. That project manager is most likely not the architect. In the traditional design/bid/ build process, the architect's drawings formed the template on which the subsequent participants introduced their refinements. All parties worked within the limits specified by the architect's design. In the new arrangement, design inputs by the various parties are virtually simultaneous. It is design by committee. Of particular concern is the loss of a design meta-concept, or parti. It is the parti that moves a building beyond the pragmatic, and into the poetic and architectural. If the design team coordinator is a project manager, and not an architect, then all parties will be approaching the design challenge as a process of suboptimization of their part of the pie. The whole that is greater than the sum of the parts will be lost.

See also: **Building information modeling: BIM • Holism • Parti (Archispeak)**

Intelligence   I

The idea is that architects use "intelligence" in a twofold way: as a specific form of practical knowledge characteristic for the profession, and in the practical way the American C.I.A. or military might want to use "intelligence." … be able to work from seemingly endless fragments of "information," rumors even, and disinformation. — Michael Speaks

The term *intelligence* is coming into use in architectural design perhaps due to the twenty-first-century War on Terror. Military metaphors are replacing sports metaphors. It is a sign of our times.

The practice of seeking *intelligence* before, during, and after design is the revival of an old tradition from the 1970s, when publications such as *Problem Seeking* (2001) by Willy Pena were in vogue. Even the National Council of Architectural Registration Boards (NCARB) adopted "problem seeking" as the model for the pre-design portion of the architectural licensing examination in the United States. The core idea was that in order to produce good and appropriate design, good *intelligence* must be sought through asking the right questions, and then supplementing the answers from a variety of other sources of information. The *intelligence* gathered was then evaluated and published in the form of an architectural program or brief. The brief was intended to launch the designer in the right direction. Later the brief was intended as the measure of the performance of the "solution." Unfortunately, the emphasis in those days was limited to pragmatic issues. Form following function, as expressed in user needs, was the formula. The entire notion of architectural design as "problem solving" proved to be devoid of the humanizing poetics that distinguish mere building from architecture.

Ironically, in the twenty-first century we are returning to the paradigm of architectural design as problem solving, as we venture ever more into parametric green architecture. Hopefully, the "problem" to be solved through the intelligence process described above by Speaks will be more inclusive and thus more acceptable to the public. After all, there is much more *intelligence* out there now.

See also: **Brief (Archispeak)** • **Chatter** • **Green building (Archispeak)**

Further sources: Lang (1987: 47)

Internationalism

The internationalism we experience today represents an internationalism of nonmaterial financial currents, of scientific and technical information, and of mass communication, with respective laws of behavior and consumption. — Vittorio Gregotti

As the developed world races towards *internationalism*, as evidenced by the formation of one European economy and parliament, the profession of architecture will follow suit. In the twenty-first century, most successful architects have already become international businessmen and women. Practice is global for the starchitect. *Internationalism* is taking the form of collaborative, multinational project teams, as well as the standardization of architectural styles and standards (within cultural limits). Before it experienced its financial downturn, Dubai was becoming an international meeting ground for architects. Beijing also served that purpose, as it prepared for the Olympics. Increasingly, innovative British and Dutch firms are eroding the dominance of American architects in the international markets. This may not be an issue in the future as architects will consider themselves to be extra-national – without one country, but of all countries. At one time, architects from Europe migrated to the United States in order to practice. Mies van der Rohe, Walter Gropius, Rem Koolhaas, Bernard Tschumi, and Daniel Libeskind are just a few of the past and present American-based non-American international architects.

Given world demographics, it will only be a matter of time before international Chinese and Indian architects outnumber all of the others. Nationality will be increasingly viewed as largely irrelevant.

See also: **Deterritorialization/reterritorialization** • **Globalization**

Further sources: Gregotti (1996: 75)

Inversion

Twentieth century architecture has resisted the creative application of inversion as a means of exploring new ideas. Modernism was entirely too serious-minded for such indulgences, and postmodernism, while more tolerant of diversity and humor, lacks the kind of intellectual rigor that can produce strong inversionist work. — James Wines

If conflict is the first law of mannerism, then the second law Wittkower identifies is "the principle of inversion." — Anthony Vidler

Inversion forbids an unequivocal reading of the façade; the eye is led to wander from side to side, up and down, and the movement thus provoked can again be called ambiguous. — Rudolf Wittkower

Inversion is a creativity technique that involves turning something upside down or inside out, in order to dislocate our relationship to it. It is a form of "strange making." *Inversion* is a technique used in art and atonal twelve-tone composition in music. The inversionist abstract art of Bauhaus teacher Wassily Kandinski was influenced by the atonal inversionist music of his long-time friend Arnold Schoenberg. Inversion in Schoenberg's music involved the reversal of the line of pitch – a descending one replaces each ascending pitch interval. Inversion in the art of Kandinski consisted of his break from representational art.

In architectural design, *inversion* is a tool of the twenty-first-century architect free of any conventions regarding the "right" way to develop architectural form. This is fairly recent, as the modernist architect did not generally have the freedom to explore composition through inversion. Even the post-modern architect was constrained by an overactive concern for embedding coded meaning into the work. Literal inversion in architecture did occur occasionally. The "Katimavik" Canadian pavilion at Expo 67 in Montreal was one such inversion (Figure 70). It remained a gimmick, rather than a breakthrough in architectural form possibilities.

A subtler example of architectural inversion is the orchestration of the entries to the Kimbell Art Museum at Fort Worth Texas by Louis Kahn (1972). Kahn chose to place the main entry at the back of the building, away from the undistinguished vehicular drop-off entry towards the street. To complicate matters even further, he placed a moat and a grove of yaupon trees between the building entry and the park next to it (Figure 71). There is no clear path to get to the park or the building. The entire entry sequence is poetically, rather than functionally, determined. The objective is to place one in the right frame of mind for contemplating the art contained in the building.

Passing from the grove on into the building, on steps up to and under the central portico, barely clearing one's head of the low branches.
— Michael Benedikt

See also: **Absence/ presence • Abstraction • Allusionism • Ambivalence • Architectural psychology •Creativity • Defamiliarization • Immateriality in architecture • Phenomenology • Sublime • Uncanny**

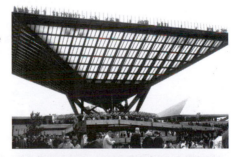

Figure 70: Inverted pavilion at Expo 67

Figure 71: Entry to the Kimbell

Junkspace

Yes, we have junk space, but we don't need architects to theorize it.
Just because it is there doesn't mean we have to love it.
— Robert Stern

Junkspace is the sum total of our current achievement; we have
built more than all previous generations together .... According to
the new gospel of ugliness, there is already more Junkspace under
construction in the twenty-first century than survived from the
twentieth. — Rem Koolhaas

Peter Blake, in *God's Own Junkyard* (1964), first pointed out the obvious –
in America we are polluting our environment with suburban sprawl and
its accompanying *junkspace*. In response, Robert Venturi, Denise Scott
Brown, and Steven Izenour in *Learning from Las Vegas* (1972) argued
for architects to stop pretending *junkspace* does not exist and embrace
it for what it is. They even compared the A&P parking lot to an Italian
piazza (Figure 72). The "emperor has no clothes" declarations by Venturi
(and group) have led to the academic discourse on *junkspace* that Robert
Stern rejects as unsuitable dinner-table conversation. Despite Stern's
objections, the "ugly and ordinary" of *junkspace* has stuck as legitimate
architectural theoretical discourse. Architects as important as Rem
Koolhaas have espoused the undeniable importance of *junkspace* as
symptomatic of our current urban malaise. His amusing diatribe of ten
dense pages in *Content* (2004) was probably inspired by the interview with
Robert Venturi that preceded the piece. In any case, the beautification of
junkspace is dishonest and futile, as there is a lot more *junkspace* than
there are architects, or paying clients, ready to take it on.

Junkspace is like being condemned to a perpetual Jacuzzi with
millions of your best friends. — Rem Koolhaas

Further sources: Koolhaas (2004: 162)

Figure 72:
Junkspace
parking lot –
a piazza?

Kitsch ▮

Kitsch **is nothing but that which has pretensions to classic status in the proliferation of voices and tastes.** — Gianni Vattimo

The notion of *kitsch* is familiar to the consumer of designed objects. Although it typically involves something that is in bad taste, in some quarters it has assumed a certain cachet. Folk art is considered to be *kitsch* by those that are not "folks" (Figure 73). Kitsch is part of the nostalgia movement in our difficult times. It smacks of a simpler world.

Is there emerging a early modernist *kitsch*? The mid-century modern bungalow is one of the most desired house types for members of the baby boom generation in America. The mythic home of their childhood, with its pink, turquoise, or avocado Formica and pre-IKEA Scandinavian teak furniture, is de rigueur *kitsch*.

The recent generation of post-contextualist, digitally based architects have few hang-ups about following classical, modern, or post-modern fashion rules. The often audacious, ugly, and awkward architecture that results from their individual artistic voices may qualify as instant *kitsch* – not a bad thing perhaps. Architects such as Will Alsop, and other blobmeisters of his ilk, are keeping things interesting. Unfortunately, most future architects will not have this luxury due to the growing popularity of integrated team design based upon discrete pragmatic parametrics, supported by a shared digital building information model or BIM. Green design by committee is unlikely to create architecture bold enough to be instant *kitsch*.

See also: **Blob architecture (Archispeak)** • **Building information modeling: BIM** • **Integrated practice**

Further sources: Vattimo (in Leach 1997: 153)

Figure 73: Folk kitsch in Souris, Manitoba

▌Late modern architecture

Late modern architecture **is pragmatic or technocratic in its social ideology and, from about 1960, takes many of the stylistic ideas and values of Modernism to an extreme in order to resuscitate a dull (or clichéd) language. Late Modern architecture, also facing the popular rejection of the "dumb box," developed after 1965 in a sculptural direction – the articulated box – and towards an elaboration of structure, services and joints: High Tech.** — Charles Jencks

Jencks seems to be referring to the early work of Renzo Piano, Richard Rodgers, and others that have been labeled "high-tech" (see *Archispeak* p. 96). The Centre George Pompidou (1977) is the poster child for late modern, high-tech architecture, as described by Jencks (Figure 74). As an apologist for the post-modern style in architecture, Jencks appears to reject technology as a desirable or appropriate inspiration for the aesthetic expression of a building. This view is consistent with the brief era of late-twentieth-century semiotic post-modern architecture de-emphasizing technology, in favor of a fragmented classical narrative.

The celebration of technology is once again on the ascendancy, as witnessed by the growing interest in the fabrication and design of building skins. Technology is also the focus of the renewed concern for environmental performance. The metaphor of the living organism has replaced the metaphor of the machine. Mechanical engineering is replaced by bioengineering. The technology suggested by the current biological metaphor is at a much higher level of technology. *Late modern architecture* is evolving into a responsive, dynamic, living architecture that is capable of mutating to optimize its performance over time. It may need a new label.

See also: **Eco-tech • Biomimicry • High-tech (Archispeak) • Responsive architecture**

Further sources: Jencks (1997: 10); Jencks (2007: 23)

Figure 74: Pompidou Center

Linguistics   ■

Linguistic theory is an important paradigm for analyzing a general
post-modern concern: the creation and reception of meaning.
— Kate Nesbitt

Linguistics is also radical because of the way it seems to overthrow
realism (the view that there is a real world out there that can be known
by the human mind) and to replace it with a linguistic relativism (what
we can know is the system of concepts generated by the arbitrary
structures of language). — Donald Palmer

Linguistics is the science of language. It was launched with the publication
of Ferdinand De Saussure's 1907 to 1911 lecture notes entitled *A Course in
General Linguistics* (Palmer, 1997: 14). Saussurian linguistics became the
core interest of the structuralists fifty years later. It was also co-opted by
mid-twentieth-century architectural avant-garde critics as the antidote
to a mute and uninteresting modern architecture. These post-modernists
hoped that by restoring a language of architecture that the public could find
meaningful, architecture would become popular again. After all, there had
been an understood classical language in architecture, as documented in
John Summerson's erudite *The Classical Language of Architecture* (1963).
The 2,000-year-old classical language was discarded by the modernist
purge of architectural history. That purge is now regarded as a mistake,
as was argued by Robert Venturi in *Complexity and Contradiction in
Architecture* (1966). This single publication was the watershed event that
marked the shift in architectural sensibilities from function to meaning.
Jencks's lively *The Language of Post-modern Architecture* (1977) was the
response to Summerson. Architectural post-modernism was eventually
devalued by its popular success. Third-rate designers found it too easy
to arbitrarily slap a classical portico on a fast-food restaurant, causing
the movement to become discredited in the eyes of the critics and the
informed public.

   Since the shift away from structuralism and post-modernism in
architecture, *linguistics* has been largely forgotten as a model for the
structure of architectural theory. Its contribution remains in that the
new modernism is more sensitive to the language understood by its
audience.

See also: **Post-modernism (Archispeak)** • **Structuralism**

Further sources: Harries (1998: 84); Nesbitt (1996: 32); Tschumi (in Ballantyne
(2002: 182)

Machines

The new artistic sensibility of the twentieth century has not only felt the beauty of the machine, but has also taken cognizance of its unlimited expressive possibilities for the arts. — Theo van Doesburg

The house... a machine for living. — Le Corbusier (Figure 75)

Architecture is a machine for the production of meaning. — Arata Isozaki

As early as Vitruvius in the first century AD, architects have had a deep interest in the machine. Michelangelo and Leonardo da Vinci designed war machines. It was seen as a legitimate aspect of architectural practice up through the Renaissance. Viollet-le-Duc, in the mid-nineteenth century, explored the marriage of the gothic with the cast iron aesthetic of the machine. It was the Victorian industrial age of "cast iron, soot and rust" (Banham 1984). The machine was the central metaphor of the modern age. Architecture did not escape the fascination with the machine. As described by Reyner Banham in his seminal book, *Theory and Design in the First Machine Age* (1960), the early twentieth century was the first in what was expected to be a series of machine ages.

The second machine age occurred in the second half of the twentieth century, and was marked by the introduction of the transistor and personal computer. It became known as the information age. Architecture briefly lost interest in the machine as it delved into the social sciences, including linguistics. However, the machine metaphor never fully disappeared. It had a resurgence of popularity after the Expo 70 world's fair in Osaka Japan. Machine-inspired "high-tech" buildings, such as the Pompidou Center (1977), Lloyd's of London (1986), and the Hong Kong and Shanghai Bank (1986), kept the machine aesthetic alive through the 1970s and 1980s.

In the twenty-first century the machine is returning to prominence in what may be called the third machine age. This time the machine is a complex bio-machine that replicates living organisms. These are the machines Deleuze and Guattari describe with earthy gusto. Although still in a beta stage, the biotechnology of today is vastly more evolved than the mechano-technology of the previous century. Our everyday machines have become smarter, smaller, more portable, global, and more personal. Our architecture will surely follow.

See also: **Biomimicry • High-tech (Archispeak) • Technology and architecture**

Further sources: Antoniades (1990: 32); Colebrook (2006: 9); Deleuze (in Ballantyne 2002: 28)

Figure 75:
Machine for
Living: Villa
Savoye

Manifestos ▮

Manifestos are poetry written by someone on the run. They have a hysterical, telegraphic quality for today as if the sender did not want to pay for extra syllables. Architects, such as Aldo van Eyck, are adept at these gnomic utterances, word trunks that collapse space-time into neologisms such as "builtform." These are directed at other Architects to hypnotize them. — Charles Jencks

I do not believe we need another manifesto in architecture .... Architecture, it seems has suffered enough from the illusion that *manifestos* matter ... — Michael Speaks

The tradition of architectural *manifestos* was in its heyday during the early twentieth century when politics and architecture were inseparable. The Marxist revolution was inspirational. CIAM, the Bauhaus, the Futurists, Le Corbusier, and Frank Lloyd Wright were among the individuals and groups that published endless *manifestos* in books, magazines and pamphlets during this period.

... a new industrial landscape, a new democratic socialism, and a new pluralistic epoch...explains , in part, the manifesto mania that soon surfaced in architecture. — James Wines

In the 1960s the *manifesto* became a gentle, and not so gentle, response to the earlier strident, and somewhat naïve, modernist declarations of ideology. Landmark publications included Christian Norberg-Schulz's *Intentions in Architecture* (1965), Robert Venturi's *Complexity and Contradiction in Architecture* (1966), the Smithsons' *Team Ten Primer* (1967), and Ian McHarg's *Design With Nature* (1969). These important *manifestos* suggested the need for a paradigm shift away from the international style and towards a more local and responsive architecture.

The flood of *manifestos* did not abate through the 1970s and 1980s. Rem Koolhaas' *Delirious New York: A Retroactive Manifesto for Manhattan* (1978), Kenneth Frampton's, *Towards a Critical Regionalism* (1983), Mark Wigley's *Deconstructivist Architecture* (1988), and Steven Holl's *Anchoring* (1989), are just a few of the important *manifestos* published during this period of realignment of architectural theory. The 1990s were a period of distancing architectural theory from the post-modern machinations of the post-structuralists. It was an era of critical theory applied to a normative direction for architecture. No longer "theory for theory's sake," *manifestos* became a forum for describing an inclusive digital and/or green architectural practice.

The turn of the century always seems to be a significant time in the evolution of western society. This "fin de siècle" is no exception. The twenty-first century seems to no longer be concerned with the critical social/cultural agendas proposed in the above late-twentieth-century *manifestos*. We are now in the early stages of a revolution that is characterized by a shift towards the technology of a globalized ethical practice. A digital architecture based upon integrated green parametric modeling is the emerging architecture of our times. The building information modeling (BIM) operating manual is the de facto *manifesto* of our times.

See also: **Building information modeling: BIM** • **Critical theory** •
Deconstructivism (Archispeak) • **Digital architecture** • **Ideology** • **Normative
theory** • **Post-structuralism (Archispeak)**

Further sources: Jencks (1997: 6); Wines (1987: 20)

▌Mannerism

**Architecture has witnessed a consolidation of anti-modern sentiment
and a settling in of mannerist preoccupations that has superseded
the self-conscious historical borrowings of postmodernism with an
intense cultivation of style ...** — P.A. Johnson

**A principally Italian movement in art and architecture between the
High Renaissance and Baroque periods (1520–1600) that sought to
represent an ideal of beauty rather than natural images of it, using
characteristic distortion and exaggeration of human proportions,
perspective, etc.** — *Collins English Dictionary*

In addition to the dictionary definition above, *mannerism* has become
associated with any adherence to a distinctively personal or affected
style. There was a debate in the mid-twentieth century about modernism
as *mannerism* which involved Colin Rowe and Nikolaus Pevsner. Rowe
contended that modern architecture had much in common with mannerist
architecture. The same argument could occur today, as the output of many
of today's starchitects could also be considered mannerist. The work of
Frank Gehry comes to mind. His exuberant, distorted forms are personal
and a cubist distortion of perspective. Other architects who complete
recognizably mannerist work are Zaha Hadid, Santiago Calatrava, Michael
Graves, Eric Owen Moss, Antoine Predock, and Richard Meier. It is as
though there is an effort for each starchitect to have their distinctive brand
of architecture. One exception might be the Renzo Piano Workshop, which
seems to sublimate a personal "style" in favor of the unique parameters

of the project at hand. The Menil
Gallery in Houston (1986) (Figure
76) is a relatively early example of
the work of Piano that bears no
resemblance to the more famous
Pompidou Center he designed with
Richard Rogers. Rogers, on the other
hand, continued in the "high-tech"
style of the Pompidou and became a
starchitect.

See also: **Baroque** • **Blobitecture** • **Blob
architecture (Archispeak)**

Further sources: Agrest (1993: 37); Vidler
(2008: 87)

Figure 76: Menil Gallery

Mask   ▮

**I think the dressing and the *mask* are as old as human civilization...
The denial of reality, of the material, is necessary if form is to emerge
as a meaningful symbol, as an autonomous creation of man.**
— Gottfried Semper

**It (architecture) constantly plays the seducer. Its disguises are
numerous. Facades, arcades, squares, even architectural concepts
become the artifacts of seduction. Like masks, they place a veil
between what is assumed to be reality and its participants. So
sometimes you desperately wish to read the reality behind the mask.
Soon, however, you realize that no single understanding is possible.
Once you uncover that which lies behind the mask, it is only to discover
another mask.** — Bernard Tschumi

**What is the beauty of a building today? ... the same as the beautiful face
of a mindless woman: something mask-like.** — Friedrich Nietzsche

The metaphor of the *mask* over the beautiful face is a powerful image for
architecture that strives to move one into an experience of mystery and
subsequent discovery. In a more negative mood, Gilles Deleuze and Felix
Guattari describe the *mask* as a negative force that hides the ugliness
and inhumanity of the face. The *mask* is seen as primitive, a ritualistic
transformation to animal.

**For there is no unitary function of the *mask*, except a negative one ...
the mask assures the inhumanity of the face.** — Deleuze and Guattari

Today, the architectural *mask* occurs most often on commercial strip
mall buildings that are lavished with expensive marble and stainless
steel fronts, while the inexpensive prefabricated metal shed lurks behind.
The deception fools no one, as one has only to peer around the corner
to see that it is a *mask*. There is no outcry, as the public is grateful that
the ugliness is shielded from their view. The complicity may even be
more overt, as in the example of the rural Florida church shown here.
The diminutive entry, with its dwarf steeple, is enough of a *mask* for the
congregation to deny the reality of the large metal building (Figure 77).

See also: **Beauty**

Further sources: Deleuze (in Ballantyne 2002: 71); Tschumi (in Ballantyne 2002:
18); Tschumi (1999: 90)

Figure 77: A mask for the believers

Meaning

Meaning in Architecture is not an analysis about the same old thing, but about difference. — José Morales

When one sees an architecture, which has been created with equal concern for form, function and technic, this ambiguity creates a multivalent experience where one oscillates from *meaning* to *meaning* always finding further justification and depth. — Charles Jencks

The search for *meaning* was the central project of post-modernism in architecture during the second half of the twentieth century. It was a reaction to the criticism that modern architecture had failed to be meaningful to the public. In order to find a way to restore *meaning*, architectural thinkers turned to the science of linguistics. The structure of language was seen as a relevant model for finding structure in architectural theory. Linguistics let to structuralist philosophy, with its belief in the importance of the underlying structure of things. Unfortunately the meaningful architecture that was attempted by post-modern architects failed to establish itself to the extent that the classical language of architecture had previously. It never gained a foothold. Despite a great deal of academic head scratching, the practitioner did not get the memos and therefore little that could be considered the new meaningful architecture was built. The post-modern architecture that did manage to be built now seems dated (Figure 78) and irrelevant, as the attention has moved to green architecture and a renewed focus on the pragmatic.

See also: **Linguistics • Post-modernism (Archispeak) • Post-structuralism (Archispeak) • Semiology (Archispeak) •Structuralism**

Further sources: Colquhoun (1991: 254); Johnson (1994: 425); Lang (1987: 94); Morales (in Gausa 2003: 426); Nesbitt (1966: 44)

Figure 78: Dated Seattle Art Museum
– Robert Venturi

Megastructure   ▌

Megastructure **form – a large frame in which all the functions of a city are housed.** — Fumihiko Maki

Megastructure has an informal and an evolving definition; its common understanding today defining excessively tall buildings, such as the Burj Kahlifa in the Arab Emirates or the Petronas Twin Towers in Malaysia. *Megastructure* can also describe a megacity, either encapsulated within a single structure or expanded additively, modular fashion and ad infinitum, in response to need. *Megastructure* is the stuff of science fiction narrative and movie sets, such as the Tyrell Corporation pyramid seen in the opening sequences of Ridley Scott's *Blade Runner* and Arthur C. Clarke's classic novel set in the twenty-second century, *Rendezvous with Rama*. However, beyond movies, there is also Buckminster Fuller's visionary megaproject – one that is still published as a novelty to this day. This is his proposed 1.6 kilometer high, 3.2 kilometer wide superdome with a footprint huge enough to envelope fifty blocks of Manhattan Island – including all of upper Manhattan's skyscrapers.

The mega-city concept was seeded at the end of the 1950s and later spawned from an ensuing 1960s pop culture. Examples include Archigram's Plug-in City (Peter Cook) and Walking City (Ron Heron), and the supersized, modular structures by the Metabolist group. There are also Constant Nieuwenhuys' New Babylon and Yona Friedman's Spatial City projects – who, seeing the modern conurbation as a redundant organism, created independent mega-structures suspended over existing cities and the landscape. A mini version of the Spatial City Megastructure can be found at the University of Winnipeg where a new science megastructure is built suspended over the historic campus (Figure 79). However, by the end of the 1960s, widespread interest in the dreams of the mega-structuralists prompted an ironic reaction from the two radical Italian architectural groups: Superstudio and Archizoom. Their respective projects, "super-architecture" and "total urbanism" came as caustic critiques of the functionalist and spatial legacies of the modern movement.

In the mid-1970s architectural critic, writer and historian of the near future Reyner Banham saw the megastructure as a way of fusing the vision of city planners and architects in their attempts to provide answers to urban sprawl and disfunctional cities. Indeed, his book *Megastructure: Urban Futures of the Recent Past* (1976) became the essential guide to the megastructure movement. A resurgence of interest has seen a 2008 exhibition and an accompanying publication *Megastructure Reloaded* (edited by Sabrina van der Ley and Markus Richter).

However, superseded by its common use, and varying from context to context, the strict definition of *megastructure* is by measure; it originally described a built structure at least 1,000 kilometers (that is, one megameter) in length, and this accounts for the origin of the term. If we apply the size yardstick, both the Channel Tunnel (50 kilometers in length) and the Great Wall of China (6,352 kilometers long) fall into the *megastructure* category.

In summary, however, the term describes any typically large, artificial, self-supporting structure or building or, using architect Ralph Wilcoxon's

1968 definition (cited in Wikipedia), a megastructure can be composed of many smaller structures grouped together. TP

See also: **Hyperbuilding**

Further sources: Colquhoun (1989: 223)

Figure 79: University of Winnipeg Sciences Building megastructure

▌Metareality

We realize that we are now seeing the emergence of a new reality in which information technologies further a way of inhabiting a networked world that requires a new approach to the conception of architecture and cities – a *metareality*. *Metareality* is the broadest most perfect interface for action in the world, the place where the physical and digital meet. — Vincente Guallart

"Meta" is a prefix used to indicate a concept that is an abstraction from another concept, used to complete or add to the latter. *Metareality* is thus a more recent iteration of the long line of "realities" that have fascinated philosophers for millennia. The idea of a *metareality* emerged from critical reality, which could be considered a branch of critical theory. It is a reality that is inclusive, embracing the cyber universe, the inner life, as well as the physical existence we have been conditioned to regard as our only trustworthy reality. *Metareality* is the reality of our combined consciousness as a networked planet. For the generation that has come of age in the Internet age, *metareality* is more real than overt "see and touch" reality. The implications for architecture and cities is profound, as community has become placeless. Our *metareality* is not supported by cities and architecture. It is deterritorialized.

Increasingly, you can't experience the built world without encountering a digital screen of some kind. They are on or in everything from airports to convenience stores – right down to the phones in our hands. They are fundamentally changing our relationship with architecture. — Christopher Hawthorne

Metareality is a relevant concern when considering the design of the twenty-first-century workplace, community building, and home. One would assume that the need for gathering is lessened, but the opposite is proving to be the case. With social networking, it is now possible to alert your social network about an event at a moment's notice. The result is that there is a greater incident of face-to-face interaction. Grass-roots political movements such as the American right-wing, ultra-conservative "Tea Party" are exploiting this capability.

See also: **Deterritorialization/reterritorialization • Hyperrealism (Archispeak)**

Further sources: Guallart (in Gausa 2003: 432)

Mimesis   █

In the future, we will see architecture doing real acts of mimicry, imitating noises, breathing or producing fog and vapor.
— Salvador Perez Arroyo

Mimesis **is a psychoanalytic term – taken from Freud – that refers to a creative engagement with an object.** — Neil Leach

The classic understanding of the term *mimesis* is that of imitation. *Mimesis* was an accepted design technique in the classical world, as is illustrated by the myth of the origin of the Corinthian capital as an imitation of acanthus leaves growing around a basket. The history of western architecture is replete with *mimesis*. Imitating the ruins of classical antiquity was an important design method for the first 4,000 years of the history of architecture. Only in the last century did it become unacceptable for architects to mimic the work of other architects. The gentleman's agreement against imitating each other's buildings prevented mimesis from being a recognized part of architectural practice – or so it seemed. The system of master and apprentice in architecture has led to many examples of the apprentice being mistaken for the master in an anonymous design competition. The most famous cases are the selection of Zaha Hadid for the Peak and Carlos Ott for the Paris Opera house. In each case, the work of the apprentice was mistaken for the work of their master, Zenghelis and Meier respectively.

As architects return to nature for their form inspirations, there will be a new round of *mimesis*. Biomimicry and bioengineering-based imitations of biological forms and processes will become more common (Figure 80).

See also: **Biomimicry • Models**

Further sources: Antoniades (1990: 171); Arroyo (in Gausa 2003: 435); Leach (in Borden 2000: 30); Ulmer (in Foster 1983: 87, 91)

Figure 80: Tree mimesis in Tartu, Estonia

Models

Generally speaking, the term "model" describes a representation, usually at a smaller scale and in another material, of a thing or a structure. It can also describe a system, such as mathematical formulae, an exemplary person, or a style or an idea. For instance, a conceptual drawing or a diagram is a graphical model of an idea; the architectural model, often described as a "physical model" to differentiate it from a computer model, being its three-dimensional equivalent.

Models have enjoyed a long history in the creation of architecture. However, it is difficult to pinpoint the advent of the scale model, as many archaeologists believe that the Greeks (and the Egyptians before them) employed the use of paradeigmata, that is, prefabricated full-sized mock-ups or specimens from which to copy and transfer dimensions on site into the actual building materials. This was because a mathematical system with a calibration fine enough to inform small-scale conversions was not yet in place. The first known scale *models* – produced as a design aid – were made in the mid-fourteenth century but achieved new status in the Quattrocento. This coincided with the Renaissance notion of the architect as sole creator of a building – when immaculately crafted small-scale *models* were made for testing both aesthetic and structural judgment and also for marketing architectural propositions. By the sixteenth century, while the architect drifted into working almost entirely by graphic means, the role of the model changed, becoming an explanatory device rather than an exploratory tool. However later, in the early twentieth century, the model reassumed its investigatory role with many of the modernist icons of the time, both realized and unbuilt, first witnessing a three-dimensional existence as 3D scale models.

Despite the awesome ability of the digital model to represent a design proposal in a photo-realistic simulation, today the physical model has not gone away. If anything, it has seen a minor resurgence as it continues to provide the opportunity for group appreciation of architectural design in the round. It has also been noted that a skillfully photographed physical model provides a more compelling representation than prints from a digital model. In addition to the widespread use of digital models for representation purposes, the digital model has taken on far greater importance as a project design and management tool. Parametrically based building information models (BIM) are becoming the industry standard, replacing traditional computer-aided drawings. An interesting development is the ability to produce physical models using three-dimensional CNC printers. Many schools of architecture now have these rapid prototyping devices at the disposal of design students. The increasing number of CNC milling machines in schools suggests that the next generation of architects will continue to keep the tradition of physical models alive.

This comparatively recent technological innovation has been pioneered by Gehry & Associates in Los Angeles to deal with the plastic complexity of their buildings. Here, physical *models* of a building idea are CAT-scanned into a computer and digitized into an electronic model. Adapting Catia software already used in the aerospace and automotive industries, the model re-emerges from the computer transformed into a new physical reality – a process rehearsed for Gehry's Guggenheim Museum of Modern Art in Bilbao

(1997). It is through this technology, and through the possibility of computer software to program the actual fabrication of building components, that we can envision the coming of a new supermodel – a building idea, via the computer, moving directly from concept to construction. It is a vision in which the architect, the model maker and the builder of tomorrow may fuse as one to become the "super-model maker." TP

Models **have moved from physical** *models* **to digital. Along with the increase in digital models there has been a renewed use of full-scale mockups, especially with the aid of CNC machines.**
— Michael Speaks

See also: **Prototyping**

Monument   ∎

The presence of the great architectural monuments of the past in the modern world... possess the task of integration of the past and the present. Works of architecture do not stand motionless on the shore of the stream of history, but are borne along by it.
— Hans-Georg Gadamer

The balance of forces between monuments and buildings has shifted. Buildings are to monuments as everyday life is to festivals...
— Henri Lefebvre

Only a very small part of architecture belongs to art: the tomb and the *monument.* **Everything else, everything that serves a purpose, is excluded from the domain of art.** — Adolf Loos

There is a distinction between a *monument* and monumentality. We tend to think of monuments as large, imposing structures that represent something important. Often they teach us something about a historic event or person. The historic Necropolis of the Arts at the Alexander Nevsky Monastery in St. Petersburg is full of works that are monuments without being monumental. They are understood to be monuments because of the important people they represent. The message is clear in the case of the modestly sized, but highly didactic, monument to the composer Pyotr Tchaikovsky. He is with the angels (Figure 81).

To qualify as an architectural *monument*, a building must have significance and presence. Significance may result from the importance of the historical period, event, or architect involved in its creation.

Figure 81: Monument to Tchaikovsky

Washington D.C. is resplendent with architectural monuments of this type. Presence is achieved by the architect's skill at providing the structure with the ability to be noticed, to have "stage presence." Typically, we associate monumentality with size. The bigger, the more monumental. Monumentality can also be achieved by smaller structures that have a formality and mystery about their purpose.

See also: **Phenomenology • Sublime**

Further sources: Gadamer (in Leach (1997: 134); Harries (1998: 244, 302); Lefebvre (in Leach 1997: 139); Rossi (in Jencks 1997: 39); Vattimo (in Leach 1997: 159)

▌Morphogenetic design

Morphogenesis involves the shapes of tissues, organs and entire organisms and the position of specialized cell types. — Michael Hensel

Morphogenetic systems generate form using internal genetic logics. — Karl Chu

A long-standing challenge that has faced architecture has been the static nature of buildings. *Morphogenetic design* addresses this problem by copying biological structures and processes in order to accommodate environmentally sensitive growth and change. It involves mimicking natural growth structures and systems, including struts, lattice systems, seeds, and cell division (mitosis). Genetic modeling is also providing inspiration for this effort. Architects are beginning to take notice of these experiments in responsive and dynamic architecture. Schools such as the AA, Harvard, and Tu Delft are involved in research work in these areas. It is at the cutting edge of twenty-first-century architectural innovation. The design of architecture is on the verge of a sea change, going from a machine-based means and methods, towards a living organism model that promises to adapt to its environment. The role of cyber tools is key to this effort, with modeling and analysis software borrowed from medicine and microbiology helping the cause. Architecture may never be the same again if these efforts succeed.

See also: **Armature • Emergence • Mimesis • Nature • Organic (Archispeak)** **•Responsive architecture**

Further sources: Brand (1994: 170; Jencks (2007: 187)

▌Multiculturalism

The practice of acknowledging and respecting the various cultures, religions, races, ethnicities, attitudes and opinions within an environment. — University of Texas at El Paso website

With the rise in globalization the challenge for architecture is to preserve multiculturalist architecture. This is particularly difficult, as architects from the West are designing much of the architecture in the East. To preserve distinctive cultures may be impossible already, as worldwide media cross-contaminates each culture. Music is a case in point. Rap music has spread from the United States to virtually every country within earshot of a radio or MP3 player. The result has been French rap, Russian rap, and Asian rap, among others. Each culture assimilates the hip-hop lifestyle in its own unique way. The lesson for architecture is that there is a commonality within the differences. *Multiculturalism* survives, not in a static pure way, but rather as evolving phenomena. The challenge is to identify and understand the elements of a culture that provide continuity and identity. Cesar Pelli, Renzo Piano, and Steven Holl, among others, have made serious efforts at mixing western and eastern cultural references in their architecture. "The international style" is giving way to "the multinational style."

See also: **Critical regionalism • Globalization**

Further sources: Jencks (2007: 16)

Myth   **I**

It is critical that we re-establish the thematic associations invented by our culture in order to fully allow the culture of architecture to represent the mythic and ritual aspirations of society. — Michael Graves

In *Language and Myth* (1946), Ernst Cassirer explores the relationship between the early interpretation of the *myth* as the vehicle for the origins of language and the development of culture. Cassirer's thesis is that man interprets his world through the use of the symbolic forms of myth, language, history, art, and science. Three of these symbolic forms are associated with the construction of space or constructed space. They are "cultural myth," "aesthetic myth," and "theoretical myth."

According to the late anthropologist Joseph Campbell (1988), "cultural myth" comments on what we believe based on faith alone, including how we should behave, how the world works, and societal structure. The constructed spaces that express cultural myths are often spaces that hold collective societal power, such as ceremonial, religious, judicial, governmental, and defensive spaces and fortifications.

The "aesthetic myth" comments on what we consider to be the ideal representation of beauty, as defined by proportion, color, deformation, materiality, scale, and position. How, and what, we consider beautiful generates vernacular architecture that defines a regional or societal identity, as well as creating monumental architecture that reflects a purposeful expression of the aesthetic myth of a culture.

The "theoretical myth" involves developing a set of predictive principles that are open to change. This is the realm of science, as is it involves a set process, and deals with the measurable. This is the most dynamic of the mythic structures, as it is not based on opinion or faith alone. The process that develops theoretical space involves perception, which leads to consciousness. Consciousness then leads to reproduction, which in turn leads to theory. MA

See also: **Aesthetics • Babel • Fictional architecture • Primitive hut**

Further sources: Leach (in Ballantyne 2002: 95); Sharr (2007: 112)

▍Naked architecture

The idea of a truly functional artifact, which is shorn of all expedient or incidental or pre-conceived impurities, is now the most difficult of all artifacts to construct. This is not to say that another development in naked architecture might come about, perhaps as a reaction to over-decorated buildings. — Robert Maxwell

Was there ever such a thing as *naked architecture*? To be naked is to be pure, with no contamination or embellishment. Architecture is always an act of compromise. That compromise cloths the architecture in the extra-functional. The notion that pure functionalism results in *naked architecture* was one of the core, unspoken beliefs of orthodox modernism. It presumed that "function" was static, definitive, and definable. What was conveniently forgotten was that "function" is dynamic, allusive, often immeasurable, and contingent upon the moment. The description of function is always an approximation of a particular point in time, usually well before the building is ready for occupancy. By the time the building is ready for occupancy, the functions to be housed in the building will have changed. Unfortunately, the building will not be able to adjust to the new functions very well unless it was initially identified as part of the "function" identification. To be naked is thus to be vulnerable to obsolescence due to change.

   In response to the dilemma posed by *naked architecture*, and its difficulty with adjusting to change over time, responsive architecture is being explored at the academy. Tu Delft, the AA, and Harvard, among others, are contemplating the design challenges presented by an architecture that accommodates moment-to-moment small incremental change. Dynamic, reflexive architecture may be the architecture of the future. It will certainly result in architecture that is fully clothed.

See also: **Morphogenetic design • Psychological needs •Responsive architecture**

Further sources: Maxwell (1993: 75)

▍Nature

It is the same for architecture as for all the arts: its principles are founded on simple *nature*, and in nature's processes its rules are clearly drawn. — Marc-Antoine Laugier

***Nature* furnished the materials for architectural motifs out of which the architectural forms, as we know them have developed.**
— Frank Lloyd Wright

Versus

Architecture, unlike the other arts, does not find its patterns in *nature*.
— Gottfried Semper

It (architecture) alone is able to make forms that have no model in *nature*. — Otto Wagner

What man makes, *nature* cannot make. — Louis Kahn

Nature has been credited with the origins of architecture. The grove of trees became the temple and the primitive hut became the genesis of architectural theory. *Nature* and architecture have been discussed together since the ancient Greeks. Opinions have varied from mimesis, that is, regarding nature as perfection that architecture should seek to imitate (Plato, Alberti, Leonardo da Vinci, Quatremere de Quincy, Frank Lloyd Wright, Richard Rogers, Santiago Calatrava), to regarding architecture as a rejection or antidote to nature (Claude Perrault, Gottfried Semper, Otto Wagner, Louis Kahn, Mies van der Rohe). Generally these architects are twentieth-century modernists. They rejected the romantic idea of nature in favor of the machine. Two notable exceptions to the modernist love affair with the machine aesthetic were Frank Lloyd Wright and Alvar Aalto. Both regarded the forest and field as their inspiration.

The view that architecture must respect and emulate *nature* has returned to the forefront with the green revolution. Sustainability, biomimicry, bioengineering, and greenscaping have become popular buzzwords since the first energy crisis in the 1970s. Form follows flora and fauna. With the current and final energy crisis, it may be too late, as there is much less that is natural remaining.

Definitely *nature* does not exist. We recently digitalized the last meter of the planet and we already have it in our artificializing pocket. — Fernando Porras

See also: **Biomimicry • Mimesis • Primitive hut • Sublime**

Further sources: Abalos (in Gausa 2003: 448) Deleuze (in Ballantyne 2002: 45); Forty (2000: 220); Jencks (2007: 36); Johnson (1994: 89); Sharr (2007: 112)

Neo-expressionism ▮

Expressionism is widespread, shifting attention from the quality of the product to the character of the producer ... — William Bartley III (1973)

Expressionism in modern architecture is generally associated with a branch of mid-twentieth-century architecture that deviated from the earlier, more dogmatic, rational efforts at expressing the machine aesthetic, and instead became more personal and expressive. Rather than treating the development of form as a science, expressionism treated it as an art. Architects as varied as Le Corbusier (chapel at Ronchamp), Erich Mendelsohn, and Eero Saarinen (Figure 82) are associated with modern expressionism.

The principles of architectural expressionism include the distortion of form for an emotional effect; the expression of inner experience; an underlying effort at achieving the new, original, and visionary; and the conception of architecture as a work of art. This prescription sounds like it would fit many of the works produced by the digital generation of

starchitects. Certainly the dramatic
and sensuous work of Zaha Hadid,
Greg Lynn, Reiser + Umemoto,
and Frank Gehry qualify as neo-
expressionistic. Perhaps the entire
crop of "fold and blob" architects
can be categorized as neo-
expressionists.

See also: **Baroque** • **Blob architecture
(Archispeak)** • **Blobitecture** •
Cosmogenic architecture • **Fold** •
Hyperbuilding

Further sources: Jencks (2007: 43)

Figure 82 Dulles Airport

Neo-functionalism

**A neo-functionalist position abandons the pendular movement that
has characterized the passage from one ideology to the next, now
represented by functionalism, now by neo-rationalism and neo-
realism.** — Mario Gandelsonas

The new functionalism, or neo-functionalism, has recast the definition
of function. Whereas classic functionalism was about responding to a
building's rational purpose, *neo-functionalism* is also very concerned
with the pragmatics of environmentalism. "Form follows function"
has been replaced by "form follows sustainable practices." The debate
between battling ideologies has been usurped by a compelling case for
getting back to the business of making an architecture that is ethical
and sustainable in our time of global challenges. A changed process of
practice drives *neo-functionalism*. Designing has become a partnership
between members of an integrated team, working with a parametric
model as the focus of their collaborative efforts. Function is defined in the
form of incremental algorithms that are the pragmatic parametric inputs
to a building information model (BIM). It is to be hoped that these new
conditions of practice will permit the neo-functional building to be more
functional, and thus more sustainable, than its earlier namesake.

See also: **Algorithm** • **Building information modeling: BIM** • **Eco-tech** •
Functionalism • **Parametric design** • **Performance-based design**

Further sources: Gandelsonas (in Mallgrave 2008: 413); Gregotti (1996: 11)

Neo-pragmatism ∎

Because all philosophical attempts to distinguish between analytical and empirical, necessary and contingent, universal and historical, reality and fiction have failed, truth and meaning are taken to be nothing but moments of specific social practices. — Richard Rorty

The denial of the absoluteness of truth and meaning has profound implications for emerging integrated and global architecture. Exporting design from one social/cultural context to another becomes problematic, as the personal and particular nature of architecture is revealed. Architectural practice involving BIM will require the almost simultaneous collaboration between "social practices," as varied as engineering and architectural disciplines, constructors, manufacturers, clients, users, financial and legal consultants, and so on. The possibility of another Tower of Babel is high.

The new pragmatism attempts to be holistic, and yet relies on a process that reduces the challenge at hand to manageable bits. The process caters to the needs of the digital tools being employed to design the architecture. At this point, the consequences of this compromise are not well understood. It may be that pragmatic agendas are met, but little else. Will it still qualify as architecture?

Architecture is not the answer to the pragmatic needs of man, but the answer to his passions and imagination. — Emilio Ambasz

See also: **Architectural positivism • Babel tower • Building information modeling: BIM • Digital architecture • Parametric design**

Normative theory ∎

Normative theory **consists of the overtly value-laden statements of philosophers, politicians, and architects, among others on what ought to be. Some people have described their normative statements as scientific. This is a contradiction in terms.** — Jon Lang

... the normative view of history must be rejected if, by setting up absolute standards outside history, it ignores the fact that architectural meaning is historically founded and that this meaning cannot be detached from those meanings which architectural forms have acquired from history. — Alan Colquhoun

Normative statements by designers are value-laden opinions on what ought to be. The sum total of normative positions held by an individual identifies their personal design ethic. Past efforts at a naïve positivist scientific basis for design decisions have denied the inevitable presence of normative thoughts by the designer. It turns out that design decisions are not entirely rational, and probably should not be. Design is inevitably a process of drawing upon rather ill-formed memories, impressions, and feelings about the challenge at hand. Not all of these inputs can be measured, or even recognized. This poses a significant problem for the purveyors of the new scientific approach to design that is required by the introduction of computers into the design process. In particular, the move towards team design, rather than relying upon one inspired genius designer, will inevitably result in a return to a positivist design process. It may mean the ascendance of engineering at the expense of architecture. Poetics will suffer at the hands of the pragmatic.

See also: **Architectural positivism** • **Autonomous architect** • **Difficult whole** • **Digital architecture** •**Elementarism** • **Integrated practice** • **Parametric design** • **American Pragmatism** • **Rational method**

Further sources: Colquhoun (1985: 19); Lang (1987: v11, 15, 219)

Ornamentalism   I

Ornament is crime. — Adolf Loos

Ornamentalism refers to the traditional practice of decoration, the term often used to denote an excess of ornament displayed on the surfaces of furniture, interiors, and exteriors of buildings. Practiced in Mesopotamia and ancient Egypt and throughout antiquity, and among the so-called "primitive cultures," the art of *ornamentalism*, through the ages, was considered the natural embellishment of surface. The main source book of ornament, of course, is nature – its inexhaustible repository of motifs being translated into pattern through a basic knowledge of geometry.

In more modern times, the advent of Art Nouveau in the 1890s was an international visual arts movement characterized by organic, highly stylized flowing curvilinear forms, especially floral and other plant-inspired motifs that soon became international in spirit. However, earlier in the nineteenth century the popularity of *ornamentalism* was already being fueled by new archeological discoveries of a highly decorative and colorful past which triggered a massive revival. In mid-nineteenth-century England, fired by the exhibits in the Crystal Palace at the Great Exhibition (1851), the demand for ornamental products sky-rocketed – an industrial revolution mass production making decorated goods not just the privilege of the wealthy but accessible to the status-seeking masses. The craving for *ornamentalism* was fed by a plethora of encyclopedias, the most important of which was *Grammar of Ornament*. Published in 1856 by the architect, decorator extraordinaire and antiquarian Owen Jones, this provided an influential reference book of ornamental language and style published in sumptuous eight-color chromolithographs and deemed appropriate to serve the new industrial age.

In his book *Ornament* (1986), Stuart Durant describes the decline or ornamentalism in contemporary architecture as paralleling the ascendancy of a modern movement austerity in the early twentieth century. For the past ninety or so years the term, rather like its synonym "decoration," has evoked negative attitudes in design circles – ornamentation being seen as adulteration of the purity of form. Anti-ornamentalists held extreme views about banishing such embellishment from objects and buildings. Indeed, in 1935 one architect, H. S. Goodhart-Rendel, considered that "A fondness for ornament is no more readily acknowledged by refined persons than would be a fondness for gin." Earlier, Adolph Loos went so far as to condemn the use of ornament as wasteful and tantamount to a criminal act. In 1908 he wrote, "As ornament is no longer organically related to our culture, it is also no longer the expression of our culture" (reprinted in Loos, 1997). Surprisingly, Loos's own architectural work was often elaborately decorated. His visual distinction was not between the complicated and the plain, but between "organic" and a superfluous, over-the-top decoration.

However, in the face of such attacks, there were architects and critics who unashamedly practiced and supported ornamentalism. For example, Louis Sullivan (1856–1924), often regarded as the "father of modernism" and creator of the modern skyscraper, was a practitioner in America's Midwest who championed its use – paradoxically seeing ornament as a requirement for a fully developed architecture and approaching the form of his buildings as a host for allusion and ornamentation. The aesthetician Herbert Read writing in his *Art and Industry* (1934), described ornamentation as a "psychological necessity" for those who have "an incapacity to tolerate empty space," and more recently the philosopher and writer Roger Scruton, in decrying the contemporary cult of the utilitarian in his televised treatise entitled *Why Beauty Matters* (BBC2, December 2, 2009), suggested that "Ornament liberates us from the tyranny of the useful."

Despite the enormous onslaught of a modernist dogma which, by 1914, had discredited Art Nouveau, *ornamentalism* still survives, flickering in revivals, such as the psychedelic graphics of the 1960s and 1970s and pluralism of movements such as post-modernism. Even folk art ornamentation takes over when the bare structure fails to deliver, as is evident from the painted houseboat door in Amsterdam (Figure 83). Post-modernism embraced the ornamentation of architecture as a device for conveying meaning, much like pre-modern architecture. TP

While it is true that Modernism rejected applied *ornamentalism*, it never abandoned ornament itself. — Robert Stern

See also: **Aesthetics • Beauty • Decoration • Iconography • Image • Meaning • Naked architecture**

Further sources: Adorno (in Leach 1997: 7); Harries (1998: 43); Scruton (1979: 125); Stern (in Nesbitt 1996: 104); Vattimo (in Leach 1997: 157)

Figure 83: Ornamented houseboat door in Amsterdam

Parametric design

Parameter: a reference or value that is passed to a function, procedure, subroutine, command, or program. — *The Free Dictionary*

Parametric design, a process based not on fixed metric quantities but on consistent relationships between objects, allowing changes in a single element to propagate corresponding changes throughout the system. — Tomoko Sakamoto

Parametric tools are doubtless among the most powerful computational devices yet to be put in service of architectural production. But parametric software is not design software and its use has failed to produce objects or worlds of interest, novelty or depth. — Sanford Kwinter

Most current CAD/CAM/CAE software utilizes parametrics. By the use of parametric equations, dimensions and other variables are linked to geometry in such a way that when the values change, the geometry may change as well. In this manner, design modifications and the creation of associated data can be performed remarkably quickly, compared with the redrawing required by traditional CAD. Parametrics are the heart and soul of building information modeling (BIM) software to the extent that *parametric design* has been used as an alternative label for BIM. It is rapidly becoming the design process of choice among "third-generation" digital architects. In *parametric design*, it is the elements of a particular design that are declared, not its shape. By assigning different values to the parameters, different configurations can be created. The overall form can be manipulated by altering specific parameters that are able to automatically adjust building data such as total gross area, total building height, total number of floors, and aspect ratio. It changes the fundamental nature of the traditional design process that architects have used since the Beaux Arts. The "equisse" and the "parti" are gone and replaced by the spreadsheet and the script, or algorithm. The romantic notion that there is an "aha" moment of clarity when one "discovers" the "solution" due to inspiration found in endless design sketching is forgotten. The designer becomes a programmer. Control over form is at the mercy of the machine – the difficult whole is abandoned. The ordering system becomes predestined, opaque and out of reach.

Architectural practice is starting to shift the role of the architect in the design process from the design of specific shapes to the determination of those geometrical/algorithmic relationships describing the project and its components. — Marco Vanucci

Recently, in the disciplinary attempts to utilize the power of the parametric process it seems as if everyone awoke from the embarrassing drunken party of post-modernism, trying to forget everything that happened. — Michael Meredith

See also: **Algorithm • Artificial intelligence • Building information modeling: BIM • Difficult whole •Digital architecture • Digital materiality**

Passive design

Nature does nothing uselessly. — Aristotle

Without light there is no architecture. — Louis Kahn

In anything at all, perfection is finally attained, not when there is no longer anything to add, but when there is no longer anything to take away. — Antoine de St Exupéry

Look deep into nature, and then you will understand everything better. — Albert Einstein

In order to reduce the consumption of our planet's finite non-renewable energy resources and the associated negative consequences such as carbon dioxide emissions, the designer or architect should optimized passive solar design strategies in creating improved thermal comfort conditions in organizing the plan, the shape of the built form, and the enclosure system. *Passive design* means that the designer takes full advantage of the resources of nature and site to improve the environmental performance of a building by using radiation, conduction, and natural convection to distribute heat and daylight for lighting. Our life on Earth tracks the cycles of the sun as it arches across the sky and so connects us with the rhythm of nature. Passive solar design does not use mechanical, electrical, or photovoltaic means to satisfy heating, lighting, or cooling loads.

Strategic awareness, understanding, and clear responses to site and place, climatic conditions, landscaping, design and construction, solar orientation, placement windows and shading devices, and thermal mass are used to redistribute the sun's energy. Passive solar design (or bioclimatic design) provides thermal comfort by using natural energy sources and sinks, such as solar radiation, thermal mass, thermal chimney effect, day-lighting, evaporation, and vegetation, depending on the local climatic conditions.

In a cold climate, passive measures would aim to design a built form so that solar gains are maximized, but in a hot dry climate, the primary aim would be to reduce solar gains and maximize natural ventilation. These principles require attention to orientation and building form. For example elongating a building in the east–west orientation provides an ideal configuration, as south-facing sunlight can be controlled as opposed to low-angle east or west-facing sunlight. Additional computer modeling of these basic principles can often help achieve further energy reductions. EL

See also: **Biomimicry • Cradle to cradle • Green design (Archispeak) • Sustainability • ZEB – Zero energy building**

Pattern language

A self-annotating solipsist.
— Rayner Banham describing Christopher Alexander

Christopher Alexander, along with Sara Ishikawa and Murray Silverstein, developed *pattern language* in the 1970s as a format for documenting timeless universal patterns of user preferences in town planning and architecture. It was documented in a series of books, starting with *The Timeless Way of Building* (1979). The language consists of many individual recipes that formed patterns for achieving places that feel good. Each pattern was reputedly derived from polling the public. Examples of patterns include such varied recipes as window seats and buildings with steeply sloped roofs. The patterns are decidedly anti-urban and nostalgic, almost medieval. The important architectural contribution of *pattern language* is not the patterns themselves, but rather the notion that architectural design is a participatory activity. Even the constructing process should involve all parties, including the architect.

In the famous 1982 Harvard University debate between Peter Eisenman and Christopher Alexander, Alexander was called a "west coast joy boy" by Eisenman, who then called himself an "Eastern intellectual." Eisenman's position in the debate was that architecture should embrace structuralist post-modern thought. Although the audience seemed to disagree, his position proved to be the more successful, based on the subsequent years of architectural discourse. Alexander argued that "feelings" were more important than one's intellectual relationship with a work of architecture. Although it remained popular on the West coast, and even formed the basis for the planning of the University of Oregon, *pattern language* never became the universal language of architecture and planning moves that Alexander intended. It languished at Berkeley for decades. It was not fashionable.

In the twenty-first century, *pattern language* may re-emerge as architectural designers return to a concern for feelings. Phenomenology is once again being discussed as the basis for achieving a satisfying architecture. One can imagine design parameters consisting of *pattern language* recipes being used in the development of a project's building information model (BIM). This would be appropriate, as Alexander's *Notes on the Synthesis of Form* (1963) contributed to the eventual development of BIM software. It would also be ironic, as Alexander recanted the strict rationalism of *Notes* shortly after its publication.

See also: **Building information modeling: BIM • Phenomenology (Archispeak)**

Further sources: Alexander (in Mallgrave 2008: 451); Brand (1994: 132); Kruff (1994: 443)

Performance-based design

Performance-based design is a systematic design method that is based on meeting quantifiable measures of performance. The performance criterion is specified upfront as part of the project brief or program, and then used in measuring the success of the design (Figure 84). This is different from the traditional building design process in which the building owner and architect create a building program that contains the functional, economic, and time requirements of the building. Typically, there are no performance goals established for the building. The architect designs the building to satisfy the program requirements, and then the project

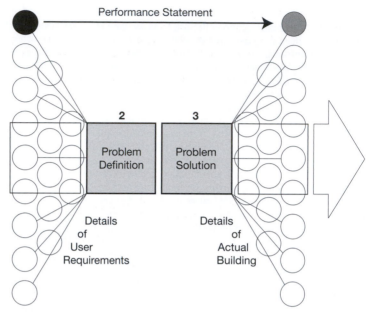

Figure 84: Performance-based design

engineers design the structural, electrical, and mechanical systems. The architect and engineers may try to design efficient systems, but with no performance goals to direct the design and little interaction, the results are usually mediocre. In a *performance-based design* approach, performance goals are developed during the initial stages of the design. The integrated design team should be involved in establishing the evaluation parameters and the performance levels desired.

The *performance-based design* method harkens back to the systems approach that grew out of the 1960s space race that launched a man on the moon. Subsequently, *performance-based design* methods were enlisted as a solution to the affordable housing shortage in the United States. "Operation Breakthrough" (1969–78) was initiated by the Department of Housing and Urban Development (HUD). It was designed to improve the process of providing housing for lower-income families by demonstrating the value of industrialized housing construction methods. Other significant systems approach projects from that period included an open systems industrialized school construction system for Southern California (SCSD).

Open systems are usually produced in response to bidding conditions requiring each subsystem to be compatible with two or more subsystems at each interface, thus assuring virtually universal interchangeability. — Educational Facilities Laboratory (1967)

Unlike the traditional space-listing program, these efforts largely failed and the use of the performance-based architectural design process faded away.

In our current climate of parametric green design, the use of a *performance-based design* method is once again relevant. It is compatible with the use of BIM as the management tool for the design, evaluation, construction and life-cycle management of buildings. The popular LEED program is a form of *performance-based design*. The challenge will be to maintain a balance between the measurable and the immeasurable. It will be a shame if architecture becomes entirely consumed by the quantifiable.

See also: **Brief (Archispeak) • Building information modeling: BIM • Green design (Archispeak)**

Pet architecture   ∎

The reader might be forgiven for thinking that *pet architecture* describes dog kennels, bird baths, aviaries and feline scratching towers, or indeed movie star and architect-wannabe Brad Pitt's design of his well-publicized and Archigram-inspired home for his offsprings' gerbils. However, although occasionally used in this context, the term actually describes an architecture of opportunity and economics, usually cheaply built, of modest scale, and encountered in the nooks and crannies of high-end real estate across the metropolis.

Pet architecture, therefore, refers to the commandeering of waste or unused urban space for its ingenious conversion into a new and imported function. Popularized in two best-selling volumes of the *Pet Architecture Guide Book* (Atelier Bow-Wow, 2002), the subject was researched by Yoshiharu Tsukamoto and Momoyo Kaijima of the Japanese architectural practice Atelier Bow-Wow, who, it is believed, also coined the term. They describe and document the urban incidence of condensed structures that range from a diminutive and ad hoc vernacular to the elegant and wafer-thin infill towers found across their native Tokyo.

However, although interest in this architectural subculture may seem to emanate from an exclusively Japanese and essentially "bonsai" approach to appropriating and squeezing into unwanted space for living and trading, such an approach is also found in architecture at large, and particularly in student projects that opportunistically "piggy-back" existing structures or cannibalize leftover space found around, between, in, or on existing structures. Designed to test the mettle of the would-be designer, *pet architecture* is the stuff of sketch designs and ideas competitions that encourage lateral thinking and sharpen design skills. Indeed, the classic habitable bridge, habitable billboard, habitable wall, together with the ubiquitous roof addition and the outdoor cinema suspended between the cheeks of adjacent city walls, all come to mind.

One realized and literal example of *pet architecture* is the birdlike "Decon" structure designed by Coop Himmelblau in 1989 and perched on the roof of Falkerstrasse 6 – a traditional apartment building in Vienna. Meanwhile, albeit confined to drawings and paper, the "freespace" interventions of Lebbeus Woods invade the Cartesian matrix of "idealized space" in existing cities such as Berlin and Zagreb. His parasitic structures hang from or burst through the fabric of existing buildings. Intentionally confrontational, they are intended to prod a re-evaluation of our occupancy of traditionally constructed space in terms of use and meaning. Although unbuilt, these Woodsian urban insertions also represent the *"pet architecture"* of this writer. TP

See also: **Ad hocism • Archigram (Archispeak)**

▌Phallocentrism

In this post-Freudian age it has become fashionable to associate such assertive buildings with masculinity; more narrowly with "the American male," and to interpret their strong verticals as phallic symbols. — Karsten Harries

Logocentrism and anthropomorphism, in particular male anthropomorphism, have underlain the system of architecture ever since Vitruvius, read and rewritten in the renaissance and through the Modern Movement. — Diana Agrest

The history of biomorphic architecture is well documented, from the pleasure palaces of the Romans to Stanley Tigerman's Daisy House (1977). The Daisy House features metaphorical references to both male and female genitalia. More common and evident in the urban landscape is the tall, vertical building as a reference to the phallus. It is no secret that with only a few exceptions, architecture is still an exclusive boys' club. That is probably why feminist literature in architectural criticism focuses on the gender associations of buildings. As an expression of power, the tall building is a popular device for establishing one's place on the world's stage, as is evidenced by the half-mile-high Dubai Khalifa, currently the tallest erection in the world. It is doubtful that the overt intention was to assert the masculinity of the developers. It is for the critics and the public at large to make the association. The Florida Capital building (1977) by Edward Durell Stone sends a clear message that it is the headquarters of the "good ole boys."

Figure 85: Florida Capitol Building

As visitors to and residents of Tallahassee have noticed over the years, from a direct view from the front, the new capitol building looks somewhat phallic, an impression aided by the delicate placement of the domed wings on either side of the base as it looms over the old capitol building. This architectural edifice has been the brunt of jokes for years, including the sale of boxer shorts with the silhouette of the building silk screened over the fly under the brand name "legislative briefs." — *Wikipedia* entry

See also: **Allusionism • Anthromorphism • Babel tower • Caricature • Morphogenetic design**

Further sources: Agrest (1993: 174); Harries (1998: 184); Scruton (1979: 27)

Phenomenology   ▮

The objects which surround my body reflect its possible action upon them. — Henri Bergson (1896)

As one of the major schools of twentieth-century philosophy, *phenomenology* has had a strong influence in architecture and many other fields concerned with the relations between ideas and things. Inaugurated in 1900 with the publication of the German philosopher Edmund Husserl's *Logical Investigations* (1900/1973), phenomenology set out to challenge the most basic assumption underlying hundreds, if not thousands of years of western philosophical history: the split between the mind and the body usually referred to as Cartesian dualism after its early-seventeenth-century formulation in the work of René Descartes. The legacy of this rationalist or "intellectualist" tradition is the idea that ultimate truths about the world are to be found – almost literally – by sitting still in a dark room and thinking very hard. In contrast to this, the phenomenological approach stresses the importance of active, embodied engagement with the world. The body is no longer to be seen as an unfortunate encumbrance and a source of error – a barrier between us and the "outside" world. On the contrary it is, as the French philosopher Maurice Merleau-Ponty suggests, the only means I have to "go unto the heart of things."

In the work of Martin Heidegger (a student of Husserl's) and even more forcibly in Merleau-Ponty, perception is not seen as producing a set of distinct and separate representations of the world (like images flashed on a cinema screen inside the head), but rather as a "way of being" – a continually unfolding temporal process of interaction between an embodied subject and a surrounding world of objects in which we are inevitably enmeshed. Inspired by Husserl's call to return to the "things themselves," the process of phenomenological description originally involved, somewhat paradoxically, a suspension of the "natural attitude" (that is, setting aside our belief in the existence of an objective reality independent of us as perceiving subjects) and a concentration instead upon the world "as it appears" to us – that is, upon the phenomena of experience, as manifest in our perception as living, moving, embodied human beings as we project ourselves towards the world in the everyday act of existing.

Much of the most important work in phenomenology was produced in the 1940s and 1950s, but it took until the 1960s before these ideas had a real impact in architecture. Christian Norberg-Schulz provides the single most important link between the philosophical tradition and architectural theory, although his earliest writings (including the dense and difficult *Intentions in Architecture* (1965)) were even more strongly influenced by Gestalt psychology, the idea that we perceive the world only insofar as it appears to us in "structured wholes" or patterns, as opposed to random sequences of sense data which the brain later "interprets." Norberg-Schulz does borrow directly from Heidegger (particularly Heidegger's 1951 essay "Building Dwelling Thinking"), and this becomes more explicit in Norberg-Schulz's later books such as *Genius Locii: Towards a Phenomenology of Architecture* (1980) and *The Concept of Dwelling* (1985), which describe the "spirit of place" as something that emerges gradually through the active process of dwelling in a particular environment, accepting the limitations of a site's natural resources and working in harmony with the local climate and traditional building patterns. It is here that the phenomenological approach in architecture becomes vulnerable to the charge of reactionary conservatism and nostalgia. A number of the architectural writers associated with this tradition (including Alberto Perez Gomez, Dalibor Vesely, and David Leatherbarrow) have been accused of this, but their work also (like that of Kenneth Frampton and Juhani Pallasmaa) retains an element of the early modernists' belief in the liberating potential of a return to the fundamental principles of form, space, and materiality. These possibilities are perhaps best evidenced in the recent work of phenomenologically inspired designers such as Peter Zumthor and Steven Holl. By focusing on the central role of the moving body in the perception of space, the sensory qualities of light, sound, temperature, and materiality can be seen as the "primordial language" of architecture – often only unconsciously experienced by the embodied observer as part of the background to their everyday existence.

There has recently been a revival of interest in many of the earlier phenomenological thinkers within contemporary work on embodied perception in philosophy, cognitive science, and computing, most notably in the writings of: Lakoff and Johnson, Andy Clark, Shaun Gallagher, and Alva Noë. Ultimately, *phenomenology* in architecture is less a design method than a discourse – a way of describing, discussing and "deciding about" architecture, from the perspective of our lived experience as embodied building users. *Phenomenology* provides a set of tools that should help remind us how to "dwell" more rewardingly within our buildings, as well as making us better at designing them. JH

See also: **Existentialism • Phenomenology (Archispeak)**

Physiognomic properties

Physiognomy is the assessment of a person's character or personality from their outer appearance, especially the face.

The term *physiognomy* can also refer to the general appearance of a person, object (architecture) or terrain (landscape and urbanism), without reference to its implied characteristics. Notions of the relationship between an individual's outward appearance and inner character are historically ancient, and occasionally appear in early Greek poetry. The first indications of a developed physiognomic theory appear in fifth-century BC Athens. The philosopher Aristotle makes frequent reference to the theory and literature concerning the relationship of appearance to character.

A recent article reported that:

...the field is undergoing something of a revival. Researchers around the world are re-evaluating what we see in a face, investigating whether it can give us a glimpse of someone's personality or even help to shape their destiny. What is emerging is a 'new physiognomy' which is more subtle but no less fascinating than its old incarnation.
— *New Scientist* (February, 2009)

Physiognomic properties in architecture explore the dialogue of the "face" in relation to the inner and outer purposes and context of a building. What does an opaque facade conceal? Does a monumental entry suggest a monumental purpose or occasion? Can one judge the character of a work from its outer appearance? Whereas most examples of classical and modern architecture would demand a clear revelation of the inner space with the exterior articulation, there are well-known exceptions. The Pantheon in Rome is one of the most moving and sublime architectural spaces ever conceived; however, the cylinder and portico composition only hints at the grandeur inside (Figure 86 and 87). Other examples of concealed physiognomic qualities are found in the complex and layered "skins" of works by Herzog & DeMeuron and Frank Gehry. CH

See also: **Abstraction • Allusionism • Beauty • Biomimicry • Character • Sublime**

Further sources: Lang (1987: 210)

Figure 86:
Pantheon
exterior

Figure 87:
Pantheon
interior

Plastic architecture

According to Theo van Doesburg , in *Towards a Plastic Architecture* (1924), a *plastic architecture* rejects existing typologies, subtractive form, inefficiency, and classical canons, including symmetry and two-dimensional façadism. It supports functionalism, economy, asymmetry, and architecture in the round. It is a recipe for modern architecture, with the added twist of rejecting Euclidean geometry and a static view of architecture. It seems to be much more in line with the new pragmatic digital architecture of the twenty-first century. Perhaps we are entering an era of neo-plastic architecture?

See also: **Façadism • Functionalism • Manifesto • Theory (Archispeak)**

Further sources: Harries (1998: 232)

Pluralism

The general tolerance of different kinds of thing, or more particularly of different and perhaps incommensurable descriptions of the world, none of which is deemed to be more fundamental than any of the others. — *Oxford Dictionary of Philosophy*

Pluralism is perhaps the best way to describe the architectural climate of the twenty-first century. The past fifty years have been a period of shedding the shackles of modernist dogma, followed by the freeing effects of the post-structuralist incursion into architectural thought. There was a further widening of architectural concern due to the influence of critical theory, and more particularly Deleuze's call for a more grounded and earthy architecture. The final result is an architectural pluralism where blobs and folds take their place next to eco-hyper-megastructures and other manifestations of the green revolution. It is a good time to be an architect. The emerging generation of architects have unprecedented tools at their disposal. One has a choice from a wide range of modes of practice and design ideologies. Architects are increasingly seen as important players in the search for a culturally valid, globally sustainable future. Although it is hard to recognize when one is in the midst of it, this is a revolutionary time in architecture. That revolution involves a greater *pluralism* in the discipline and practice of the profession of architecture.

See also: **Deleuzianism • Globalization • Internationalism • Multiculturalism • Technology and architecture**

Further sources: Jencks (2007: 23)

Post-functionalism

Post-functionalism ... is a term of absence. In its negation of functionalism it suggests certain positive theoretical alternatives – existing fragments of thought which, when examined, might serve as a framework for the development of a larger theoretical structure ...
— Peter Eisenman

Eisenman rejects the term post-modernism and prefers the term *post-functionalism*, as he claims that modernism never arrived to architecture, but functionalism did. The assertion that we have been in a classical period in architecture right up to the end of the twentieth century appears to be counter-intuitive at first. At a theoretical position it can be argued that not much had changed since the ancient Greeks invented Western architecture. We were still caught in the grips of "commodity, firmness, and delight" expressed through Euclidean geometries. The emphasis may have changed over the centuries, but not the basic formula. With the emergence of post-structuralist deconstructivism, that conceptual framework was revealed for what it was, an artificial construct, just an invention, and not something that is intrinsic to architecture. Functionalism was simply that phase of classical architecture that placed an emphasis upon "commodity." The short-lived post-modern phase in architecture was merely an emphasis upon "delight." In the current post-functionalist period, function is still considered, but it is not a driving force. Now architecture is more holistic, yet egalitarian, in its search for an inspiration to drive the design process forward. Critical theory has shown us that limiting the scope of what, and whom, is considered is undesirable and unproductive in the larger project of improving the conditions of humanity as a whole. The post-functionalist era is an era of rebuilding the conceptual framework for architecture to establish one that suits the conditions and challenges of the twenty-first century.

See also: **Archi-philosophy • Architectural theory • Critical theory • Deconstructivism (Archispeak) • Post-structuralism (Archispeak)**

Further sources: Eisenman (in Jencks 1997: 266); Eisenman (in Mallgrave 2008: 414); Nesbitt (1998: 78)

Primitive hut   ∎

The very first building structure must have occurred when our ancestors – either as a result of a population explosion or following the retreat of the glaciers, and after a nomadic foraging phase, began to establish agrarian settlements. Leaving the safety of their cave dwellings, they would have been forced to protect themselves from the elements and the dangers of the night. *Primitive hut* describes a range of theories exploring the origin of humankind's first adventure into shelter building. The earliest of these theories was expounded by the Roman writer, architect and engineer Vitruvius (c.80–70 BC to c.15 BC) in his *Ten Books on Architecture*. He described two conceptual primitive constructions: one built log-cabin style on a square footprint using horizontal mud and moss-caulked poles topped with a pyramidal roof; the other a conical construction over a circular mud-walled pit using vertical poles tepee fashion and covered with reeds and brushwood. Vitruvius would recognize the vernacular Florida farmhouse shown here as a direct descendant of his notion about primitive constructions (Figure 88). In the seventeenth century, Marc-Antoine Laugier conceived his cabane primitive – the primitive house in a forest composed of four living trees forming corner columns, with sawn log lintels and branches frame working an elementary pitched roof. It is the image of this basic skeletal structure that provides the popular archetypal image of the origins of architecture; one perceived as prototypical of all great architecture, including the classical temple.

Further theories that reflect on the generating architectural idea include those proposed in the mid-nineteenth century by Gottfried Semper and Viollet-le-Duc. While Viollet-le-Duc's account of the origins of the first house, documented in his *Histoire de L'habitation Humaine Depuis Les Temps Préhistoriques Jusqu'à nos Jours* (1875), and couched in the narrative of legend, bears a strong similarity to Vitruvius's tepee version, Semper's *The Four Elements of Architecture* (from 1851) was a study of the origins of ornament and style. However, by the end of the century, this, like Le-Duc's, was overtaken by a technological proto-modernist sensibility bent on looking toward an industrial age rather than any nostalgic return to an organic past.

Embedded in the respective timescales of all these theories is a need to re-examine architectural first principles, this archaeological detective work seeking to establish a model – a standard from which to re-evaluate and cleanse a perceived decline in a contemporary architecture. Furthermore, apart from challenging issues concerning structural purity versus an imposed architectural style, they seek, especially in the case of Vitruvius, to account for the historical missing link: that is, the incidence of nature carved into the stone and marble of the later architectural orders. For example, it was Vitruvius who proposed that it was a subconscious mental concept of the primitive hut that informed the ancient Greek artist-artisan-architect in the creation of the temples. TP

See also: **American pragmatism • Naked architecture • Technology and architecture • Unselfconscious form**

Figure 88:
Nineteenth-century
primitive hut

Principle of consistency

Often today the *principle of consistency* has become a race towards vulgar practicality. But even where this has not occurred, the idea of consistency appears to be leaning toward such an extreme generalization of functional relationships that it deprives them of the material resistance of aims, techniques, and site, which the project ought to encounter, discuss and organize.
— Vittorio Gregotti

The fundamental architectural *principle of consistency*, including consistency between parts, between the exterior and interior, between content, subject, and meaning, between form and construction, is a burden that has come with modernist dogma. Aesthetic rules regarding "part to whole" relationships, proportional systems, rhythm, balance, and harmony are an aspect of the *principle of consistency*. Beyond aesthetics, the benefit of employing consistency has been that it can expedite the task of designing, and the subsequent manufacture and erection of the architecture. The ability of digital tools, such as building information modeling (BIM) and CNC fabrication, to make each aspect of architecture unique has removed the economic need for consistency. What then remains as the justification for making the compromises that are required in order to be consistent? Perhaps the answer is in our human nature, our innate need for order. After all, biological organisms seem to display adherence to the *principle of consistency*, as is evident from fractals and the self-similarity aspects of chaos theory. Even the sacrosanct entropy principle suggests the importance of form consistency in natural systems as they move towards greater levels of order. But then again, is not each snowflake unique?

In the spirit of the new skepticism about rules regarding how one should design, the *principle of consistency* is seen as arbitrary, an invention by those who seek order for purely aesthetic and economic reasons. Without consistency, each aspect of design has the freedom to be exactly what is optimum for it, and it alone. The result may be disturbing to those who are uncomfortable with indeterminacy and disorder. Adherence to a "principle of inconsistency" in architecture would result in endless innovation, and thus healthy confusion for the public. The shared language of architecture will have been thrown away, to be restored at some point in the future as a reinvented art form. Meaning will become entirely personal and contingent upon individual bias, not a bad thing perhaps.

See also: **Ad hocism • Accident • Building information modeling: BIM • Biomimicry • Digital architecture • Heterogeneity • Indeterminate architecture • Self-similarity**

Further sources: Gregotti (1996: 12)

Profane–sacred ∎

The profane is the place in front of the sanctuary... The concept of the profane always presupposes the sacred. — Hans-Georg Gadamer

In terms of space, the Sacred delineates the demarcation between sacred and profane and thus locates the axis mundi as center. — Randal Cummings

Western architecture originated in the form of the temple, and that the change by which temple fronts were in turn applied to churches, palaces, villas, and banks, exactly parallels the historical process of secularization that we have ascribed to the evolution of culture in general. — Robert Maxwell

As described by Maxwell above, architecture has moved from the sacred to the profane over its history. It made its reputation with the sacred and lost it with the profane. The influence of the sacred is still felt, each time a temple front is placed on a bank or government building. Even the wealthy class still adorn their homes with sacred porticos. The single-family home in Natchez, Mississippi shown here is a case in point (Figure 89). The process of secularizing architecture continues to this day. With the gradual demise of classical references, eventually architecture and the rest of western culture will have all but eliminated the sacred. Even as the numbers of sacred places are in decline, spirituality is on the increase. The new sacred places are in the cyber-world. The worship is of consumer goods and eBay is the temple.

See also: **Axis mundi (Archispeak)**

Further sources: Gadamer (in Leach !997: 130)

Figure 89: Home with sacred front

▮ Prototyping

The most innovative practices today use rapid *prototyping* as a way of design thinking and not as a way to move more quickly to a final design. — Michael Schrage

With capabilities provided by digital design technologies, *prototyping* is becoming a powerful architectural design technique for the development of building assembles, in particular the skin. CAD/CAM devices allow the quick design and manufacture of prototypes for full-scale evaluation and testing by designers and clients. Increasingly, schools of architecture are investing in CNC milling machines for this purpose. ETH Zurich is even employing robotics to give students real-time experience in a nearly simultaneous design/manufacture process.

The technology that has now emerged has been forecast for some time, as is evidenced by the cartoon by Donald Winkelmann that appeared in the 1973 *AIA Journal* (Figure 90). The caption reads "The architect of the future describes his idea to a secretary, who feeds the information to a computer. The machine goes to work, and a robot builds the three-dimensional structure." What appeared to be amusing science fiction at the time has become fact. It will not be long before the forecast is that every architectural office will be able to produce three-dimensional full-scale holographic virtual environments, or at the very least photo-realistic "Second life" simulations in which their clients can "inhabit" the proposed architecture as avatars. Work on this is already well underway at Harvard. Stay tuned.

See also: **Digital materiality**

Further sources: Litwell (2003: 158); Muller (in Gausa 2003: 502)

Figure 90: 1973 Forecast of the future of architectural production process

Psychological needs

Something is needed for some end if the end cannot be achieved without it. — *Oxford Dictionary of Philosophy*

The needs of man are ignoble and disgusting, like his poor weak nature. — Theophile Gautier

The architect can only aim at generalized satisfaction of averaged social needs, and it may satisfy nothing.
— Reyner Banham

Humans are social animals. We associate, belong; we join, influence, dominate, control, like love people. Do we have a "herd instinct," which draws us together? Are there psychic dynamic forces which pull us, or gradually acquired drives we develop for survival purposes? Are we to talk of a few basic general drives which energize our behavior, or a vast number of motivating influences directed towards the satisfaction of our goals?

These are some of the questions to which psychology and evolutionary biology have failed to provide clear answers. Whether the human needs that express these drives are basically physiological, or basically psychological, or a fairly even mixture of the two, remains uncertain. The extent to which such needs can be explained simply in terms of territory alone is also far from settled. Research on defensible space (Oscar Newman, 1972) and *Designing Out Crime* (current UK legislation and directives) are examples of this approach.

F. F. Darling (1952) suggested that the provision of territory satisfies not only our physiological needs but also our psychological ones. In this "castle and border" interpretation of territory, the nest site provides for security (as opposed to anxiety), and at the border, the periphery, for stimulation (as opposed to boredom). R. Ardrey, in his book *The Territorial Imperative* (1966) added a third need, that of identity (the need of the animal to defeat anonymity and to differentiate itself from all others of its species).

Kurt Goldstein, followed by Abraham Maslow, adopted as man's main driving-force the idea of self-actualization developed earlier by Carl Jung – the drive to make actual realization of one's potentialities. Maslow (1954) believes that there is a "natural unfolding; of our needs in a gradual and progressive fashion from the 'lower needs' to the 'higher needs.'" Individuals follow this development as they mature, ideally arriving at self-actualization. In hierarchical order, the five basic need levels are physiological, safety, belonging, esteem, and self-actualization.

Over the past 30 years various architects have considered human *psychological needs* as an integral part of their design. For example in the Pågens bakery in Malmo, Sweden, Ralph Erskine has considered occupants' psychological needs such as the balance between "contact" and "privacy" as well as "identity" and "personalization," while remaining very much aware of the occupants' differences in terms of personality and values.

Herman Hertzberger's (2002) attempt to get people involved with their surroundings, with each other and with themselves, is another such approach. Lucien Kroll's dictum, "no inhabitant participation, no plans," is yet another. The late Charles Moore's observation that "buildings, if they are to succeed, must be able to receive a great deal of human energy and store it and even repay it with interest" is a genuine attempt to consider, interpret, and translate the concepts of human need, aesthetics and wellbeing into designs.

On the understanding that such approaches do not claim to have developed an adequate theory about the complex nature of personality, lists of psychological needs such as Maslow's are helpful as simple practical guides for checking and identifying needs within the context of a defined problem. Further research on the relative strength of such needs between cultures could provide us with useful information leading to greater understanding about the nature of human needs and the way in which the environment can facilitate their expression.

Missing from these modernists' approach to *needs* are the following questions. Are human needs objective? Are they distinguishable from wants? Are they universal or culturally relative? In considering self-esteem and self-actualization, it is hard to posit that these needs are understood objectively, or that one can draw the line between needs and wants. The implication is that wants are somehow less deserving of consideration, yet the essence of architecture, versus mere building, is likely found in the accommodation of wants. Other than the question of life or death, needs and wants are really the same thing on a continuum. Having said that, needs and wants are clearly culturally and geographically relative.

In the twenty-first century the consideration of "user needs" has been overshadowed by user entertainment. Satisfying the desire for self-esteem and self-actualization is the focus of the contemporary architect.

It is to be hoped that that focus can be maintained as the onslaught of pragmatic green design grows. BM

Architecture is not the answer to the pragmatic needs of man, but the answer to his passions and imagination. — Emilio Ambasz

See also: **Modernism (Archispeak)** • **User**

Further sources: Johnson (1994: 324); Lidwell (2003: 106); Mikellides (1980); Scruton (1979: 31)

Purism ∎

Generally "purity" in the arts has been associated with form: Kant understands a pure or free beauty as one that pleases by virtue of its form alone. — Karsten Harrries

... everything in architecture is expressed by order and economy. — Le Corbusier

De Stijl's insistence upon elementary form was not only a return to some anachronistic purity but also a deliberate regression to a secure order. — Bernard Tschumi

Purism is generally associated with the modern art and architectural movement of the 1920s and 1930s. De Stijl and Le Corbusier are perhaps most closely identified with purist architecture. The hallmark of purism was the use of primary colors and forms, devoid of extraneous features. It was never a popular form of architecture, outside of a small group of early-twentieth-century artists and architects. The purist tradition was continued for a short period in that second half of the 1960s with the work of the "New York Five." It included some of the leaders of the post-modern movement – Richard Meier, Peter Eisenman, John Hejduk, Michael Graves, and Charles Gwathmey. Of that group, Richard Meier has continued to practice purist architecture, only without the color. A neo-purism is emerging with the work of contemporary digital architects. Their work, as exemplified by Will Alsop, is colorful, exuberant, and all about form. *Purism* is reinvented as blobitecture.

Form does not follow function. Form does not arise out of its own accord. It is the great decision of man to make a building as a cube, pyramid, or a sphere. — Hans Hollein

See also: **Abstraction** • **Beauty** • **Plastic architecture**

Further sources: Harries (1998: 230); Tschumi (1994: 83); Tschumi (in Ballantyne 2002: 174)

Rational method

Rationalism is the metaphysical view that everything in reality is logically consistent with everything else in reality, and that this logical consistency can be grasped by the human mind because the human mind reflects the logical structure of reality. — Donald Palmer

On the longest view, modernism in philosophy starts out with Descartes' quest for knowledge self evident to reason and secured from all of the demons of skeptical doubt. — *Oxford Guide to Philosophy*

Following Descartes, architects such as Laugier (1753) described the process of designing as one of decomposing a problem, solving these components, and then synthesizing these partial solutions into whole ones. They referred to this as the *rational method*. — Jon Lang

The rational became the moral and aesthetic basis of modern architecture. At this point ... reason turned its focus on itself and thus began the process of its own undoing. Questioning its own status and mode of knowing, reason exposed itself to be a fiction.
— Peter Eisenman

The *rational method* is most closely associated with the scientific method. It was embraced by pre-modern and modern architects of the nineteenth and twentieth centuries as the route to legitimization and acceptance in a world that had come to value the utility of science above the arts. It promised to give architecture a rationally defensible footing and respectability as a quasi-science. Unfortunately, the *rational method* rejects the irrational, an important human dimension. It also fails to acknowledge the immeasurable – a significant part of our existence. Because of these limitations, and its reliance on "function" as the authority for form, the public vilified the barren modern architecture that resulted. The assault was relentless from all quarters. In response, some architects turned away from their reliance on rationalism, and embraced the merging of the mind and body in the form of phenomenology.

Phenomenology is still an important influence on architectural designers, however its application proved to be mostly limited to the personal agenda of the designer. Architectural rationalism survived by co-opting the philosophy of structuralism and the science of linguistics. Concern for function was replaced by concern for meaning. The experiment seemed to be working initially, as post-modern architecture reintroduced an element of humanity that was missing with modern architecture. Unfortunately, the movement devoured its own tail with the nihilism of deconstructivism. All rational methods proposed by structuralism were rejected as arbitrary fictions. The vacuum was short lived. With the emergence of digital parametric design tools, rationality is making a comeback. In order to be compatible with the digital world, once again the architect must reassume the guise of a solely rational being. The difference this time will be that the technology has advanced to the point that the resulting architecture will be more entertaining, with its blobs and folds. Eventually architectural design and production technology will be capable of dealing with the irrational and immeasurable. It will mean the restoration of the total architect.

A great building must begin with the un-measurable, must go through measurable means when it is being designed and in the end must be un-measurable. — Louis Kahn

See also: **Abstraction • Architectural positivism • Building information modeling: BIM • Modernism (Archispeak)**

Further sources: Antoniades (1990: 132); Harries (1998: 9); Kruff (1994: 445); Lang (1987: 37); Palmer (1997: 145); Perez-Gomez (1984: 7); Schonfield (in Borden 2000: 30); Scruton (1979: 117); Tschumi (1994: 89)

Representation

The user's space is lived – not represented. — Henri Lefebvre

The Real is "in place" and all forms of *representation* are "out of place," necessarily deflected from the Real, which is that in experience which resists all *representation*. — Donald Palmer

Modern architecture claimed to rectify and liberate itself from the Renaissance fiction of *representation* by asserting that it was not necessary for architecture to represent another architecture...
— Peter Eisenman

According to Charles Jencks in *The Language of Post-modern Architecture* (1977), the modern architecture that rejected the duty of representation died on 15 July 1972, with the demolition of the Pruitt-Igoe housing project in St. Louis. It was replaced by post-modern architecture that was essentially about restoring meaning to architecture using cliché representations from the past. Architecture ceased to be about itself, and assumed the mantle of being about something other. Michael Graves seized on post-modern architecture as a style that reflected the commodification of architecture (Figure 91).

Michael Benedikt ascribes the subsequent failure of post-modern architecture to this burden. As he points out, "buildings designed on the notion that architecture is a medium of communication cannot hope to create satisfying, if any, direct esthetic experiences of their own reality" (1987: 16). Post-modern architecture has been replaced by a restored and more potent modernism. The new modernism is also not concerning itself with *representation*. It is instead focusing on exploiting an expanded array of technology within the context of a generally elevated concern for the environment.

The new technology has had a significant impact on representations of architectural proposals still under development. Design representation has become more complex due to the modeling capabilities of twenty-first-century digital tools. With the ability to construct architectural "second life" cyber worlds, *representation* becomes tangled up with issues of "virtual" versus "real." Architectural *representation* is thus more complex and layered. Your client's avatar can now inhabit your unbuilt architecture. There is a new arsenal of design *representation* aides that should ensure that clients know exactly what they are getting – a first in the history of architecture. The architecture needs only to represent itself, the ideal that Benedikt and other phenomenologists originally espoused.

Thus an essential issue before us today is "how the representational techniques and technologies of the information age do and will affect architecture." Eluding this question means to fall into the trap of an uncritical utilization of the new tools of depiction. Trying to answer it requires us to frame our inquiry carefully.

See also: **Algorithm • Digital architecture • Hyperspace • Phenomenology**

Further sources: Benedikt (1985: 16); Eisenman (in Nesbitt 1996: 213); Tschumi (1999: 93)

Figure 91: Applied representation – Dolphin Hotel Orlando

Responsive architecture

Man will live in living, intelligent machines or cognitive physical environments that can immediately respond to his needs or wishes or whims. The possibilities are unlimited and a challenge to any imagination. — Nicholas Negroponte

We are accustomed to thinking about architecture as static, immovable and unresponsive. This has been the plight of buildings since the beginning of human habitation. With the exception of only few minor ways that change can be easily accommodated, architecture is incapable of adapting smoothly to demands placed on it. We can turn lights off and on, we can move partitions, but the structure, vertical circulation, and outer skin of the building have remained largely unavailable for adjustment. That situation is in the process of changing. The potential of a *responsive architecture* that is modeled after biological systems is unlimited. Biomimicry, utilizing bioengineering, holds the promise of architecture that can smoothly adjust to accommodate incremental changes, changes in internal demands and the external environment. The Institut du Monde Arabe (1987) by Jean Nouvel was an early experiment in *responsive architecture*. The entire south wall is covered with metal lenses that open and close in response to the sun. Unfortunately, it turned out to be the most expensive wall in the world, and no longer functions. Future buildings will be more successful, as the technology of building skins advances to mimic natural skins. Other responsive systems are already well established in today's smart buildings. Sensors turn lights on and off, heating and cooling systems continuously optimize energy use. It is only a matter of time before buildings themselves will grow and shrink as needed. Buildings will become analogous to living organisms.

See also: **Biomimicry** • **Eco-tech** • **Technology and architecture** • **Vitalism**

Rhizomatic   ∎

The rhyzomatic project is ecological. It proceeds, associating heterogeneities; from the atmosphere in general as well as from the culture it meets. — José Morales

Here in the West, the tree has implanted itself in our bodies, rigidifying and stratifying even the sexes. We have lost the rhizome, or the grass. — Gilles Deleuze

Rhizomes are plant organisms that grow and reproduce without a central body or telos. They send out roots in a decentralized manner from nodes that develop sporadically. Grasses, bamboo, ferns, and so on are *rhizomes*, but trees are not. The rhizome is a powerful metaphor for the nature of emerging architectural practice. With the increase in integrated practice using building information modeling (BIM), the practice is no longer a tree structure. Now, loose networks of firms and individuals that have no clear hierarchy can complete projects. Each joins the decentralized project as the need arises. The common thread is the shared parametric model of the project. Members of this loose confederation of project participants could be located anywhere in the world. Christopher Alexander wrote in a 1965 *Architectural Forum* article, "The City is not a Tree." Perhaps now we can expand that to include architecture.

See also: **Globalization** • **Integrated practice** • **Internationalism** • **Vitalism**

Further sources: Deleuze (in 2002: 25); Morales (in Gausa 2003: 529); Tafuri (1976: 11)

Romanticism   ∎

Romanticism **was a reaction against the stiff rationality of the Enlightenment and its official, static neo-classical art, in favor of the spontaneous, the unfettered, the subjective, the imaginative and emotional, and the inspirational and heroic.**
— *Oxford Dictionary of Philosophy*

Romanticism was a movement in art and philosophy from about 1775 to 1830. It was overrun by modernism and retreated to the background, only to re-emerge once modernism became vulnerable to reconsideration. As early as 1941, Sigfried Giedion observed in *Space, Time, and Architecture* that modern architecture had given way to "a kind of playboy-architecture" – an architecture treated the same way that playboys treat life, jumping from one sensation to another and quickly bored with everything. If Giedion had hoped that this turn to "playboy-architecture" would prove to be a passing fad, such hope remains unfulfilled. Today, the "romantic orgy" he deplored shows no sign of abating. In fact, the blob and fold architecture of the day is rife with playboyness. It jumps from one sensation to another in a never-ending spiral of one-upmanship. The reintroduction of vibrant color, the introduction of complex non-Euclidean geometries, and the race to be the biggest, or the greenest, are all symptoms of an architecture caught up in a romantic frenzy.

See also: **Blobitecture • Blob architecture (Archispeak) • Neo-expressionism**

Further sources: Ballantyne (2002: 21); Brand (1994: 147); Colebrook (2006: 82); Harries (1998: 6); Sharr (2007: 72)

▌Ruin

The decision to build a *ruin* or give buildings a ruinous look betrays a crisis of confidence in the architect's ability to provide shelter.
— Karsten Harries

Why are we drawn to ruins? Is it because of their historic significance – or is it because they are incomplete? They allow us to imagine their previous form and potential completeness. A *ruin* is self-referential – it does not mask anything; it reveals space. There is an innate strength in ruins, as they persist over time (Figure 92).

There are process-oriented behaviorist theories that discourage an architecture of "timeless artifacts"; however, one could argue that building well allows ruins to emerge as important spatial-cultural fragments and markers, and from the Egyptian pyramids to Machu Pichu are not just remnants from extinct cultures, but living archeology that continues to exert architectural influence over our imagination.

The *ruin* also conveys a romantic idea of nature and the inevitable decay of man's works. Joseph Michael Gandy completed for Sir John Soane in 1832 an atmospheric watercolor of the architect's vast Bank of England rotunda as a picturesquely overgrown *ruin*. The painting is an icon of Romanticism.

The notion of a *ruin* can be used as a rhetorical wall that has spatial identity apart from the enclosure of a building volume. A well-known example is Louis Kahn's unbuilt Salk Meeting House. Ruin-like planes wrap the various solids of the building and provide structure + solar shading for the balconies and terraces. CH

Figure 92: Ruin in Tartu, Estonia

Scaffolding   ▮

Scaffolding can provide architects with a new field of action. Its constantly changing image makes it a pretext for experimental action.
— Bea Goller

Scaffolding as a theoretical position suggests that an open framework for ideas is more useful than a specific reductive position. The open framework is a process and methodology of indeterminacy and adaptation. In lieu of a narrowly focused limiting ideology, a theoretical scaffold establishes general reference points for experimentation. Ideas and investigations may fill in, extend, or oppose the initial geographic, culture, language, philosophical, technological, social, political, or economic framework.

As a tectonic idea, many works of architecture are more engaging during construction than when they are complete. The temporary bracing and *scaffolding* generates a layered complexity – a network of accommodation and possibility.

In design, *scaffolding* is an approach that supplants permanent construction with a temporary ad hoc framework. The farmers' market and shoppers' bazaar are indigenous scaffolds that easily mutate in response to changing dimensions, weather, and market conditions. The Pompidou Center (Piano and Rogers) is an example of adapting the scaffold as a permanent urban backdrop that dissolves into a system of lighting, signage, and circulation. CH

See also: **Ad hocism • Ambivalence • Armature • Indeterminate architecture**

Further sources: Ballasteros (in Gausa 2003: 535)

Scenographic   ▮

... the actual meaning of the word is "to describe something on stage."
— P. Howard

... between 1979 and 1984 ... *"scenographic* attitude" towards building in general spread through architectural education and practice.
— Michael Benedikt

... the primary principle of architectural autonomy resides in the tectonic rather than the *scenographic*. — Kenneth Frampton

Its detractors have described post-modern architecture as the equivalent of theatrical scenery. Projects such as Charles Moore's Piazza d'Italia in New Orleans, and several projects by Robert Venturi, have given credence to this view. Despite the continuing support of the post-modern style of architecture by Charles Jencks, the general consensus appears to be that architecture as *scenography* had become passé by the mid- 1980s. It was accused of devaluing architecture to merely an exercise in applying two-dimensional decoration to a building – the decorated shed syndrome. For a while there was an effort to legitimize post-modernism in architecture by introducing structuralist philosophy, and the science of linguistics, as the conceptual underpinnings of post-modern architecture. Despite copious academic writing that made many successful academic careers, the effort was never embraced by practicing professionals.

The emergence from this rather short-lived chapter in the history of architecture has seen a shift towards the tectonic and pragmatic. With the relatively recent introduction of digital tools into the design process, the challenge has become that of achieving meaningful architecture while "solving the problem" of sustainability. History repeats itself. Perhaps the last cycle during the twentieth century taught us that it is important to combine the functional with the *scenographic*.

See also: **Aesthetics • Allusionism • Decoration • Facadism • Image • Post-modernism (Archispeak) • Representation**

Further sources: Frampton (in Foster 1983: 27); Jameson (in Leach 1997: 251); Mallgrave (2008: 538); Ruiz-Geli (in Gausa 2003: 538)

▊ Self-similarity

In mathematics, a self-similar object is exactly or approximately similar to a part of itself (i.e. the whole has the same shape as one or more of the parts). Many objects in the real world, such as coastlines, are statistically self-similar: parts of them show the same statistical properties at many scales. *Self-similarity* is a typical property of fractals. — Wikipedia

Self-similarity: when the parts, no matter how small they might be, resemble the whole. — Benoit Mandelbrot

The unit to whole relationship is a formative idea that relates units to other units and to the whole in specific ways to create built form. — Roger Clark and Michael Pause

The principle of *self-similarity*, as described within chaos theory, is promising to be a new twist in the age-old relationship of "part to whole" in architecture. Fractals in particular have been inspirational to those architects who believe that the detail should somehow generate the whole. The current interest in the rapid prototyping of building elements that consist of highly repetitive parts has brought fractals and *self-similarity* to the forefront. As robots and CNC machines manipulate the parts to create the whole, the occurrence of *self-similarity* between those parts and the whole is likely.

Another type of architectural *self-similarity* is the relationship between plan and section or elevation. The basic geometry of the plan and section can be the same, as is demonstrated by the Pantheon in Rome. The circular plan has the radius as the circle created by the dome in section.

Self-similarity is a feature of nature, and as such, will be an aspect of the current movement in architecture that is trying to mimic natural systems and processes.

Just as a single hair is not sufficient to make a hair-do, so too a single element in architecture will never reveal the rich organizational possibilities inherent when greater quantities come to play.
— Jesse Reiser

See also: **Chaos theory (Archispeak)** • **Complexity (Archispeak)** • **Fractal (Archispeak)**

Further sources: Clarke and Pause (1985: 161); Gausa 2003: 543); Jameson (in Leach 1997: 250); Johnson (1994: 422); Knights (in Borden 2000); Lidwell (2003: 176); Reiser + Umemoto (2005: 46)

Sensitivity analysis method   ∎

A method for producing logic free curved surfaces closer to those drawn by the architect. — Mutsuro Sasaki

The *sensitivity analysis method* is an engineering process that utilizes self-organizing trial and error to produce the structure required to achieve the exact curved surface that has been envisioned by an architect's sketch. It was developed by Mutsuro Sasaki in order for the free-form work of Arata Isozaki and Toyo Ito to be realized. It is but one of the many new techniques that will be needed to bring the process of design using a computer closer to the manual processes that have been followed since the beginning of architecture. The rough sketch, the parti diagram, the conceptual model, and so on are currently difficult to fold into a digitally based design process. That will change very soon with the development of artificial-intelligence-based personal design software. Personal design software will "think" like the designer, rather than the other way around.

See also: **Digital architecture** • **Prototyping** • **Tessellating** • **Tooling**

Silence   ∎

Silence to Light and Light to Silence. Light, the giver of presence, casts its shadow, which belongs to Light – what is made belongs to Light and Desire. This making occurs at the threshold of the Treasury of Shadow. — Louis Kahn

In Kahn's metaphysics, Silence is the unmeasurable (desireless) desire to be, the desire to express, the source of new need. To know one's art is to understand the "order of the shadow" (the threshold of realization) – what lies between idea and reality, between Silence and Light.

What Kahn called Silence, Lao Tzu called the nameless. What Kahn called Light, Lao Tzu called the named. Like Lao Tzu, Kahn was in touch with the eternal Tao of architecture. — John Lobell

Architecture can be thought of as a spiritual path and a practice of meditation and reflection. An architecture of spirit responds to place and explores the spatial aspects of the mystical and eternal. It seeks to give architectural expression to that which we cannot name or know. This is sensed in the works of Kahn, Tadao Ando, and some of the later buildings by Le Corbusier. It is also found in ruins and works from antiquity that time has layered with spiritual meaning.

In architecture, there are passages back to the unmeasurable (Silence). If one stands before the Parthenon or looks down the ribbon of water in the courtyard of the Salk Institute, they gain access to the eternal. They may not pursue it, but the spiritual passage is there. CH

A work is made in the urging sounds of industry, and when the dust settles, the pyramid, echoing Silence, gives the sun its shadow.
— Louis Kahn

See also: **Absence/presence • Architectural presentness • Betweenness • Emptiness • Existential space • Sublime**

Further sources: Benedikt (1985: 54)

▌Simultaneity

We are witnessing a change of times, from a culture of the successive to a culture of the simultaneous. — Willy Muller

Simultaneity has influenced design by providing near-instant gratification to the designer. Technological advances in digital design and representation have reordered the time sequence for the current generation of architecture from a cumbersome linear process to an efficient, nearly simultaneous, one. Computer-based design utilizing building information modeling (BIM), linked to computer-aided manufacturing (CAM), promises to reduce the building delivery timeframe even further, as the technology evolves beyond its current near-beta status. The concern might be that this rush to occupy might cause a tyranny of the pragmatic. The poetics of architecture may have a hard time squeezing into the script. Some critics feel that the architect will become superfluous in a world where computers have automated the entire design/manufacture/assemble process into a near-simultaneous enterprise.

See also: **Building information modeling: BIM**

Further sources: Guallart (in Gausa 2003: 551)

▌Soft architecture

Hard Ware to soft Form. — Winka Dubbeldam

Soft architecture – Living spaces with few fixed items or partitions, instantly controlled by computers as required.?

Nicolas Negroponte coined the term *"soft architecture"* in 1974 to refer to cyber-manipulated architecture – an architecture born of the computer's ability to sense and react to changing demands and conditions. Thus, cyber-controlled devices are central to the achievement of a useful *soft architecture*. Sensors that trigger the opening and closing of doors and windows, the movement of walls, and even the lowering and raising of floors and ceilings produce the personalized spaces that characterize *soft architecture*. Theatrical stages have had this capability for some time, and thus have a lot to teach the designer seeking to produce *soft architecture.*

Traditional Japanese architecture is an early version of *soft architecture*. The ability to change the use and "feel" of a space by simply moving a rice paper screen and rearranging the mats on the floor is a manual, low-tech version of *soft architecture*. A more recent manifestation of softness was attempted with the Centre Georges Pompidou in Paris (1977) (Figure 93). It was to have an interior in which many walls and floors were movable. Unfortunately that degree of flexibility was unjustified. Consequently the building was renovated in 2000 to increase its capacity and efficiency by "hardening" it.

In *soft architecture* each force applied to it creates content that has form, as "water poured into a vase has form" (Ezra Pound). The water-generated Blur building by Herzog and Meuron poetically illustrates the new frontier of soft or reflexive architecture. The term now refers to any architecture that is not finite or fixed.

See also: **Blur** • **Responsive architecture** • **Flexibility**

Figure 93 Pompidou Center

Space

The classical questions include: is space real, or is it some kind of mental construct, or an artifact of our ways of perceiving and thinking?
— *Oxford Dictionary of Philosophy*

If architecture can be understood as the construction of boundaries in *space*, this *space* must be understood as commonsense space, a *space* that possesses meaning and speaks to us long before the architect goes to work. — Karsten Harries

The ethereal thing about architecture is this thing called *"space." Space*, as a central design concern for architects, has the interesting quality of being invisible to the untrained eye. Clients and beginning architecture students seldom know what architects or teachers are referring to when they are talking about *space*. For the initiated space is not an abstraction, it has substance. For the uninitiated, it remains an abstract concept. Architects often tout space making as their design objective, yet what that really means is seldom examined beyond the level of a slogan. It is assumed that everyone at the table lives in the same world of spatial awareness. Little is understood about our spatial awareness and understanding. Only in extreme cases of pathologies such as agoraphobia or claustrophobia is one's relationship to *space* overtly addressed. In the early 1970s the nascent quasi-science of Man–Environment Relations (MER) attempted to broach the topic with attitudinal and preference studies. The notion of "spatial style" variability among various subsets of the population was examined in one study in which this author was a subject. The study appears to conclude that geographers preferred horizontality, whereas architects preferred verticality. It pointed out that architects do not necessary have the same spatial preferences and biases as their clients and building users. Unfortunately, architects unconsciously assume that everyone inhabits their specialized spatial world. This can result in buildings that only the architect can love. The rest of the world wonders what the fuss is about.

The pleasure of *space* can not be put into words, it is unspoken... it is the presence of absence... leans towards the poetics of the unconscious. — Bernard Tschumi

See also: **Absence/presence • Abstraction • Behavior and environment**

Further sources: Agrest (1993: 173); Certeau (in Ballantyne 2002: 74) Gausa (2003: 561); Harries (1998: 125, 180; Heidegger (in Leach 1997: 122); Jencks (2007: 174); Johnson (1994: 383); Sharr (2007: 53); Scruton (1979: 43); Tschumi (1999: 29, 84)

▌Spirit of place

Not to be confused with the late Charles Moore's or Christopher Alexander's use of the term "sense of place" – which concerns a reinforced spatial occupancy or imbuing particularly urban space with special meaning – *spirit of place* describes a more profound degree of supernatural awareness. Usually applied to a rural or a natural, unspoiled place, its original meaning is embedded in a Roman mythology: that is, the concept of every human being having two guardian spirits in the form of fallen angels (genii) that give life or spirit to people or places. Generally speaking, the modern world has shed such beliefs, and rather than a guardian spirit, the term now refers to the distinctive atmosphere of a particular site. More superficial versions of a contemporary superstition of place still exist, such as a flickering of interest in ley lines and feng shui.

The development towards assigning a modern concept of the "extraordinary ability" to a place is complex – invisibly intertwined in a cultural weave of folk stories, memories, belief systems, and so on – but it seems to have been connected with the idea of "spirit" through a notion of "inspiration." The alternative term for *spirit of place*, that is, genius loci, however, refers back to the original meaning of genius as "essence."

Thus, in geography and, following Alexander Pope's (1688–1744) poetic insistence on respecting the genius of wild, natural locations, particularly landscape architecture and garden design, genius loci is now accepted as denoting "spirit or essence of place." In his groundbreaking book, *Genius Loci: Towards a Phenomenology of Architecture* (1980), Christian Norberg-Schultz set the stage for this shift from the quantitative to the qualitative in architectural theory discourse. Indeed, some environmental designers now regard the essential role of architecture as that of making place in a spiritual sense versus that of solely creating a physical space.

As a consequence of the resurgence of interest in phenomenology during recent decades, *spirit of place* (genius loci) has become a popular and somewhat trite expression in architectural circles, especially in the design studio. It now refers to any quality that defines the experience of a place. Common examples of the genius loci tend to describe a unique or dramatic natural landscape, while an architecturally inspired genius loci might be Andrea Palladio's Villa Capra (Villa Rotunda) in Vincenza. TP

See also: **Aura • Genius loci (Archispeak) • Ley lines (Archispeak) • Phenomenology (Archispeak)**

Further sources: Sharr (2007: 1)

Starchitect   **▮**

Starchitecture culture... – characterized by the premature coronation of designers based on flashy forms and blowout press coverage.
— Philip Nobel

... if we keep on stamping our own personal mark or "signature" on each building we design, each city will end up having a fish building, a Meier building, a Jahn building, until each city will be a bit like a Woolworth's, with a sample of everything and with no character of its own. — Cesar Pelli

We live in an age of star worship. In every field of endeavor a great deal of attention is played to a few individuals who have achieved fame by whatever means. Witness the star making of Susan Boyle. The most surprising is the plethora of "reality stars" we are now forced to endure. Architecture is no exception. Although this is not a new development, increased access to the media, plus the more recent emergence of more dramatic and even bizarre buildings, have resulted in architects joining the ranks of Paris Hilton for their fifteen minutes of fame. The development of fame as a brand-name architect does not just happen. Architects have resorted to publishing their monographs as catalogues of project stories and fragments of design theory, or intelligence. What was at one time a slick marketing brochure of firm work has now been reinvented as a pseudo book. OMA's *SMLXL* and *Content* series (Koolhaas, 1995, 2004), or in a more subtle form Reiser and Umemoto's *Atlas of Novel Tectonics,* are examples. *Starchitects* have also been more aggressive in courting the press. Even individual projects have become stars. Witness the extensive coverage of Dubai's Burj Khalifa. Even during the Beijing Olympic games as much attention was paid to the "bird's nest" and "swimming cube" as to the athletes.

Pundits are suggesting that the era of the starchitect is coming to a close. Now that Frank Gehry is designing hats for Lady Gaga the decline is certainly well under way. In any case, he has always hated the label, as he should.

See also: **Intelligence**

▌Structuralism

An interdisciplinary movement of thought which enjoyed a high vogue through the 1960s and early 1970s – when it acquires a certain radical cachet. — *Oxford Guide to Philosophy*

Structuralism **– the theory of social reality that applies the principles of science of linguistics to all social phenomena.** — Donald Palmer

Structuralism **as a system began to fall out of favor as its limitations became exposed.** — Neil Leach

Structuralism is a way of looking at the world that focuses on the permanent structures or relationships between things, rather than the things themselves. In that way it is ahistorical (synchronic) and organic, as opposed to historical (diachronic) and atomistic. *Structuralism* follows in the tradition of the classical rationalist philosophers – Plato to Kant. They shared the general belief that there are permanent innate structures that are unchanging and thus constitute the universals of reality. In this way *structuralism* is opposed to empiricism, and architectural phenomenology in particular. *Structuralism* found its most comfortable home in the science and philosophy of linguistics.

Structuralism was co-opted by twentieth century anti-modernists, as they searched for a "scientific" basis for restoring meaning to architectural works. It was a rich source for the academy to mine in the pursuit of a respectable architectural theory. In addition to moving the agenda of architectural design forward, the goal was to establish architectural theory as a legitimate academic discipline. Linguistics was particularly appealing as it came complete with arcane French and German philosophers and a whole new esoterica. The effort was embraced principally in East coast Ivy League universities. Because of its disconnect from the realities of practice, *structuralism* never caught on with the practicing architectural community, except as the most evident and trivial expression of post-modern kitsch. Today the word *structuralism* is seldom heard, other than in a history of theory class.

See also: **Diachronic • Kitsch • Phenomenology (Archispeak) • Post-structuralism (Archispeak) • Synchronic**

Further sources: Colquhoun (1991: 246); Gelernter (1995: 265); Hale (2000: 132); Knights (in Borden 2000: 77); Leach (1997: 163); Mallgrave (2008: 459); Nesbitt (1996: 33); Perez-Gomez (1984: 6); Scruton (1979: 160)

Style

Architecture is like literature; the simple style is preferable to an inflated style. — J.F. Blondel (1771)

There is a word we should refrain from using to describe contemporary architecture – "style." The moment we fence architecture within a notion of "style," we open the door to a formalistic approach. — Nikolaus Pevsner (1949)

Sixty years after Pevsner's statement, *"style"* is still a difficult concept for architects to embrace. It normally comes up when a client wishes a building to reference a certain historical period. The general public recognizes several styles that are a puzzle to architects. What is meant by "contemporary style"? The extensive identification and elaboration of architectural styles has been perpetuated as a marketing tool by the real estate industry. This emphasis upon recreating a supposed historic style is one more step in the commoditization of architecture. Few of the styles that are attached to developer generated housing are those that an architectural historian would subscribe to.

Designing to create a *"style"* implies that the architect is merely following the dictates or canons of a historic *style*. *Style* devalues design as "Disneyfication" in that it fails to recognize unique circumstances of time and place, as well as available technological advances. Neoclassical architecture was perhaps the last *"style"* to be recognized by the profession. Everything since then has been a "movement," that is, the "modern movement," the "post-modern movement," the "green movement," and so on. That may change as blobitecture is threatening to become a *style*.

With the breakdown of consensus, with the end of national styles or modernist ideology, we have reached a paradoxical point where any style can be, and is, revived or continued. — Charles Jencks

See also: **Blob architecture (Archispeak) • Blobitecture • Disneyfication**

Further sources: Antoniades (1990: 162) Gregotti (1996: 90); Harries (1998: 88); Johnson (1994: 407); Reiser + Umemoto (2005: 45); Scruton (in Ballantyne 2002: 62)

Sublime

The sublime refers to the mingled terror and pleasure inspired by the ruins, Alpine passes and storms that became the standard imagery of the Gothic novel. — *Dictionary of Critical Theory*

The concept of the *sublime* is most associated with Edmund Burke's *Philosophical Enquiry into the Origin of our Idea of the Sublime and the Beautiful* (1756). Kant continued the debate about the sublime versus the beautiful in *The Critique of Judgment* (1790). According to Kant, the *sublime* "raises the soul above the height of vulgar commonplace." The *sublime* was resurrected in the phenomenology literature of the twentieth century as an important aspect of aesthetics. It was posed as a somewhat uneasy opposition to beauty. It was attractive to the detractors of modern architecture because it relied upon direct experience, and not rationalism and function. The uncanny and the grotesque are aspects of the sublime that extend the notion that the *sublime* is concerned with the profoundly moving aesthetic experience. Peter Eisenman and Anthony Vidler, among others, seized on this new critique of aesthetics born of the Gothic novel.

With the decline in interest in phenomenology, and theory in general, the term *sublime* may once again go into hibernation until the next cycle of reaction to the new rationalism that is sweeping architecture today.

See also: **Aesthetics • Beauty • Emptiness • Phenomenology • Phenomenology (Archispeak) • Uncanny – unheimlich**

Further sources: Colebrook (2006: 51, 148); Deleuze (in Ballantyne 2002: 6); Forty (2000: 229); Harries (1998: 8, 247, 306) Nesbitt (1996: 30); Thomas (in Borden 2000: 111)

Superdutch

You know, you Dutch people, you only build diagrams. — Stan Allen

The term *"Superdutch"* entered the public consciousness with the 2000 publication of Bart Lootsma's coffee table book *Superdutch, New Architecture in the Netherlands*. It was a portfolio of the work of twelve successful and well-known Dutch firms. Since then, it has become a code word for the pragmatic, digitally generated, second coming of modernism that is generally associated with the progeny of Rem Koolhaas. The work has become viral, with followers in ever corner of the globe. As described by Lootsma, characteristics of superdutch architecture are: "inventiveness, whimsy, the creative use of materials, and dynamic formal experimentation." Schools in the Netherlands are also leading the way in architectural education. The Berlage Institute has become the Harvard of Europe. TU Delft has become the MIT.

See also: **Datascapes • Responsive architecture • Technology and architecture**

Super-modernism

There has been a debate in the media and the academy about what to call the architecture after modernism. Eisenman will argue that modernism never existed, as classicism never left. Most others accepted the term architectural post-modernism for a short period of time, until it degenerated into a parody of classicism. One of the last holdouts is Charles Jencks, who still clings to his invention – post-modernism in architecture. Most academics have been referring to this post-modern period in architecture as critical modernism. Other labels are: *super-modernism*, ecological postmodernism, PoMo, deconstructive post-modernism, post-structuralism, and so on. This name game is ultimately meaningless and a bit silly. Whatever the label, architecture seems to have returned to basics in a sophisticated way. The attention paid to program and tectonics, while slighting theory, seems to be the hallmark of most twenty-first-century architecture.

Charles Jencks has taken the position that post-modernism is more up-to-date modernism – modernism plus one (*super-modernism*). In response to Jencks and his attack on the "Modernists," Conrad Jameson wrote the book *Super-Modern Architecture*. It was an obvious reference to the seminal 1975 work by Jencks, *Post-Modern Architecture*. Super-modernism will not survive as the dominant label for the architecture of the fin de siècle, as it is has mostly been critically ignored.

See also: **Critical modernism • Post-modernism (Archispeak) • Post-structuralism (Archispeak) • Tectonic form**

Sustainability   ▮

But the care of the Earth is our most ancient and most worthy and, after all, our most pleasing responsibility. To cherish what remains of it, and to foster its renewal, is our only hope.
— Wendell Berry, *The Art of the Commonplace*

If we keep going the way we are going, we are going to end up where we are headed. — Groucho Marx

I just need enough to tide me over until I need more.
— Bill Hoest, *The Lockhorns*

Society is a partnership, not only between those who are living, but between those who are living, those who are dead, and those who are to be born. — Edmund Burke

The notion of *sustainability* is a broad, far-reaching and critically important term addressing the possibility and ability of humans and other life to endure and flourish on this planet forever. We as a society cannot continue down the current destructive path we are on. Each year we see increasing amounts of energy, water, and materials being used and the resultant pollution and waste created. The question of sustainability asks of each of us, what kind of world will we leave to future generations? What is our responsible role?

The Brundtland Commission of the United Nations in 1987 resulted in the most widely quoted definition of *sustainability* and sustainable development, that "sustainable development is development that meets the needs of the present without compromising the ability of future generations to meet their own needs." This usually requires understanding the three mutually reinforcing pillars of *sustainability*: the environmental, social, and economic needs. Not only must we maintain and endure, as the dictionary defines sustainability, we must work collectively to restore. As our human population has increased, natural living systems have weakened. To live sustainably, requires society to reach for a balance between environmental protection, social improvement, and economic development, while working in harmony with Earth's ecosystems.

Ways of living more sustainably are: to reduce our dependence on fossil fuels, underground metals, and minerals, to reduce our dependence on synthetic chemicals, to reduce our encroachment on nature, and to meet human needs fairly and efficiently. EL

See also: **Green design (Archispeak)** • **Sustainability (Archispeak)**

▌Synchronic

Synchronic linguistics views a particular state of a language at some given point in time. — Donald Palmer

... relating to or studying something, especially a language, as it exists at a certain point in time, without considering its historical development. — *Encarta® World English Dictionary*

When Art is the norm it's dead. — Manfredo Tafuri

Tafuri is taking the avant-garde position in making architecture that believes every work is unique, and needs to be invented anew. This theoretical position is one in which the architect is trying to make a unique statement in their design, often ignoring tradition and any existing architectural language. The intent of the work is to make architecture primarily a work of art. As such, the process of making architecture often relies on the architect making intuitive design decisions, as opposed to relying on reason. The inspiration for the design might be something beyond architecture, for example, a work of music, an event in history, or a set of compositional rules.

Synchronic architecture, when it does use symbols or traditional elements, will often place them in an unexpected position, or might change the scale of the element, possibly making it larger or smaller than would be expected. The manner with which this architecture engages nature is to manipulate and control it. Architecture that is *synchronic* might result in a work that is machine-like in that it utilizes the physics embedded in nature rather than the literal form or materiality of natural elements. Examples of architects who make synchronic architecture are Zaha Hadid, Frank Gehry, Peter Eisenman, Daniel Libeskind, and Thomas Mayne. MA

See also: **Autonomous architect** • **Creativity**

Tabula rasa   ∎

The fresh start, is a well-known formula in human affairs ... a *tabula rasa* against whose clarity all false logic, unjustified assumptions and simple irrelevancies will stand out and be eliminated.
— Robert Maxwell

... nothingness – the no thing – is the starting point of design: *tabula rasa* is where it begins. With no preconceptions. Starting off thinking that one is going to design something can put up barriers to being creative. But once the decision is taken about what should be designed, then a whole range of ideas and concepts about how design should be done may come into play. — Conway Lloyd Morgan

The beginnings of everything start with a blank sheet of paper, don't they? — Will Alsop

The moment an idea is transferred from a designer's mind into some external presence is a critical moment in the life of any design concept. This occurs when ideas become so complex that they have to be externalized for clarification, assessment, and development. Their emergence can take different forms, as ideas can be expressed by metaphor, a word, or lines of prose. They can also be encapsulated in a scribble, sketch, illustration, or be rooted in a diagram. This manifestation process usually involves a language of abstraction in which the pictures in the mind begin to be mapped and processed using descriptive symbols or annotation, which combine to chart the potential relationships between concept and reality. The resultant marks appear most useful in these critical moments for, often functioning as a constructive doodle, they are clearly more concerned with the essence of ideas than any premonition of appearance. Indeed, unlike objective drawing which decodes our impression of the perceived external visual world, conceptual drawing is an internal process that draws from our creative imagination which, in turn, is fed by our memory, past experience and, indeed, by our fantasies.

Tabula rasa, of course, exists in the mind of the designer. It is broken when a concept passes through its mental space to be translated into some form of descriptive external model, which will allow the designer to experience the externalized nature of his or her idea. These newly represented marks then act as the basis for further development, inspiring the creative imagination on to the externalization of successive mental images, which in turn are realized for evaluation. This chain of representation – one newly emerging idea informing and leading to another – forms a two-way language of design. This is a continuous, cyclical dialogue between concept and mode of expression – the sequence alternating until the creative process has been exhausted. TP

See also: **Metaphor (Archispeak)** • **Representation** • **Tabula rasa (Archispeak)**

▌Technology and architecture

The term "technology" is a generalization, displacing the "scientific" study of the so-called "practical arts" by the whole apparatus of specialized production and methods, and their products.
— Paul-Alan Johnson

Technology is morally, socially, and politically neutral, though its exploitation may require adjustments of social and political structure, and its consequences may call moral attitudes in question.
— Reyner Banham

... building technology is changing at a frightening rate and architects have a duty to act as midwives of this change. — Tom Heath

Architecture has always depended heavily on technology. For most of the history of architecture, that technology has been stuck in its primitive stage, that of sticks and bricks. Only a few technological advances occurred during the first 4,000 years of building – the arch, dome, concrete, steel, and glass. However, in recent years technology has dramatically changed architecture. That change has come from several directions. Perhaps the most profound has been the introduction of the computer. It has revolutionized not only the process of design and the representation of those designs, but also what it is possible to build. New materials have also been introduced at an accelerated rate in recent years. Nanotechnology, composite fiber materials, recycling technology, advances in communications, and sustainable energy production technologies have all made an impact.

... five innovative material concepts that architects should watch in the coming years: plastics made from renewable materials such as chicken feathers and soybeans; optically colored fibers that mimic butterfly wings and thus need no pigmentation; photovoltaic thin films (rendered as "leaves that flutter along building facades"); high-fidelity woods souped up with sugar-industry biowaste; and composites made by digital fabrication to integrate form and performance capabilities.
— *Architecture Magazine*

Rapid prototyping and other gains in the efficiency of manufacturing and assemblage of building elements using parametric design tools are also beginning to impact on the process of design at a profound level. Responsive architecture is a new frontier that is now possible due to advances in technology. The dream that one day buildings will dynamically and automatically tailor themselves to the needs and wishes of their users as they occupy them is closer to being realized thanks to technology. It will be a brave new world of the best kind.

We must ask the bat-eyed priests of technology what on earth they think they are doing. — Lewis Mumford

See also: **Parametric design • Prototyping • Responsive architecture**

Tectonic form   ▮

In general the term refers to an artisan working in hard materials except metal. In the fifth century B.C. this meaning undergoes further evolution, from something specific and physical, such as carpentry, to a more generic notion of making, involving the idea of poesis.
— Kenneth Frampton

The current mood in architectural theory is to focus on the tectonic. Having exhausted the form possibilities presented by the metaphor of language, the metaphor of biology is coming to the forefront. The question becomes "What are the *tectonic form* implications of an architecture based on biology?" The green revolution is providing the impetus for this paradigm shift. Biomimicry, as an aspect of this green form tectonic, calls for the technology of architecture to be capable of responding to changing external and internal demands placed on it over time. The skin, as the first line of defense, becomes an important preoccupation of the designer. Structure takes on a different role, that of infrastructure – analogous to the armature in sculpture, or the skeleton of a living organism. Components of the *tectonic form* are tasked with specific behaviors that are programmed to anticipate their role in the architecture. The notion of "form" has evolved from a reference to an ideal and static Platonic shape, to that of a constellation of technical responses to parameters that various designers have contributed. The result is more of an assembly than a singular form. The exception is blobitecture, which references the natural forms of the whole organism, rather than its parts.

See also: **Armature • Biomimicry • Form • Skin (Archispeak)**

Further sources: Frampton (in Mallgrave 2008: 535)

Tessellating   ▮

A tessellation is created when a shape is repeated over and over again covering a plane without any gaps or overlaps. — *mathforum.org*

Tessellating is a form of tiling with no gaps between the tiles. Tessellations can produce flat or curved surfaces. Architect-produced tessellations have been around for a very long time. The mosaics and masonry walls of the ancient world are examples of tessellation. In the past decade *tessellating* has become of great interest as digital design and fabrication permit architects to propose complex, curved surfaces. *Tessellating* opens up endless architectural form possibilities, as building envelopes are no longer limited to orthographic geometries. Non-Euclidean geometry consisting of topological manipulations of tessellated surfaces is resulting in cutting non-edge blobitecture. Well-publicized examples of tessellated architectural surfaces include the Expo 67 Geodesic dome by Buckminister Fuller, and the Beijing swimming venue – the "bubble."

Along with repetition and modularity, the characteristic of tiling that provides such inspiration to tectonics is the issue of adjacency.
— Benjamin Aranda and Chris Lasch

Tiling can be three-dimensional, as is demonstrated in the work of Aranda and Lasch (2006), and documented in *Princeton Press Pamphlet Architecture27: Tooling*.

See also: **Blob architecture (Archispeak)** • **Blobitecture** • **Topology (Archispeak)**

Further sources: Iwamoto (2009: 42)

Tooling

Tooling is about what rules exist within the "pre-material" state – before ideas coalesce into a definitive form free of any organization. — Benjamin Aranda and Chris Lasch

Based upon the above definition, the design phase of digital architectural design is a form of *tooling*. If the design process consists of pre-design, design, and post-design phases, then *tooling* is principally involved in the pre-design phase. Architectural *tooling* during pre-design consists of amassing the intelligence necessary to input the building information model (BIM) that becomes the basis for the construction of the building. Architectural *tooling* during the design phase includes the development and graphic realization of the various algorithms that can produce geometries of interest. Architectural *tooling* may also include the rapid prototyping of those geometries or building elements. Just as the tool and die artist/technician prepares the machines in the factory for manufacturing the desired artifact, the architect prepares the necessary digital model for constructing the building. During post-design, *tooling* is less evident.

Interestingly, the physical tool and die maker is a becoming extinct in this age of CNC machines that only require a digital design and related instructions in computer code. The machine must be fed.

The objective of tooling is … establishing very coherent, pre-material rules that can be used with mathematics and geometry... the job of designing begins. — Benjamin Aranda and Chris Lasch

See also: **Algorithm** • **Associative design** • **Building information modeling: BIM** • **Prototyping**

Total design

What does "total design" mean today … say after postmodernism? Total design is a fantasy about control, about architecture as control. — Mark Wigley

Wigley goes on to describe two meanings associated with the term *"total design."* The first involves the design of everything in a particular work of architecture, down to the napkins on the dining room table. The second meaning of *total design* involves the expansion of design to include everything in a culture.

The first meaning was a sentiment shared by many modern architects, including Gio Ponti. Ponti expressed this sentiment when he proclaimed that "the full and total time of architecture awaits us still. It will mean a perfect civilization." Ponti not only designed everything from basins to buildings, but also put out an arts and architecture magazine. Other architects famous for designing napkins and teaspoons are Frank Lloyd Wright, Alvar Aalto, Michael Graves, and Frank Gehry. The idea started with the Bauhaus. Furniture designed by Bauhaus-associated architects such as Marcel Breuer and Mies van der Rohe can still be purchased to complement architectonic interiors.

The second meaning of *total design* finds architects hoping to be involved in the design of cities, and other non-architectural aspects of modern life. This remains mostly an unfulfilled desire, which may be a good thing when we consider the unrealistic and inhumane visionary city designs of Le Corbusier and Wright.

In the current age of integrated practice and team design, total design by an individual architect seems like an archaic idea. However, total design endures in the form of starchitects designing consumer objects.

The most remarkable thing about this relentless drive towards total design ... is its constant failure. — Mark Wigley

See also: **Commoditization • Detail • Difficult whole • Fetishization**

Further sources: Lang (1987: 240); Wigley (1998)

Trope   **I**

Derived from the Latin word *tropus*, *trope* is a form of metaphor, a simile, and is used to develop associations that link different entities that otherwise have no relationship to each other.

John Hersey, in *The Lost Meaning of Classical Architecture* (1992), explores the use of troping in architecture. According to Hersey, the ancient Greeks used this form of metaphor to symbolize the reincarnation of sacrificial animals in their temple ornamentation. Another symbolic representation use of *trope* is in the analogical representation of different types of trees in the development of the classical orders. Early Greeks worshiped in sacred groves of trees that were thought to be representative of the physical attributes of the god in question. Eventually, when permanent temples where built for the various gods and goddesses, there was an attempt to emulate these physical attributes in the architectural proportions and sensibility of the work.

More contemporary use of *trope* in making architecture might be seen in Frank Gehry's museum in Bilbao, where in plan and elevation the work resembles a ship, a conscious echoing of the previous use of the site as a dock for ships. Another more famous use of *trope* might be found in the Swiss architect Le Corbusier's famous dictum "A house is a machine for living." MA

See also: **Allusionism • Associative design • Biomimicry • Mimesis • Myth • Nature • Ornamentalism**

Further sources: Gausa (2003: 641); Hersey (1992: 1)

█ Ugly and ordinary

Daniel Libeskind's angular new addition to the Royal Ontario Museum in Toronto, called "the Crystal," was placed at No. 8 on a list of the world's ten ugliest buildings assembled by Virtual Tourist.com. The rationale mentions its stark incongruity with the original museum's Romanesque architecture. — *Toronto Star*

Daniel Libeskind's extension of the Royal Ontario Museum in Toronto beats any Wal-Mart with its ugliness because it is "both ugly and useless." Curators seem to have trouble hanging art on its canted walls. "And it cost only $250 million." — *Washington Post*

When Robert Venturi penned his famous "Part Two" of *Learning From Las Vegas – Ugly and Ordinary Architecture, or the Decorated Shed*, he seemed to be presenting a defense of some of his firm's recent work, such as the Guild House and the fire station in Columbus, Indiana. Unfortunately, the effort was read as a license for architects and clients to accept ugliness as a valid aesthetic for architecture. It opened the door to a lowering of standards for beauty in architecture. With the resulting "no rules" architecture, experimentation became much more prevalent than during the short-lived era of dogmatic modern architecture. Deconstructivism further eroded any remaining standards of beauty to the point where it is no longer part of the conversation about architecture. The new aesthetic is techno bio-grunge.

See also: **Aesthetics • Atopia • Beauty • Disneyfication • Junkspace • Sublime**

█ The uncanny – *unheimlich*

The sublime's darkside – the uncanny. — Kate Nesbitt

In general we no longer understand architecture ... beauty entered the system only secondarily, without impairing the basic feeling of uncanny sublimity ... at most the beauty tempered the dread – but this dread was the prerequisite everywhere. — Friedrich Nietzsche

Heimlich equals homely and unheimlich equals uncanny.
— Sigmund Freud

For Freud the Heimlich contains the unheimlich repressed within it.
— Neil Leach

The uncanny is the rediscovery of something familiar that has been previously repressed. It is the uneasy recognition of the presence of an absence. The mix of the known and familiar with the strange surfaces in unheimlich, the German word for the uncanny, which literally translated means "unhomely." This uncanny is the terrifying side of the sublime. — Kate Nesbitt

The uncanny can be understood as an unsettling disorientation that destabilizes human beings, casting doubt on their certainties and causing a subtle, sudden feeling of anxiety or estrangement. In architecture it can be identified with the sensation aroused by spaces without a specific identity, where the apparent familiarity or recognizability of the place is at the same time compromised by sudden, unexpected changes of perspective or by visible features that are perceived as out of place, because they are located in a context not in keeping or not consistent with their identity. There are non-places such as large stations, airports, ferry terminals, and large town parks, as well as city business districts, where architectural styles devoid of identity are repeated, equal to themselves and reflected in each other, annihilating features recognizable as familiar. They communicate a feeling of alienation and bewilderment that lead human beings to lose their bearings, finding themselves at the mercy of insecurity and distress, without being able to make out the reason for these sensations.

At the same time, however, *the uncanny* can be the guiding element of a design that goes against the common codes, creating dynamic volumes and spaces designed to contradict a banal, monotonous and repetitive architectural language. This can arouse a feeling of disorientation and "displacement" and confer identity and energy on an anonymous area. AO

Architecture since the romantic period has been intimately linked to the notion of the uncanny. — Anthony Vidler

See also: **Absence/presence • Aporia • Emptiness • Heterotopia • Sublime**

Further sources: Bachelard (in Leach 1997:85); Leach (in Ballantyne 2008:94); Nesbitt (1996:574); Vidler (in Nesbitt 1996:174)

Universal design   ∎

Objects and environments should be designed to be usable, without modification, by as many people as possible. — William Lidwell

Accessible environments are typically designed with only one type of person in mind – the disabled. Often people without disabilities utilize accessible spaces without realizing that they have. These spaces have been designed as universal. The practitioners of *universal design* believe that unobtrusive measures that provide accessibility for everyone are preferable to those measures that are especially designed for the disabled. Many *universal design* objects already exist in our environment. We don't pay any attention to them because they don't seem to be special. Most elevators have universal controls. The public drinking fountain that is lower, with space for a wheelchair, seems normal. It has been designed for everyone to use equally.

The *universal design* movement is expected to accelerate in the United States over the next ten years, as 80 million "baby boomers" reach the age at which they begin to have mobility and other disabilities. Industrial designers are already immersed in universal design practices. Architects need to do the same. After all, universal design is consistent with a larger change in attitude brought about by critical theory and its concern for inclusivity.

See also: **Constraints • Critical theory • Ethics • Flexibility • Ideogram • Inclusive architecture • Integral design • Psychological needs • Sustainability • Wayfinding**

Unselfconscious form

The *unselfconscious design* ... evolved in response to an unformulated cluster of desires and needs, and achieved a realization unmediated by thought or reflection. — Roger Scruton

Several notable architects derive form unselfconsciously. Through devices such as gesture sketches (Gehry), abstract water colors (Holl), and painting (Alsop), these architects avoid thinking about the specifics of a design challenge until their unselfconscious "warm-up" exercises give them a feeling for the direction they would like the form to go as the conscious specifics of the project are addressed. This exercise goes beyond the intuitive and reaches back into the total experience of the designer, both real and imagined. In *Architecture Without Architects* (1964), Rudofsky makes the argument that vernacular architecture is based upon cultural traditions that have evolved as conscious responses to environment. As such, vernacular architecture is not synonymous with unselfconscious architecture. Christopher Alexander is a proponent of unselfconscious design as somehow more valid than the design solutions that result from self-conscious aims that lead to inadequate concepts. Thinking too much about a project is considered to be a process of distancing oneself from its true nature. Giving a "quality without a name" a name fundamentally changes it. Reducing it to a "problem" that needs a "solution" further increases the distance. As we abdicate our designing process to the computer, what may remain as the unique contribution of the architect might be the creative, yet unselfconscious, overall *unselfconscious form* inspiration.

See also: **Accident • Ad hocism • Creativity • Defamiliarization**

Further sources: Colebrook (2006:99); Scruton (1979:28)

Urbanism

Urbanism in English gains its contemporary meaning as a translation of the French expression *l'urbanisme,* which can be translated as "town planning." However, it has implications which go beyond this translation.

Urbanism suggests an approach which comprehends the city as a whole and contains a theory which seeks to explain urban relations.
— Lincoln Allison

Leon and Rob Krier have been in the vanguard of the movement to respond to urban history and fabric in a more positive and less destructive way than was proposed by international modernism, the Athens Charter, and CIAM. The Kriers and their colleagues argued that context was important where sites were being redeveloped, and that it was not just a question of one building, but streets, urban spaces, and ultimately whole towns that needed careful design to avoid the visual chaos imposed so destructively on so many cities since 1945: they argued in favor of a sensitivity to townscape that had been so thoroughly rejected by modernists. *Urbanism* also rejects the concept of separate single-use zoning, and embraces complex hybrid mixed-use districts (for the pleasures of urban life suggest a plurality of activities), and accepts the necessity of keeping the automobile at bay. According to Jane Jacobs and others, people should live in cities, use them, and walk in them, not clutter and pollute them with cars and other vehicles. *Urbanism* implies recapturing quality, beauty, pleasure, and the "civic art" of living in cities. It embraces density, multi-ethnicity, community space, multi-modal transportation, human scale, proximity, permeability.

Urbanism is also an approach to urban design that responds to urban morphologies. It follows that settlement patterns evolve over time according to a dominant urban form; and that there are clear typologies that include organic/topographic, grid, formal/baroque, planned/ideal, and modernist. However, based on the sprawling chaotic growth patterns of urban development since the mid-twentieth century and more recently the impacts of digital and communication technology; one could argue that traditional patterns of *urbanism* are no longer relevant. Current and emerging forms of *urbanism* suggest new morphologies including: superimposition, fragmentation, hybridization, mega structures, mega scale, and a universal "logo culture."

In the recent past, architects such as Rem Koolhaas, OMA, and Bernard Tschumi have explored these patterns primarily at the architectural scale. Systematic research and urban/environmental design that investigates the human place and "civic art" among these newer forms/non-forms has not coalesced into a clear way forward. An authentic "new urbanism" may be just around the corner? CH

See also: **Atopia • Cultural theory • Datascapes • Deterritorialization/ reterritorialization**

Further sources: Deleuze (in Ballantyne 2002:89); Sharr (2007:3)

User   ∎

The word "user" has something vague-and vaguely suspect about it... the users space is lived not represented. — Henri Lefebvre

One would not talk about "using" a work of sculpture. — Adrian Forty

It is common practice when preparing an architectural brief or building program to refer to the eventual occupant as a *user*. It is a convenient, yet meaningless, grouping of a diverse and dynamic constituency. The *user* is someone who utilizes the resulting architecture rather than inhabits it. In the mechanistic worldview of modern architecture this made sense. Users were considered to be anonymous consumers who occupy buildings in an impersonal, generic manner. The alternative of humanizing the *user* was considered to be impractical. If a potential inhabitant of architecture were to be considered in totality, the task of discovering and describing the needs, aspirations, and biases of that individual would be insurmountable. Thus, future inhabitants cannot be treated as individuals, unless the building is a private home. The research required to move beyond considering the generic user into understanding the inhabitant is a service for which the architect would seldom be compensated. Thus the *user* becomes the stand-in of convenience. To round out an understanding of the user's needs and desires, the architect generally draws upon their own personal experiences. The difficulty is that it has been shown that designers exhibit unique spatial preferences and understandings of terms related to architecture. As a result, they may be misinterpreting the expressed wishes of the client.

The term *user* may already be passé when applied to architecture due to its popular usage in other settings. For example, the term has become most associated with drug abusers and computer "user groups."

See also: **Brief (Archispeak) • Psychological needs**

Further sources: Forty (2000:312)

▌Utility

Architecture is a useful art, not a fine art – absolved therefore from taking on the burden of fine art, which is to trace the destiny of mankind through its myths. — Aristotle

Considering it only from the point of view of *utility*, architecture surpasses all the arts. — Quatremere de Quincy, 1778

Utility has been the bane of architecture in the nineteenth and twentieth century, and it threatens to do the same for the twenty-first. Vitruvius started it with his prescription of "utilitas" (loosely translated as *utility*) as one of the three cornerstones of an architecture that would appease the emperor Augustus and everyone else in the ancient world. Years later, the devaluation of the art of architecture as a utilitarian enterprise was rediscovered. The emergence of modern architecture in the nineteenth century followed decades of largely non-utilitarian, classical architecture. This new emphasis upon *utility* was popularized by the slogan "form follows function," a sentiment that originated with the American artist Horatio Greenough. When Louis Sullivan eventually wrote, "form ever follows function – this is the law" fifty years later (1924), he was referring to the natural forms in the ornamentation applied to his buildings. The Art Nouveau entrance to the Carson Pirie Scott department store in Chicago perhaps best demonstrated this. For Sullivan, the dictum meant that in nature form follows the utility of the "functions." Examples that he listed included open apple blossoms, branching oaks, and winding streams. Clearly the notion that function should shape the form of a building was a misunderstanding of what Sullivan intended. After all, none of his buildings were formed by function, but rather by technology and historicism. The modern utilitarian interpretation of the dictum led to a modern architecture that failed to gain the favor of the general population. Its failure was largely due to its emphasis upon *utility* at the expense of beauty and meaning. Despite a short-lived effort by late-twentieth-century post-modernists to correct this situation, there is a good chance that a new age of architectural utilitarianism is emerging.

In our age of renewed and invigorated pragmatism, the danger looms that utility will again be the dominant influence in architecture. With pressure to create environmentally responsible and functionally efficient buildings, architects will be coerced into giving pre-eminence to *utility*. The danger is magnified by a growing reliance upon parametric modeling and digital materialization that favors the solving of "problems" that can be quantified.

Architecture is whatever in a building did not point to *utility*. — Hegel

Hegel's definition of architecture should be heeded if architecture is to survive. It should be posted on every design architect's computer.

See also: **Digital materiality • Neo-pragmatism • Parametric design**

Further sources: Harries (1998: 29); Johnson (1994: 79); Scruton (1979: 244)

Visionary architecture

Many architects in the past established their reputations well before they had produced any buildings of note. Seen as "paper architects" who produce a *visionary architecture*, their drawings remain forever trapped in a two-dimensional phase of visible non-existence. Such a visionary was a young Ludwig Mies van der Rohe, whose series of five large charcoal drawings, drafted between 1921 and 1923 and exhibited throughout post-First World War Germany, not only projected his prophetic vision of a new architecture, but established him in the public's mind as a leader of the modern movement.

Similar visions of an unbuilt architecture have appeared continuously through time. Indeed, from the extraordinary dreams of Piranesi to Boullee and Nicholas Ledoux, through to Franco Purini and Lebbeus Woods, the thinking behind their pictorial "castles in the air" is as valid as that underpinning any radical built edifice. However, detached from the business of making real buildings, their images function to question the very nature of accepted architectural thinking and push the boundaries of possibility. Consequently, such illustrated visions represent a form of architecture, in its purest, most essential sense.

One celebrated visionary was the late Cedric Price, whose entire career represented an onslaught against convention, and one that sought to marry available technology with the provision of new opportunities. He was at the time undoubtedly one of the major forces in British architecture. His enormous contribution to the architectural debate stemmed not from realized works, but mainly from an endless flow of innovative "outside of the box" ideas that consistently excited, influenced, and provoked his peers. As an "agent provocateur" Price did much to undermine orthodoxy and complacency by his heretical insistence on rethinking each problem, not necessarily in building terms. His seminally most significant building remains unbuilt, however, despite remaining an icon of modern architecture in the imaginations of countless designers. It is the acclaimed and "architecture-free" Fun Palace project of 1961 – a concept to which, to paraphrase Robin Middleton, much ensuing architectural thinking owes such a debt, and without which much of Archigram and the Pompidou Center would have been unthinkable.

A literary version of *visionary architecture* is found in Italo Calvino's accent on the intangible qualities of cities in the imaginary conversations between Marco Polo and Kubla Khan – when in poetic terms Polo recounts his memories of faraway cities. Rather than using prosaic, travelogue prose, his descriptions refer to the spirit of each place – that is, its genius loci. This is what the book *Invisible Cities* is all about: the failure of quantification to describe quality. Indeed, in the words of Conway Lloyd Morgan (2000), Calvino's classic narrative (1972) represents "a subtle assault on particular conventions of Modernism that place the formal and physical values of architecture and urbanism above the human experience." TP

See also: **Archigram (Archispeak)** • **Genius loci (Archispeak)**

Vitalism   ∎

Life and reality, in so far as it is living, consists of movement and becoming, rather than static being. Reality is organic, not mechanical. Life is known empirically or by intuition, rather than by concepts and logical inference. — *Oxford Guide to Philosophy*

Classical *vitalism*, as originally postulated by Aristotle, speculated that there is a life force – a psyche beyond the physical and chemical make-up of living organisms. Since then, the biological sciences have failed to find this force, and have found instead molecular genetics that appear to explain the mechanics of life – but not its source. *Vitalism* has been redefined as a philosophy. It draws upon biology to understand the nature of reality in our time of concern for living things, including the planet. *Vitalism*, is an appropriate "ism" for the twenty-first-century architect, as it rejects the primacy of the machine analogy and all that it represents. It is in many ways the yin/yang of western philosophy. As proposed by Fritjof Capra in *The Tao of Physics* (1975), East meets West. The acceptance of *vitalism* as an appropriate philosophy for twenty-first-century avant-garde architecture gives the discipline the ontological foundation it needs in order to sustain a direction in its evolution. The acceptance of overtly organic architectural forms by the younger generation of digital architects heralds the future of design. Even starchitects are drawing upon *vitalism*. When starchitects speak, the rest of the profession eventually listens, even if it is about justifying blobs and folds.

See also: **Blob architecture (Archispeak)** • **Blobitecture** • **Digital architecture** • **Fold** • **Starchitect**

Further sources: Colebrook (2006: 101); Johnson (1994: 8, 85, 109)

Wayfinding

The process of using spatial and environmental information to navigate to a destination. — Kevin Lynch

Since the 1960s, *wayfinding* has been seen as the purview of the graphic designer rather than the architect. Overt measures such as signage that are meant to facilitate *wayfinding* are often an afterthought that signals the failure of the architecture itself to assist the user in navigating the building or urban environment in an intuitive manner. As universal design becomes more commonplace, the provision of unobtrusive *wayfinding* measures will become increasingly important. The person with partial sight, or mobility challenges, will need clear and direct path clues that are not relying upon signage. The design of large hospitals, and other institutions that cater to the elderly or disabled, is a special *wayfinding* design challenge. Unobtrusive *wayfinding* is a particular challenge for twenty-first-century designers, as the structures that are now possible due to digital fabrication are potentially more complex. Even blobitecture will not be exempt. Fortunately architectural color is now acceptable, as are the hyper-surface and richly textured facades. This expansion of the architectural palette makes the achievement of successful integrated *wayfinding* possible. The advent of responsive and reflective soft architecture, with integrated media walls, complete with participant-activated sound, promises to be a brave new world where architecture personally greets and guides the visitor. *Wayfinding* will then become the responsibility of the architecture itself on a case-by-case, need to know basis.

See also: **Blob architecture (Archispeak) • Blobitecture • Soft architecture • Universal design**

Further sources: Lidwell (2003: 208)

Weak architecture

Modern western philosophy was built on a belief in "strong thought," that is, that there are fundamental truths and universals that will eventually be revealed through the rigorous application of reason and logic. Post-modern philosophy, on the other hand, challenged this notion as unrealistic. It proposed instead that there are no universal fundamentals to seek. The here and now is our only real existence in the world. This form of nihilism has a long history of champions, from Nietzsche to Derrida. One of those champions, Gianni Vattimo, has described post-modern philosophy as "weak thought." In "The end of modernity" (1988), he proposed that the recognition of weak thought changes the position of the architect from a "deductive rationalist serving as a functionary of humanity" to that of a less definitive, somewhat messy, and complex arbitrator of the various cultural traditions of the community in question. This refocuses the work of the architect to that of an agent of cultural change, well beyond the role of the modern architect as a problem solver charged with providing shelter. It provided the grounding for the various critical theory movements that have opened up the arena of legitimate architectural concern to include social equity for the disenfranchised. Thus, weak thought forms the philosophical underpinning for *weak architecture*. As Michael Speaks describes it (1998), the confident modernist manifesto has given way to uncertain attempts at seeking the intelligence necessary to design critically. Architects of the twenty-first century are faced with a more complex challenge than the naïve architects of the previous century. They must reject the lure of historicism in all its forms, including thinking about reality as knowable and measurable. The resulting *weak architecture* is situational, contingent, elusive, and provisional. It may even be reactive, dynamic, reflexive, and biomorphic, rather than mechano-morphic. It harbors no greater agenda than what it is. It is phenomenological and ultimately more of a cultural intervention than a Utopian technological construction. Marxism has given way to Deluzeanism.

See also: **Critical theory** • **Deleuzianism** • **Feminism** • **Intelligence**

Further sources: Hale (2000: 221); Sola-Morales (in Mallgrave 2008: 476); Vattimo (in Leach 1997: 147)

Weaving   ▐

Weaving **is the synthesis of two different materials, interlocking in order to give self-supporting form to their combined whole.**
— Benjamin Aranda and Chris Lasch

Weaving **may have contemporary architectural applications ...**
— Toshiko Mori

Toshiko Mori's seminar at Harvard in 2001 has demonstrated convincingly that today's most successful digital design algorithms are actually based on weaving. — Sanford Kwinter

Weaving in architecture is most associated with the large woven structural frame of the "Bird's nest" stadium built for the 2008 Beijing Olympics. The dramatic structural tour de force of intersecting diagonal columns and beams would not have been possible without the aid of the computer. It marked the public arrival of digital, parametric architecture. In parametric design, *weaving* is accomplished by the development of equations or algorithms that organize sine and cosine curves in space. Unlike traditional *weaving* that involves a loom and a material such as wool, computer-based *weaving* produces woven figures that can easily be manipulated and refined through successive iterations. The potential for the development of new building assemblies that employ sustainable materials such as bamboo and recycled plastics is unlimited.

Woven materials can offer greater freedom to produce non-Euclidean architectural forms, perhaps replacing the titanium panel as the technology of choice for the blobmeisters. Leadership will come from the schools. Lisa Iwamoto produced "Digital Weave" with her 2004 U.C. Berkeley graduate studio. It was a demonstration of "sectioning" as a technique for digital fabrication of surfaces. Using CAD/CAM technology, the resulting structure consisted of woven ribs combined with aluminum plates and plastic sign material. Similar experiments are occurring in well-equipped schools of architecture throughout North America and Europe. It represents a future for architectural form unencumbered by traditional methods of designing and fabricating architectural enclosure systems.

See also: **Algorithm • Blob architecture (Archispeak) • Parametric design**

Further sources: Iwamoto (2009: 17)

ZEB – Zero energy building █

What is the good of having a nice house without a decent planet to put it on? — Henry David Thoreau

Denial ain't just a river in Egypt. — Mark Twain

Designing and constructing energy efficient buildings, combined with a massive harnessing of renewable energy, makes it not only possible but also profitable for buildings to operate without fossil fuels.
— Edward Mazria, Architecture 2030

The building sector is responsible for a large share of the world's electricity consumption and raw material use. In the United States, commercial and residential buildings together account for over 72 percent of electricity use and over 38 percent of carbon dioxide emissions. Building construction worldwide is responsible for over 40 percent of material use. Buildings can last for 50–100 years so we are facing the looming obsolescence of our non-green current building stock. An energy retrofit of an existing building can cut energy use and bills by over 50 percent, but we need to design our buildings to use less energy at the outset. The construction and real estate industries are driving a wave of reform by recognizing that "going green" is future-proofing their financial assets.

There is enormous potential for reducing energy use in buildings, and the many-headed monster of climate change is the paramount reason to do so. Dramatically increasing the efficiency of our buildings is vital if we hope to steady the Earth's climate. Ed Mazria, an architect from New Mexico, launched the 2030 Challenge to architects to design buildings by 2030 that use no fossil fuels, stating, "It is the architects that hold the key to turning down the global thermostat." His goal is to transform architectural design from the mundane reliance on fossil fuels to an architecture intimately linked to the natural world in which we live. The architectural concepts and construction technologies available today enable architects easily to design new buildings with half the energy requirements of existing ones. Among the design technologies used are: natural lighting, natural ventilation, rooftop solar water and space heating, rooftop solar electric cells (photovoltaic), ultra insulation, ground source heat pumps, waterless urinals, and more efficient lighting technologies and windows.

The pioneers in the green building world are those attempting *zero-energy buildings* by pushing the envelope to drive technological improvements and initiatives to provide the comfort and services that people expect with the least adverse impact on natural resources and natural systems. There is much confusion about the term *zero-energy building* (ZEB), but at the heart of the concept is the idea that buildings can meet all their energy requirements from low-cost, locally available, non-polluting, renewable sources. A stricter level is that a ZEB generates enough renewable energy on site to equal or exceed its annual energy use. Four commonly used definitions are net zero site energy, net zero source energy, net zero energy costs, and net zero energy emissions. Typical renewable technologies available today include PV, solar hot water, wind, hydroelectric, and bio-fuels, which are all favored over conventional energy sources such as coal and natural gas. EL

See also: **Conservation • Cradle to cradle • Gaia architecture • Green design (Archispeak) • Hannover principles • Sustainability (Archispeak)**

List of terms

absence/presence
abstraction
accident
ad hocism
aesthetics
aletheia
algorithm
allusionism
alterity
ambivalence
American pragmatism
anthropomorphism
aporia
architectonic
archi-philosophy
architectural determinism
architectural positivism
architectural presentness
architectural psychology
architectural theory
architecture
armature
artificial intelligence
associative design
atopia
aura
authenticity
autonomous architect
Babel tower
banal
baroque
beauty
behavior and environment
betweenness
Bilbao effect
building information modeling:
    BIM
biomimicry
blobitecture
blur
bracketing
braids

branding
caricature
cartooning
catastrophe theory
cave
character
chatter
classicism
cliché
closure
commoditization
communitarianism
conservation
constraints
contextualism
continental philosophy
cosmogenic architecture
cosmopolitan architecture
cradle to cradle
craft
creativity
critical humanism
critical moderism
critical regionalism
critical theory
criticism
cryptodeleuzian materialism
cultural theory
datascapes
de-architecture
decentering
decomposition
decoration
deep structure
defamiliarization
Deleuzianism
dematerializations
deontic
design
detail
deterritorialization/
    reterritorialization

responsive architecture
rhizomatic
romanticism
ruin
scaffolding
scenographic
self-similarity
sensitivity analysis method
silence
simultaneity
soft architecture
space
spirit of place
starchitect
structuralism
style
sublime
superdutch
super-modernism
sustainability
synchronic

tabula rasa
technology and architecture
tectonic form
tessellating
tooling
total design
trope
ugly and ordinary
uncanny – unheimlich
universal design
unselfconscious form
urbanism
user
utility
visionary architecture
vitalism
wayfinding
weak architecture
weaving
ZEB – zero-energy building

Further reading

Abercrombie, S. (1984) *Architecture as Art*, London: Harper & Row.

Agrest, D. (1993) *Architecture from Without*, London: MIT Press.

Alexander, C. (1977) *A Pattern Language*, New York: Oxford University Press.

—— (1965) "The City is not a Tree," *Architectural Forum*, Vol. 122, No. 1, April, pp. 58–62 (Part I), Vol. 122, No. 2, May, pp. 58–62 (Part II).

—— (1963) *Notes on the Synthesis of Form*, London: Harvard University Press.

Alexander, C. et al. (1979) *The Timeless Way of Building*, Berkeley, Calif.: Center for Environmental Structure.

Antoniades, A. (1990) *Poetics of Architecture*, New York: Van Nostrand Reinhold.

Aranda, B. and Lasch, C. (2006) *Tooling*, New York: Princeton Architectural Press.

Ardrey, R. (1966) *The Territorial Imperative*. Kingsport, Tenn.: Kingsport Press.

Argyle, M. (1997) *The Psychology of Interpersonal Relationships*, London: Pelican.

Asensio, N. (ed.) (2002) *Great Architects*, Mexico City: Atrium.

Atelier Bow Wow (2002) *Pet Architecture Guide Book*, Tokyo Institute of Technology: Tokyo.

Avery, A. E. (1966) *History of Philosophy*, New York: Barnes & Nobles.

Bachelard, G. (1969) *The Poetics of Space*, Boston: Beacon Press.

Ballantyne, A. (ed.) (2002) *What is Architecture*, London: Routledge.

—— (2007) *Deleuze & Guattari for Architects*, London: Routledge.

Banham, R. (1984) *The Architecture of the Well-Tempered Environment*, Chicago: University of Chicago Press.

—— (1976) *Megastructure: Urban Futures of the Recent Past*, London: Thames & Hudson.

—— (1969) *The Architecture of the Well-Tempered Environment*, London: Architectural Press.

—— (1960) *Theory and Design in the First Machine Age*, New York: MIT Press.

Barker, R. (1963) "On the Nature of the Environment," *Journal of Social Issues*.

Benedikt, M. (1991) *Deconstructing the Kimbell*, New York: Lumen Books.

—— (1987) *For An Architecture of Reality*, New York: Lumen Books.

Benyus, J. (1997), *Biomimicry: Innovation Inspired by Nature*, London: William Morrow.

Bergson, H. (1988) *Matter and Memory*, trans. N. M. Paul and W. S. Palmer. New York: Zone Books.

Blackburn, S. (2008) *Oxford Dictionary of Philosophy*, London: Oxford University Press.

Blake, P. (1964) *God's Own Junkyard: The Planned Deterioration of America's Landscape*, New York: Holt, Rinehart & Winston.

Bloomer, K. C. and Moore, C. W. (1977) *Body, Memory and Architecture*, New Haven, Conn.: Yale University Press.

Borden, I. and Rendell, J. (eds.) (2000) *Intersections*, London: Routledge.

Brand, S. (1994) *How Buildings Learn*, New York: Penguin.

Broadbent, G. (1973) *Design in Architecture; Architecture and the Human Sciences*, Toronto: John Wiley & Sons.

Brundtland Commission (1987) *Our Common Future*, Oxford: Oxford University Press.

Burgin, V. (1986) *The End of Art Theory, Atlantic Highlands*, N.J.: Humanities Press International.

Burke, E. (1756/1909) *Philosophical Enquiry into the Origin of our Idea of the Sublime and the Beautiful*, New York: P. F. Collier & Sons.

Calvino, I. (1972) *Invisible Cities*, Turin: Giulio Einaudi Editore.

Campbell, J. (1988) *The Power of Myth*, New York: Doubleday.

Canter, D. (1974) *Proceedings of the Dalandhui Conference 1970*, Surrey Conference.

Canter, D. (ed.) (1974) *Psychology for Architects*, London: Applied Science.

Capra, F. (1975), *Tao of Physics: An Exploration of the Parallels Between Modern Physics and Eastern Mysticism*, Berkeley, Calif.: Shambhala.

Cassirer, E. (1946) *Language and Myth*, Toronto: General Publishing.

Casey, E. (1997) *The Fate of Place: A Philosophical History*, Berkeley, Calif.: University of California Press.

Clark, A. (1997) *Being There: Putting Brain, Body and World Together Again*, Cambridge, Mass.: MIT Press.

Clark, R. and Pause, M. (1985) *Precedents in Architecture*, New York: Van Nostrand Reinhold.

Cold, B. (2001) *Aesthetics, Wellbeing and Health: Ethnoscapes*, Kent, UK: Ashgate.

Colebrook, C. (2006) *Deleuze: A Guide for the Perplexed*, London: Continuum.

Coleman, A. (1989) *Utopia on Trial*, London: Hilary Shipman.

Colquhoun, A. (2002) *Modern Architecture*, Oxford: Oxford University Press.

—— (1991) *Modernity and the Classical Tradition*, London: MIT Press.

—— (1985) *Essays in Architectural Criticism*, London: MIT Press.

Cook, P. (1967) *Architecture: Action and Plan*, London: Studio Vista/Reinhold.

Cullen, G. (1995) *The Concise Townscape*, New York: Elsevier.

Curtis, W. (1996) *Modern Architecture Since 1900*, 3rd edn, London: Phaidon Press.

Dennett, D. C. (1993) *Consciousness Explained*, London: Penguin.

Descombes, V. (1983) *Objects of all Sorts: A Philosophical Grammar*, trans. L. Scott-Fox and J. Harding, Oxford: Blackwell.

Dietsch, D. (2002) *Architecture for Dummies*, New York: John Wiley.

Diprose, R. and Reynolds, J. (eds.) (2008) *Merleau-Ponty: Key Concepts*, Chesham, UK: Acumen.

Dreyfus, H. and Wrathall, M. (2009) *A Companion to Phenomenology and Existentialism*, London: Wiley-Blackwell.

Durant, S. (1986) *Ornament: A Survey of Decoration since 1830*, New York: Macdonald.

Eco, U. (1986) *Travels in Hyperreality*, New York: Harcourt Brace Jovanovich.

Eisenman, P. (2007) *Written into the Void: Selected Writings, 1990–2004*, New York: Yale University Press.

—— (1984) "The end of the classical: the beginning, the end of the end," in K. Nesbitt (ed.), *Theorizing a New Agenda for Architecture an Anthology of Architectural Theory 1965–1995*, New York: Princeton Architectural Press.

—— (1982) *House X*, New York: Rizzoli International.

Fawcett, P. (2003) *Architecture Design Notebook*, 2nd edn, London: Architectural Press.

Fenton, J. (1985) *Pamphlet Architecture: Hybrid Buildings*, New York: Princeton Architectural Press.

Forty, A. (2000) *Words and Buildings: A Vocabulary of Modern Architecture*, New York: Thames & Hudson.

Foster, H. (ed.) (1983) *The Anti Aesthetic: Essays on Postmodern Culture*, Seattle: Bay Press.

Frampton, K.(1995) *Studies in Tectonic Culture: The Poetics of Construction in Nineteenth and Twentieth Century Architecture*, ed. John Cava, Cambridge, Mass.: MIT Press.

—— (1990) "Rappel a l'ordre: the case for the tectonic," *Architectural Design*, 3–4.

—— (1983) "Towards a critical regionalism" in H. Foster (ed.), *The Anti-Aesthetic: Essays on Postmodern Culture*, Port Townsend: Bay Press.

Friedman, M. (ed.) (2002) *Gehry Talks*, New York: Rizzoli.

Gallagher, S. (2005) *How the Body Shapes the Mind*, Oxford: Clarendon Press.

Gannon, T. (ed.) (2004) *UN Studio: Erasmus Bridge*, New York: Princeton Architectural Press.

Gausa, M. et al. (2003) *The Metapolis Dictionary of Advanced Architecture*, Barcelona: Actar.

Gautier, T. (1825), *Mademoiselle de Maupin*, New York: A. A. Knopf.

Gelernter, M. (1995) *Sources of Architectural Form*, New York: St. Martin's Press.

Gibson, J. (1979) *Ecological Approach to Visual Perception*, Boston, Mass.: Houghton Mifflin.

Giedion, S. (1941) *Space, Time and Architecture*, Cambridge, Mass.: Harvard University Press.

Goffman, E. (1963) *Behaviour in Public Places*, London: Free Press.

Gonchar, J. (2007) "Transformative tools start to take hold: a critical mass of building information modeling projects demonstrates the technology's benefits and its potential for redefining practice," *Architectural Record*, April.

Gregory, R. L. (1998) *Eye and Brain*, London: World University Library.

Gregotti, V. (1996) *Inside Architecture*, London: MIT Press.

Hale, J. (2000) *Building Ideas*, New York: John Wiley.

Hall, E.T. (1966) *The Hidden Dimension*, London: Bodley Head.

Harbison, R. (1997) *Thirteen Ways*, London: MIT Press.

Hard, A. (2009) *The NCS Colour Order and Scaling System*, Stockholm: Svenskt Forgcentrum.

Harries, K. (1998) *The Ethical Function of Architecture,* London: MIT Press.

Hasiotis, A. and Isreal, J. (ed.) (2002) *Reproduction and Production,* Thesholds 24, Cambridge, Mass.: MIT Press.

Hauptmann, Deborah (ed.) (2006) *The Body in Architecture,* Rotterdam: 010 Publishers.

Hays, M. (ed.) (2000) *Architecture Theory Since 1968,* London: MIT Press.

Hearn, F. (2003) Ideas that Shaped Buildings, London: MIT Press.

Heidegger, M. (1977) *The Question Concerning Technology and other Essays,* New York: Harper & Row.

—— (1971) "Poetically Man Dwells," in *Poetry Language Thought,* trans. A. Hofstadter, New York: Harper & Row.

—— (1962) *Being and Time,* trans. John Macquarrie and Edward Robinson, New York: Harper & Row.

—— (1951/1971) "Building dwelling thinking," in *Poetry Language Thought,* trans. A.Hofstadter, New York: Harper & Row.

Hellman, L. (2000) *Archi-Tetes, the Id in the Grid,* London: Wiley Academy.

—— (1988) *Architecture for Beginners,* London: Writers and Readers.

Herdeg, K. (1983) *The Decorated Diagram,* London: MIT Press.

Hersey, G. (1992) *The Lost Meaning of Classical Architecture,* London: MIT Press.

Hertzberger, H. (2002) *Articulations,* London: Prestel.

Heschong, L. (1979) *Thermal Delight in Architecture,* Cambridge, Mass.: MIT Press.

Holl, S. (1996) *Intertwining,* New York: Princeton Architectural Press.

—— (1991) *Anchoring,* New York: Princeton Architectural Press.

Honderich, T. (ed.) (2005) *The Oxford Guide To Philosophy,* New York: Oxford University Press.

Howard, E. (1902) *Garden Cities of To-Morrow,* London: S. Sonnenschein.

Hubbard, W.(1996) *A Theory for Practice,* London: MIT Press.

—— (1980) *Complicity and Conviction: Steps Toward an Architecture of Convention,* London: MIT Press.

Humphrey, N. K. (1978) *The Illusion of Beauty, Perception,* Vol. 2, London: Pion.

Husserl, E. (1973) *Logical Investigations,*trans. J. N. Findlay, London: Routledge.

Iwamoto, L. (2009) *Digital Fabrication: Architectural Material Techniques,* New York: Princeton Architectural Press.

Jameson, C. (1990) *Super-Modern defense: An open letter to C. Jencks,* in Architectural Design No. 3-4 (1990), p. 26-33

Jencks, C. (2007) *Critical Modernism,* New York: Wiley Academy.

—— (1995) *The Architecture of the Jumping Universe,* New York: Academy.

—— (1977) *The Language of Post-Modern Architecture,* New York: Rizzoli.

—— (1973) *Modern Movements in Architecture,* London: Doubleday Anchor.

Jencks, C. and Kropf, K. (ed.) (1997) *Theories and Manifestos,* New York: Academy.

Johnson, M. (2007) *The Meaning of the Body: Aesthetics of Human Understanding,* Chicago: University of Chicago Press.

Johnson, P. A. (1994) *The Theory of Architecture,* New York: John Wiley.

Jones, J. C. (1970) *Design Methods,* London: John Wiley.

Jones, O. (1856) *Grammar of Ornament,* London: Day & Sons.

Kant, E. (1790/1987) *Critique of Judgement,* trans. W. S. Pluhar, London: Hackett.

Kearney, R. (1994) *Modern Movements in European Philosophy*, Manchester: Manchester University Press.

Knevitt, C. (ed.) (1986) *Perspectives*, London: Lund Humphries.

Kockelmans, J. J. (1967) *Phenomenology: The Philosophy of Edmund Husserl and its Interpretation*, Garden City, N. Y.: Anchor Doubleday.

Koestler, A. (1964) *The Act of Creation*, New York: Dell.

Köhler, Wolfgang (1992) *Gestalt Psychology: An Introduction to New Concepts in Modern Psychology*, New York: Liveright.

KoolHaas, R. (1995) *S,M,L,XL*, New York: Monacelli Press.

—— (1978) *Delirious New York: A Retroactive Manifesto for Manhattan*, New York: Oxford University Press.

Koolhaas, R. (ed.) (2004) *Content*, London: Taschen.

Krautheimer, R. (1942) "Introduction to an iconography of medieval architecture," *Journal of the Courtaid and Warburg Institutes 5* (New York: New York University Press reprint, 1969).

Kroll, L. and Blundell-Jones, P. (1987) *An Architecture of Complexity*, New York: MIT Press.

Kruft, H. (1994) *A History of Architectural Theory*, New York: Princeton Architectural Press.

Kuhn, T. (1962) *The Structure of Scientific Revolutions*, 2nd edn, London: University of Chicago Press.

Küller, R. and Mikellides, B. (1993) "Simulated studies of colour, arousal and comfort," in R. W. Marans and D. Stokols (eds.), *Environmental Simulation*, New York: Plenum Press.

Lakoff, G. and Johnson, M. (1999) *Philosophy in the Flesh: The Embodied Mind and its Challenge to Western Thought*, New York: Basic Books.

Lang, J. (1987) *Creating Architectural Theory*, New York: Van Nostrand Reinhold.

Le Corbusier (2007) *Towards an Architecture*, trans. J. Goodman, Los Angeles, Calif.: Getty Research Institute.

—— (1986) *Towards a New Architecture*, New York: Dover.

Leach, N. (ed.) (1997) *Rethinking Architecture,* London: Routledge.

Leatherbarrow, D. and Mostafavi, M. (2002) *Surface Architecture*, Cambridge, Mass.: MIT Press.

Leopold, A. (1949) *A Sand County Almanac*, New York: Oxford University Press.

Lidwell, W., Holden, K., and Butler, J. (2003) *Universal Principles of Design*, Beverly, Mass.: Rockport.

Lifchez, R. (1987) *Rethinking Architecture*, Berkeley, Calif.: University of California Press.

Lloyd-Morgan, C. (2000) *Twentieth Century Design, A Reader's Guide*, London: Architectural Press.

Loos, A. (1997) *Ornament and Crime*, Calif.: Ariadne Press.

Lootsma, B. (2000) *Superdutch, New Architecture in the Netherlands*, London: Thames & Hudson.

Lynch, K. (1960) *The Image of the City*, London: MIT Press.

Lynn, G. (1993) "Folding in architecture," in G. Lynn (ed.), *Architectural Design Profile,* London: AD Magazine.

Macey, D. (2001) *Dictionary of Critical Theory*, London: Penguin.

Macrae-Gibson, G. (1989) *The Secret Life of Buildings: An American Mythology for Modern Architecture*, London: MIT Press.

Mallgrave, H. F. and Contandriopoulos, C. (eds.) (2008) *Architectural Theory Vol 2*, Oxford: Blackwell.

Mann, T. (2007) *Abbe´ Boulah*, USA: Xlibris.

—— (2004) *Time Management for Architects and Designers*, New York: W. W. Norton.

—— (ed.) (1999) *EDRA 30/1999*, Edmund, Okla.: EDRA.

Marans, R. W. and Stokols, D. (1993) *Environmental Simulation, Research and Policy Issues*, New York: Plenum Press.

Marble, S. et al. (eds.) (1988) "Architecture and body," *Columbia Architecture Journal*, New York: Rizzoli.

Maslow, A. (1954) *Motivation and Personality*, New York: Harper & Row.

Matthews, E. (2002) *The Philosophy of Merleau-Ponty*, Chesham: Acumen.

Maxwell, R. (1993) *Sweet Disorder and the Carefully Careless,* New York: Princeton Architectural Press.

McDonough, W. and Braungart, M. (2000) *From Cradle to Cradle: Remaking the Way We Make Things*, New York: North Point Press.

McGreight, T. (1996) *Design Language,* Portland, Maine: Brymmorgen Press.

McHarg, I. (1969) *Design With Nature*, New York: John Wiley.

Merleau-Ponty, M. (1982) *Phenomenology of Perception*, trans. C. Smith, London: Routledge.

—— (1968) "The intertwining – the chasm," in *The Visible and the Invisible*, trans. A. Lingis, Evanston, Ill.: Northwestern University Press.

Mikellides, B. (1980) *Architecture for People*, London: Studio Vista.

Mitchell, W. (1999) "Urban life, Jim – but not as we know it," in *E-Topia*, London MIT Press, pp. 148–9.

—— (1989) *The Logic of Architecture*, London: MIT Press.

Molnar, J. M. and Vodvarka, F. (2004) *Sensory Design*, Minneapolis, Minn.: University of Minnesota Press.

Moore, C. and Bloomer, K. (1977) *Body, Memory, and Architecture*, New Haven, Conn.: Yale University Press.

Mostafavi, M. and Leatherbarrow, D. (1993) *On Weathering*, New York: MIT Press.

Nesbitt, K. (ed.) (1996) *Theorizing a New Agenda for Architecture*, New York: Princeton Architectural Press.

Newman, O. (1965) *Defensible Space*, London: Architectural Press.

Newman, O. (1972) *Defensible Space: Crime Prevention Through Urban Design*, New York: Mcmillan.

Nobel, Philip (2007) "Editorial," *Metropolis,* June.

Noe, A. (2004) *Action in Perception*, Cambridge, Mass.: MIT Press.

Norberg-Schulz, C. (1985) The Concept of Dwelling: On the Way to Figurative Architecture, New York: Rizzoli.

—— (1980) *Genius Loci: Towards a Phenomenology of Architecture*, New York: Rizzoli.

—— (1975) *Meaning in Western Architecture,* London: Studio Vista.

—— (1971) *Existence, Space and Architecture*, London: Studio Vista.

—— (1965) *Intentions in Architecture*, Cambridge, Mass.: MIT Press.

Olgyay, V. (1973) *Design with Climate*, 2nd edn, New York: Princeton Architectural Press.

Oosterhuis, K. (2003) *Hyperbodies: Towards an E-motive Architecture,* Basel: Birkhauser.

Otto, F. (1982) "Natural constructions" in IL 32.

Palladio, A. (1738) *The Four Books of Architecture*, London.

Pallasma, J. (2005) *The Eyes of the Skin: Architecture and the Senses*, Chichester: Wiley-Academy.

—— (2001) *The Architecture of Image: Existential Space in Cinema*, Helsinki: Rakennustieto Oy.

Palmer, D. D. (1997) *Structuralism and Poststructuralism*, Danbury, Conn.: Writers and Readers.

Papdakis, A. (ed.) (1990) *New Architecture: The New Moderns & The Super Moderns*, London: Academy.

Pawley, M. (1974) *The Private Future*, New York: Random House.

Pena, W. (2001) *Problem Seeking: An Architectural Programming Primer*, New York: John Wiley & Sons.

Perez-Gomez, A. (1984) *Architecture and the Crisis of Modern Science*, Cambridge, Mass.:MIT Press.

Pevsner, N. (2005) *Pioneers of Modern Design*, London: Yale University Press.

Porter, T. (2004) *Archispeak*, London: Spon Press.

Porter, T. and Mikellides, B. (2009) *Colour for Architecture Today*, London: Taylor & Francis.

Porter, T. and Neale, J. (2000) *Architectural Supermodels*, Oxford: Architectural Press.

Prak, N. (1984) *Architects: The Noted and the Ignored*, London: John Wiley.

—— (1977), *Perceptions of the Visual World*, Delft: Delft Universty Press.

—— (1976) *The Visual Perception of the Built Environment*, Delft University Press.

Proshansky, H. M., Ittelson, W. H., and Rivlin, L. G. (1970) *Environmental Psychology*, New York: Holt, Rinehart & Winston.

Rasmussen, S. E. (1962) *Experiencing Architecture*, Cambridge, Mass.: MIT Press.

Rattenbury, K. and Bevan, B. (2004) *Architects Today*, New York: Harper Collins.

Read, H. (1934) *Art and Industry*, London.

Reiser, J. and Umemoto, N. (2005) *The Atlas of Novel Tectonics*, New York: Princeton Architectural Press.

Rowe, C. (1994) *The Architecture of Good Intentions*, London: Academy.

Rowe, C. and Koetter, F. (1976), "Collage city," in K. Nesbitt (ed.), *Theorizing a New Agenda for Architecture an Anthology of Architectural Theory 1965–1995*, New York: Princeton Architectural Press.

Rowe, P. (1994) *Design Thinking*, London: MIT Press.

Rosa, J. (2003) *Next Generation Architecture*, New York: Rizzoli.

Rudofsky, B. (1964), *Architecture Without Architects, a short introduction to non-pedigreed architecture*, Albuquerque: University of New Mexico Press.

Sakamoto, T. and Ferré, A. (eds.) (2008) *From Control to Design: Parametric/ Algorithmic Architecture*, New York: Actar-D USA.

Sartre, J.-P. (1948) *Existentialism and Humanism*, London: Methuen.

—— (1945) *Being and Nothingness*, London: Washington Square Press.

Sausmarez, M. (1964) *Basic Design: the Dynamics of Visual Form*, London: Studio Vista/Reinhold.

Scruton, R. (1995) *A Short History of Modern Philosophy*, 2nd edn., London: Routledge.

—— (1979) *The Aesthetics of Architecture*, Princeton, N. J.: Princeton University Press.

Semper, G. (1989) *The Four Elements of Architecture and Other Writings*, trans. H. F. Mallgrave and W. Herrmann, Cambridge, UK: Cambridge University Press.

Sharr, A. (2007) *Heidegger for Architects*, Abingdon: Routledge.

Smith, P. F. (2006) *Sustainable Architecture*, London: Routledge.

—— (2003) *The Dynamics of Delight – Architecture and Aesthetics*, London: Routledge.

Smithsons, A. (1967) *Team Ten Primer*, London: Studio Vista.

Steenbergen, C. et al. (eds.) (2000) *Architectural Design and Research: Composition, Education, Analysis*, Delft: Thoth.

Stevens, G. (1990) *The Reasoning Architect*, New York: McGraw-Hill.

Sommer, R. (1970) *Personal Space*, New York: Prentice Hall.

Speaks, M. (2010) in A. Sykes (ed.), *Constructing a New Agenda for Architecture*, New York: Princeton Architectural Press.

Speaks, M. (1998) "It's out there ... the formal limits of the American avant-garde," *Architectural Design*, Vol. 68, No. 5/6 (May–June), pp. 30–1.

Sullivan, L. (1924) *The Autobiography of an Idea*, New York: Press of the American Institute of Architects.

Summerson, J. (1963) *The Classical Language of Architecture*, Cambridge, Mass.: MIT Press.

Symes, M. (1989) *Journal of Architecture & Planning Research*, Vol. 6, No. 3, special issue on Architectural Education for Architecture Practice.

Tafuri, M.(1992) *Sphere and the Labyrinth*, London: MIT Press.

—— (1976) *Architecture and Utopia*, London: MIT Press.

Thiis-Evensen, T. (1987) *Archetypes In Architecture*, London: Norwegian University Press.

Thoenes, C. et al. (2003) *Architectural Theory,* London: Taschen.

Tschumi, B. (1994) *Architecture and Disjunction*, Cambridge Mass.: MIT Press.

Tschumi, B. and Cheng I. (2003) *The State of Architecture at the Beginning of the 21st Century,* New York: Monacelli Press.

Tzonis, A. and Lefaivre, L. (1981) "The grid and the pathway," in *Architecture in Greece 15*, pp. 176–8.

Unwin, S. (2003) *Analysing Architecture*, London: Routledge.

Van der Lay, S. and Richter, M. (2008) *Megastructure Reloaded*, Ostfildern, Germany: Hatje Cantz.

Van Doesburg, T. (1924/1975) "Towards a plastic architecture" in C. Ulrich (ed.), *Programs and Manifestoes on 20th-Century Architecture*, Cambridge, Mass.: MIT Press.

Varela, Francisco J., Thompson, E., and Eleanor, R. (1991) *The Embodied Mind: Cognitive Science and Human Experience*, Cambridge, Mass.: MIT Press.

Vattimo, G. (1988) "The end of modernity, the end of the project?" in N. Leach (ed.), *Rethinking Architecture: A Reader in Cultural Theory*, London: Routledge.

Venturi, R. (1977) *Complexity and Contradiction in Architecture*, 2nd edn., New York: Museum of Modern Art.

Venturi, R., Brown, D., and Izenour, S. (1977) *Learning From Las Vegas*, London: MIT Press.

Vesely, D. (2004) *Architecture in the Age of Divided Representation: The Question of Creativity in the Shadow of Production*, Cambridge, Mass.: MIT Press.

Vidler, A. (2008) *Histories of the Immediate Present*, London: MIT Press.

Viollet-le-Duc, E.-E. (1875) *Histoire de L'habitation Humaine Depuis Les Temps Préhistoriques Jusqu'à nos Jours*, published in English in 1876 as *Habitations of Man in All Ages*.

Vitruvius (1999) *Ten Books on Architecture*, trans. and ed. I. D. Rowland and T. N. Howe, Cambridge, UK: Cambridge University Press,

Wagner, R. (1981) *The Invention of Culture*, London: University of Chicago Press.

Wernick, J. (2008) *Building Happiness*, London: Black Dog.

Whiteman, J., Kipnis, J., and Burdett, R. (ed.) (1992) *Strategies in Architectural Thinking*, London: MIT Press.

Wigley, M. (1998) "Whatever happened to total design?" *Harvard Design Magazine*, no. 5, Summer, London: MIT Press.

Wigley, M. (1988) *Deconstructivist Architecture,* New York: Little, Brown/ New York Graphic Society Books.

Will, G. (2004) "Facadism", *Vancouver Review*.

Wines, J. (2000) *Green Architecture*, New York: Taschen.

—— (1987) *De-Architecture*, New York: Rizzoli.

Wittkower, R. (1962) *Architectural Principles in the Age of Humanism*, London: W. W. Norton.

Zevi, B. (1978) *The Modern Language of Architecture*, London: University of Washington Press.

Zumthor, Peter. (1998) *Thinking Architecture*, trans. M. Oberli-Turner, Baden, Germany: Lars Muller.